# THE ISSUE IN LITERARY
## CRITICISM

# THE ISSUE IN LITERARY CRITICISM

BY

MYRON F. BRIGHTFIELD

GREENWOOD PRESS, PUBLISHERS
NEW YORK                    1968

University of California Press
Berkeley, California, 1932
Reprinted with the permission of the
University of California Press

*Reprint edition, 1968*

Library of Congress catalogue card number: 68-23278

Printed in the United States of America

# CONTENTS

[v]

# PREFACE

This book aims to give organic and systematic expression to the working principles of literary criticism. It does not, therefore, seek new materials; its contribution must be the organizing and methodizing of principles well known. It may, indeed, be viewed as an extended commentary on the *Poetics* of Aristotle—the chief extensions being two in number. The first is predicated on the position that a literary judgment is inevitably an aesthetic and a philosophic judgment—so that the road to literary criticism necessarily lies through the fields of aesthetics and philosophy. The second is that any formulation of scientific principles must be made in face of the inexorable opposition of the idealist, the romanticist, and impressionist.

The traversing of a territory so huge as that which comes within the scope of this work is possible only through a determined maintenance of proportion and a rigorous exercise of suppression. At each re-writing, during the five years I have been engaged on this work, it is these two necessities which have been in command. My critic will therefore allow me to present a topic or a position by citing a small number of what I have believed to be the most typical or most important elements of it, or by quoting a few only of its proponents. He will not think me ignorant of the hosts of additional materials or authorities which will spring to his mind—unless, indeed, those additional items would force a material alteration in my views.

It may be that some students of philosophy will consider me an interloper in their field. I wish to say, accordingly, that I have endeavored, in my second chapter, to identify myself completely with the position of orthodox pragmatism. I have studied pragmatism under A. W. Moore and B. H. Bode. I have heard lectures, or courses of lectures, from G. H. Mead, J. H. Tufts, and John Dewey. In the interests of compression I have usually cited as authority the writings of Professor Dewey. But I know that I have incorporated in that chapter many of the opinions of the others I here mention.

As originally planned, this work was to have contained an Appendix in which was to be outlined the character which a scientific History of Literary Criticism must assume. Such a topic, however, deserves separate and independent attention, and this I hope to devote to it in the near future. I think, moreover, that I have sufficiently indicated my position in this matter in the text of the present work. I have declared (pp. 290–92) that the status of any critical formula of the past depends (among other things) upon (1) those elements in it which are integrally expressive of the empirical attitude at all times toward literature; and (2) those elements which constitute the "literary tradition" of its day. My position on the question of the organic status of literary tradition does not differ essentially from that set down by Mr. T. S. Eliot ("Tradition and the Individual Talent," in *The Sacred Wood*):

[W]hat happens when a new work of art is created is something that happens simultaneously to all the works of art which preceded it. The existing monuments form an ideal order among themselves, which is modified by the introduction of the new (the really new) work of art among them. The existing order is complete before the new work arrives; for order to persist after the supervention of novelty, the *whole* existing order must be, if ever so slightly, altered; and so the relations, proportions, values of each work of art toward the whole are readjusted; and this is conformity between the old and the new. Whoever has approved this idea of order, of the form of European, of English literature, will not find it preposterous that the past should be altered by the present as much as the present is directed by the past.

I have also, I trust, made clear my attitude toward literary history (pp. 285–87).

For the Appendix thus planned I had also written an essay surveying the present situation in literary criticism. But there seemed little use in pointing out in works of the past decade the same principles that I had already discussed in connection with writers of the more distant past. If my reader will turn, for example, to such works as Max Eastman's *Enjoyment of Poetry,* Lascelles Abercrombie's *Theory of Poetry,* J. L. Lowes's *The Road to Xanadu,* F. C. Prescott's *The Poetic Mind*—he will see the idealist at work precisely in the ways I have described in the present volume. He will be impressed not only with the eternal sameness of the idealistic attitude toward literature, but he will also marvel at the fact that the same ancient and unvarying idealistic principles, repeated almost in the same words, are offered as brilliant discoveries year after year in a steady succession of books on literary criticism and aesthetics.

In connection with literary criticism of the present day, I should, I think, make clear my attitude toward the "neo-humanists"—Irving Babbitt, Paul Elmer More, and Norman Foerster. Their position, as I see it, is that of those whom I have called (pp. 98–102) the "difficult" idealists. They, like Kant, Hegel, and the mature Goethe, wish to occupy a middle ground between the "easy" idealist (the romanticist, the impressionist) on the one hand, and the empiricist on the other. They are idealists because their real aesthetic values are spiritual and static; but they assert the necessity of arriving at them through the rigid discipline of talented achievement, or through an ethical ideal. They stand thus in an (as I believe) untenable position between the two great world attitudes, one or the other of which every man *must* and *does* accept (whether he admits the fact or not). We see, for example, Mr. More (in his *The Demon of the Absolute*) cursing both houses in the following terms:

But it will not be amiss to indicate by way of summary the two main currents of influence from the same fountain head of naturalism. On the one hand we have the illicit usurpation of science which came to a climax in the mid-nineteenth century, and which taught us to believe that the world runs forever in a set groove under some complex of mechanical laws, and that man like the animals is no more than a cog in the huge fatalistic machine. The modern form of this hypothesis is what our psychologists call behaviorism; its outcome in literature is the sort of realism that still actually dominates our fiction. On the other hand we are haunted by a suspicion that this world of ours, so far from exhibiting the tight regularity of a machine, is an infinite flux of accidents without calculable plan or meaning. From this creed derives the literature that undertakes to represent man as the merely passive channel for an ever-flowing stream of sensations. It might appear that these two views were mutually exclusive one of the other, and the distraction of the age is indeed due to the fact that they are in one sense contradictory. But it is to be observed that they have a common origin in the denial of that element in man which is outside of nature and is denoted by consciously directive purpose; they are alike in being anti-humanistic, and they both end in the morass of "futilitarianism" by depriving life of any serious interest or deep emotions for representation.

Now the "easy" idealist, who is placed at one extreme of Mr. More's classification, will scarcely concur in what is here said about him. He does not deny "that element in man which is outside of nature." On the contrary, his entire system is based on what he thinks to be that element. What he does deny is that an absolute can be "denoted by consciously directive purpose." An absolute is perfect and self-sufficient. It cannot be combined with, or attained by, the "earthly" or talented efforts of men. When it appears, by its own choice, the "conscious processes" (reason, intelligence) must totally abdicate. And a man who expresses his spiritual experience of the absolute must necessarily become a "passive channel." The absolute is itself the guaranty of the perfection of the result. Impressionism, in short, is pure and consistent idealism.

Moreover, the "easy" idealist will continue, the "new humanists" do not deny the nullity of reason in the face of the absolute. "Humanism," declares Professor Foerster (*American Criticism*, 242), "seeks to press beyond reason by the use of *intuition* or *imagination*, following the example of the most poetical of Hellenic philosophers" (Plato). Professor Babbitt speaks continually of "imagination," of "insight," of "truths above the reason." Yet he condemns the attaining of aesthetic values after the manner of the romantic idealist. On what grounds does he base his condemnation? What is the source of the desire of "neo-humanists" to dictate rules to absolute beauty? Obviously they cannot be holding a brief for the "reason," of whose "earthly" nature and utter inadequacy they are convinced. Accordingly, the "easy" idealist will declare, only one source remains. They are condemning the Beautiful, an absolute, in the name of the Good, another absolute (see my discussion, pp. 270–76, of the conflict between the beautiful and the good). They appeal not to the aesthetic, but to the moralistic, Plato. The writings of (for example) Professor Babbitt lend color to this accusation. "The solution," he writes (*Rousseau and Romanticism*, 380), "of this problem as to the relation of humanism and religion, so far as a solution can be found, lies in looking upon them both as only different stages in the same path. Humanism should have in it an element of religious insight.''

The empiricist, who has been placed at the opposite end of Mr. More's division, must call attention to the fact that the controversy between impressionists and ''humanists''—whether over the question of genius and talent, or of the eternally beautiful and the eternally good—is a private war for idealists. For his part, the empiricist feels unable to reply to Mr. More's assertion that science forces us to believe that ''man like the animals is no more than a cog in the huge fatalistic machine''—or to Mr. Foerster's declaration that empiricism leads to ''naturism.'' He feels unable to reply because, since ''humanists'' are idealists, there exists no basis whatever for debate. A ghost intervenes. Upon what grounds can one enter a discussion with writers who have extracted from human experience all the humanistic values it contains, who give these to an absolute, and who are then scandalized to observe that what remains has the ''tight regularity of a machine''? Their entire case against the scientist reposes on this initial arbitrary dualism. One notes Mr. More's assertion that the curse of science is that it is an *absolute* system. This is strange language for an idealist to use toward an empiricist. One notes, too, the dual character of the accusation against science. Not only is it to be condemned as an absolute; it is also abhorrent because it is purely relative and sets no standards! Not only is the scientist ''in one sense'' the opponent of the impressionist, but he is also basically united with him!

When the ''neo-humanists'' fight against the romanticists and impressionists (and it seems to me that this has been their main battle), I am enthusiastically of their number. But they can make no effective stand until they become empiricists. They cannot be empiricists until they abandon their absolute and their thoroughly false definition of science. Although I have attempted to make emphatically clear in this volume my definition of scientific method, it may be not unwise to repeat in this place that scientific thinking means to me what it did to Huxley:

The method of scientific investigation is nothing but the expression of the necessary mode of working of the human mind. It is simply the mode at which all phenomena are reasoned about, rendered precise and exact.

Bliss Perry had the kindness to read over the manuscript of this work. I am indebted, also, to three colleagues at the University of California. W. R. Dennes and V. F. Lenzen read intently the chapter on philosophy (Chapter II) and made many valuable suggestions. Walter Morris Hart did not read the work in manuscript; but he has on many occasions given me the benefit of his keen-sighted comments during discussions of literary problems. His kindly encouragement often enabled me to surmount the baffling crises which arise during the writing of a work of this kind. These gentlemen are not responsible for my mistakes; nor are they to be considered, because of my mention of them, as in agreement with the views I expound.

MYRON F. BRIGHTFIELD.

BERKELEY, CALIFORNIA,
July, 1932.

# Chapter I

# SCIENCE AND LITERARY CRITICISM

The appearance of the *Origin of Species* in 1859 inaugurated a general recasting of aims and methods in many fields of human knowledge. To this movement literary criticism was not unresponsive. It was in France that criticism most flourished at the time; it was there, too, that the positivism of Auguste Comte had prepared a fertile soil. Consequently it was among the French critics that the word "science" was soonest and most frequently heard in connection with judgments in literature.

Edmond Scherer wrote in 1862:

> The importance which criticism has acquired in our days may seem exaggerated. Its rôle answers, however, to a need of our times. And, indeed, criticism has changed. We demand to-day that it explain to us men, things, and actions. Criticism is no longer a simple reflection upon works of genius; it has become one of the numerous instruments, or, one may say, one of the applications, of modern science. As such it tends each day to enlarge its sphere.[1]

H. A. Taine's well-known introduction, in 1863, to his *Histoire de la littérature anglaise* breathes this new spirit. "Virtue and vice," he writes, "are products, like vitriol and sugar; and every complex phenomenon has its springs from other more simple phenomena on which it

---

[1] Essay on Sainte-Beuve, in *Etudes sur la littérature contemporaine*. My translation.

hangs. Let us then seek the simple phenomena for moral qualities as we seek them for physical qualities.'' When one finds the underlying moral phenomenon in the history of a man, a tribe, or a nation, one possesses the key to social development. For: ''In each case the mechanism of human history is the same. One continually finds, as the original main-spring, some very general disposition of mind and soul, innate and appended by nature to the race, or acquired and produced by some circumstance acting upon the race.''[2] To expose this basic principle by an internal and external examination is thus to explain all social phenomena—religion, philosophy, art. Of the last named Taine writes: ''A work of art is determined by an aggregate which is the general state of the mind and surrounding circumstances.''[3]

Ferdinand Brunetière wished to be the Darwin of literary criticism and thus to supersede its Cuviers.[4] ''You all know, at least in general,'' he tells his hearers in 1889, ''the meaning of the word and the idea of *evolution,* the success it has achieved—that it has, within a score of years, invaded, one after the other, all the provinces of learning and science, transforming or renewing them.'' A principle so fertile seems eminently applicable to literature: ''. . . . since we know what profit natural history, history, philosophy, have already drawn from it, I should like to discover whether the history of

---

[2] Translated by Henri Van Laun (A. L. Burt Company).

[3] *Lectures on Art,* first series, trans. John Durang (Holt, 1899), p. 87. Taine's words are: ''L'oeuvre d'art est determinée par un ensemble qui est l'état général de l'esprit et des moeurs environnants.''

[4] *L'évolution des genres dans l'histoire de la littérature: L'évolution de la critique depuis la renaissance jusqu'a nos jours* (Libraire Hachette), p. 18: ''. . . . nous pourrions dire qu'à la critique fondée sur les analogies qu'elle présente avec l'histoire naturelle de Geoffroy Saint-Hilaire et de Cuvier, nous nous proposons de voir si l'on ne pourrait pas substituer ou ajouter pour la compléter, une critique à son tour qui se fonderait sur l'histoire naturelle de Darwin et de Haeckel.''

literature and criticism cannot, in their turn, utilize it also."[5]

Sponsored thus by critics of eminence, the design of applying scientific methods to criticism was much discussed and found considerable favor in the closing decades of the century. The ''esthopsychology'' of Emile Hennequin, as propounded in his *La critique scientifique* of 1888, was designed to explain a work of literature ''from the point of view of the relations which unite its peculiarities with certain psychological and social phenomena, thus revealing the author's mind or nature.''[6] In Germany, Ernst Grosse attempted to view literature in accordance with the principles of Herbert Spencer in his *Die Literatur-Wissenschaft* of 1887. In England, John Mackinnon Robertson took up the question of a scientific criticism in his *Essays Towards a Critical Method* of 1889, and returned to it, in 1897, in his *New Essays Towards a Critical Method*. The visit of Bruntière to America, wrote Professor William P. Trent in 1899,[7] has caused the following question to be uppermost in the minds of our critics: ''Is there such a thing, men are asking themselves, as a science of criticism, or is all criticism at bottom merely the expression of an individual opinion, unsupported, or supported in varying degrees, by other individual opinions?'' In France again, in 1900, appeared G. Renard's *Méthode scientifique de l'histoire littéraire*. Moreover, writers on general aesthetics also felt the impulsion of the new methods. The idea of a scientific aesthetic is present in Herbert Spencer's *Principles of Psychology*, in Grant Allen's *Physiological Aesthetics* (1877), in Léon Dumont's *Théorie scientifique*

---

[5] *Ibid.*, 1 f. My translation.

[6] *La critique scientifique* (ed. 2; Paris, 1890), p. 21. My translation.

[7] *The Authority of Criticism, and Other Essays.*

*de la sensibilité* (1875), in Eugène Véron's *L'esthétique* (1878).

Before the year 1900 there were, then, numerous indications that literary criticism, following the example of many other branches of knowledge, was striving toward the adoption of more exact methods—was attempting, in short, to become a science. If the movement had succeeded, there would have been erected a system of criticism so definite and clearly marked that there would now be general agreement as to its character and principles. But no such result was effected. After the beginning of the present century, little was heard of further serious attempts. The entire project had very definitely failed.

Nothing could be more clearly demonstrative of this failure than the complete lack of agreement at the present time about the use of the term "science" in connection with literary judgments. Almost every variety of criticism has pretended to be or has been called "scientific"— by its friends or by its enemies. It is sometimes asserted that scientific criticism is merely exact and discriminating criticism of any sort. According to such a view, it is a degree and not a method of criticism. Sometimes, on the contrary, it is declared that the scientific critic refuses to discriminate—that he merely records everything he sees with aloof impersonality. Occasionally he is upbraided because he disavows all judgment upon a work of literature, contenting himself with pointing out its extra-literary relations; at times he is denounced because he *does* pass judgment—because he imagines that works of art can be ticketed and classified in a precise scale of merit.

Usually scientific criticism is declared to be the exact opposite of appreciative and impressionistic criticism. And the scientific critic is often accused of following in blind reverence the methods of the chemist and the biologist, and thus foolishly imagining that dogmatic, abstract, impersonal formulae, imposed from without, can be made to measure the unique and individual spirit which the author has breathed into his work. Yet Professor Irving Babbitt, in 1906, declared that "scientific" and impressionistic critics are fundamentally in agreement:

Now nearly all recent criticism . . . . may be roughly classified as either impressionistic or scientific; and it is in this doctrine of relativity that both impressionistic and scientific critics unite. To be sure, the doctrine assumes with the impressionist a form closer akin perhaps to true criticism than in the case of the scientific critic, whose method tends only too often to dehumanize the study of literature completely. . . . . The scientific critic for his part is interested solely in the way a book is related as a phenomenon to other phenomena, and when it is the culminating point or the point of departure of a large number of these relationships, he says that it is "significant". . . . . If the scientific critic in turn is urged to get behind the phenomena and rate a book with reference to a scale of absolute values, he absconds into his theory of the "unknowable".[8]

It is surely, one may say, a strange sort of "science" which has no other basis than chance, fleeting, personal impressions, and which evades attack by postulating an "unknowable"! Certainly, in every other field of knowledge, "science" means the direct opposite of tactics like these.

Yet Professor Babbitt's words find support. "Scientific" criticism has frequently been defined in terms of impressionistic or appreciative methods. In his *Shakespeare as a Dramatic Artist* (which bears the subtitle, *A*

---

[8] "Impressionist versus Judicial Criticism," *Publications* of the Modern Language Association of America, 1906:690 f.

*Popular Illustration of the Principles of Scientific Criticism*), the late Richard G. Moulton, after proclaiming himself an appreciative, as opposed to a judicial critic,[9] writes of his critical method: "Interpretation in literature is of the nature of a scientific hypothesis, the truth of which is tested by the degree of completeness with which it explains the details of the literary work as they actually stand." Such a method does not differ in any appreciable respect from that proposed by Professor Thomas Munro's *Scientific Method in Aesthetics* of 1928:

> Broadly conceived, an experimental attitude in aesthetics would imply making use of all possible clews to the nature of aesthetic experience, from a variety of sources and modes of investigation. It would imply putting all these clews together and on that basis working toward tentative generalizations through induction and the testing of hypotheses.[10]

Similarly, Miss Edith Rickert, in her *New Methods for the Study of Literature*, uses the term "scientific" in connection with her endeavors to discern within a work of literature various "thought patterns" and "tone patterns" whose discovery is to provide the following result: "The increased activity of the mind in the process of analysis will inevitably produce increased sensitiveness in the mental areas adjacent to the central activity."[11] Yet Walter Pater, the prince of impressionists, declared that the critic must always remain "at the focus where the greatest number of vital forces unite in their purest energy." There appears to be no distinct difference between these attitudes.

---

[9] For example: ". . . . the judicial attitude of mind is itself a barrier to appreciation, as being opposed to that receptiveness which is a first condition of sensibility to impressions of literature and art."

[10] Mr. Munro's essay is a volume in a collection called *An Outline of Aesthetics*, edited by Philip N. Youtz (Norton, 1928).

[11] P. 22.

In view of this entire situation, one is inclined to the conclusion that science and literary judgments are mutually antipathetic. Every opportunity, one may hold, has been afforded the project of a scientific criticism. Critics of eminence have attempted it; adequate time has been afforded for a definite result. The present complete disagreement over the very first principles of a scientific literary method merely emphasizes the failure of the whole project. One may add that it is wisest to avoid the term altogether. For "scientific" (like "psychological") has become obnoxiously popularized—so that one experiences a slight intellectual nausea at the very mention of the word.

Yet it is difficult to dismiss the question in this fashion. For science has successfully entered almost every department of human knowledge. The principles it establishes are clear and explicit. They are recognized by all workers in each field; they are taught to all who enter it. Accordingly, one feels that if literary criticism is an independent and reputable department of knowledge, then it too should be capable of receiving a scientific method. At any rate, there should be general agreement about the character of the demands a scientific criticism imposes. After these demands are known, then the possibility or impossibility of bringing criticism under their authority can be intelligently discussed. Then scientific criticism could be accepted or rejected; but there would at least be agreement as to *what* was being advocated or opposed.

We are led to believe, accordingly, that the present confusion is to a great extent the product of superficial, partial, popular, or incorrect notions of the character of general scientific method on the part of those who have attempted to apply such a method to literary criticism. Consequently the first step of all—if the project of a

scientific criticism were to be seriously undertaken—
would be to gain from those who have written on the
subject, a hint of the basic connotations of scientific procedure. The following excerpts appear to serve this purpose not inadequately:

The scientific investigator convinces others not by the plausi-
bility of his definitions and the cogency of his dialectic, but by
placing before them the specified course of experiences of search-
ings, doings and findings in consequence of which certain things
have been found. His appeal is for them to traverse a similar
course, so as to see how what they find corresponds with his
report.—John Dewey.[12]

Science is that unique human enterprise whose aim is precisely to correct and extend our knowledge of the general laws,
the truth of some of which we are assuming whenever we think.
To view science in this light is to appreciate its supreme importance in the advancing life of humanity. Reflection is the most
effective method of solving all human problems; scientific knowledge is the only sound foundation of reflection.—E. A. Burtt.[13]

Any concern or occupation, sufficiently important, purposive,
practical, explicit, and rational, which is based on knowledge or
its pragmatic equivalent, is science. This knowledge . . . . may
be the knowledge of natural phenomena either mechanical or
vital, of emotion, will and thought, of human affairs; of ways
and means, methods and procedures; of abstract relationships;
of God. It is a very loose term, yet it has a sharply distinctive
flavor: that of matter-of-factness and of detached rationality.—
Frederick Barry.[14]

The primary concern of these passages is obviously
to point out that scientific method is of the broadest and
most inclusive scope. It is not a trick, not a formula, not
an adventitious adornment. To employ it means no cring-
ing, obsequious aping of natural science. The chemist and

---

[12] *Experience and Nature* (1925), p. 35 f.
[13] *Principles and Problems of Right Thinking* (1928), p. 259.
[14] *The Scientific Habit of Thought* (1927), p. 7.

the biologist have no prescriptive right to it. They may indeed have obtained the most striking and readily apparent results by its use. But to think only of them when considering scientific method is to yield to a grossly popular specialization of the meaning of the term. Basically, then, scientific knowledge is that arrived at by open methods, so that any succeeding experimenter may review the steps by which it was attained. This implies, moreover, that it is knowledge based upon a standard as impersonal and as free from private whim or prejudice as is humanly possible—for only such knowledge can be verified adequately by another.

The desirability of erecting such a method within the realm of literary judgments is obvious. There need be little wonder that numerous critics have seriously gone about the task. It occasions little surprise, also, that the attribute of ''scientific'' has been claimed on behalf of numerous kinds and types of criticism. It is not surprising, finally, that experienced critics and writers on general aesthetics still harbor the hope of succeeding in giving a scientific character to their labors. Those hopes find frequent and ardent expression at this day. Thus T. M. Mustoxidi, in the introduction to his *Histoire de l'esthétique française,* wrote in 1920:

All the sciences have passed through an unsystematic and unverifiable state. We believe, without risk of being mistaken, that aesthetics also is certain in the near future to enter into a period in which actual experience will no longer contradict the conclusions of the mind. All systems evolve toward the only legitimate system, the scientific system—in one word, *science.* We shall call *aesthetics* that scientific system which the future will see—in which the facts of aesthetics will be patiently analyzed and explained.[15]

---

[15] My translation.

Writers like M. Mustoxidi see clearly that the benefits of applying scientific method to the fine arts would be immense. Furthermore, they are aware of nothing in the character of the method which would render such an application impossible. Their beliefs may be accepted as a favorable augury with which to initiate an attempt to formulate a scientific literary criticism. What, now, is the next step? For further guidance one may make a general survey of some department of knowledge which has been successfully invaded by a scientific method in order to observe the character of the conquest and the nature of the method erected. The natural sciences would be of little aid for this purpose. The labors of the chemist appear to differ so radically from those of the judge of literature that analogies between their two subjects would hold little significance. Between history and literature, however, one feels a closer connection. The two have a number of problems in common. Accordingly, it is interesting to view, even briefly and sketchily, the circumstances under which the department of history was won for the methods of science.

From its beginnings in what are now called myths and legends, history, during many centuries and in spite of many setbacks, came gradually to define its purposes and to mark the boundaries of its realm. In 1824 Von Ranke declared that history "will blos zeigen wie es eigentlich gewesen." Truth to fact in events of the past, and truth to fact only; here is the province of history. Such truth can be seriously approached only if the historian makes every effort to be unprejudiced and disinterested—to view his documents impersonally, to acquire a method external to the vagaries of a temperament, to arrive at results by methods which can be tested by others. The *Origin of Species* gave the historian a vastly extended conception of his subject matter. History was no longer to be the narrative of military actions displayed against a pictorial background. Its subject matter was clearly seen to consist of the study of the past actions of men living amid an entire environment of physical and social forces. And it is futile to attempt to describe human events except in terms of this entire environment. Thus it follows that, although its aim of recovering truth to fact concerning the past gives history an independent position in relation to human knowledge, the results of historical research must nevertheless be closely inter-woven with results attained in other fields of scientific knowledge—geology, biology, sociology, economics.

His purposes, his attitude, his subject matter thus defined, the historian was able to erect his working method. Its nature need be only sketchily indicated here. The historian wishes to reconstruct, in accordance with the demands of truth to fact, an incident of the past. The materials for the task are documents which are of vary-ing degrees of trustworthiness and which are often woe-fully incomplete in testimony. Nevertheless, by various recognized tests the historian labors to discover what he may pronounce to be all the known facts relative to the incident. By connecting these facts he reconstructs the incident. The gaps which are inevitably present are openly confessed and are allowed to remain as genuine elements of the situation, qualifying all judgments drawn therefrom. Finally, the historian has to classify his recon-structed incident, that is, to indicate its relations and its significance with respect to other incidents closely related in time or causal sequence, to events, situations, or social groups before and after and of greater or lesser impor-tance, and—according to the nature and importance of the incident—to closely connected subjects or fields of more inclusive scope. His entire task may, in fact, be said to consist of the establishment of successive series of *liaisons,* both of the facts within the incident, and of the incident itself with other incidents and, possibly, with more extensive subjects involving other divisions of human knowledge.

The new method met determined opposition from numerous history writers of the time. Carlyle, Macaulay, and Froude had other aims and other methods. They followed Sir Walter Scott, a novelist. They did indeed express high regard for historical records, and they wished, usually, to remain faithful to the facts as they saw them. Yet they desired something more. The materials in the sources were to be the foundation for dramatic and narrative re-creations of the past, in which would naturally appear the suspense, the swift movement, the vivid descriptions, which are the glories of literature. It was the aim of these writers to transport the delighted reader bodily into the past by creating for him a complete milieu, in the midst of which, in their habits as they lived, move famous characters actuated by human motives and torn by human passions. That their endeavors met frequent success is attested by the graphic vigor of many of their scenes—the flight of Louis XVI and of James II, the battle of the Boyne, the execution of the Queen of Scots.

It was soon recognized that the issue lay between two fundamentally opposed ideas, those of scientific history and of literary or romantic history. The objections raised by the literary historians and their followers fell into two general divisions. They contended, in the first place, that scientific history is scarcely history at all. For, since the days of Herodotus, there has been a glorious line of narrative historians. From it, history writing has acquired its aims and its character. Scientific history means the condemnation and extinction of this line; it means the death of Clio the Muse. And what has it to offer as a substitute? Scientific method causes the great figures of the past to appear as dull abstractions and musty documents, not as the living, breathing men which they actually were. It means the disappearance of great literary historians before a crowd of patient, uncomprehending grubs capable only of lifeless, technical monographs on minute subjects. It means, therefore, the extinction of history as a subject of popular interest with millions of delighted readers. They asserted, in the second place, that scientific history is, on its own terms, impossible of attainment. The historian himself is inextricably bound to numerous personal and group interests which cause all his judgments to become in some degree biased and prejudiced. More important still, the materials he works with are of such a nature that any definite, dependable knowledge is out of the question. The records of the past are themselves prejudiced, incomplete, and conflicting. It is ridiculous to speak of science in connection with them— to pretend that the historian, like the chemist, is able to work impersonally with unvarying and readily observable data.

The scientific historian was not demolished by these attacks. The first one, he noted, has been echoed in all fields whenever more exact methods were being established; it is the cry of the alchemist against the chemist, of the astrologer against the astronomer, of the phrenologist against the psychologist. If history would hold up its head among other departments of present day knowledge, it must adopt the soundest possible methods for attaining verifiable and cumulative knowledge. Otherwise history is merely an inferior imitation of the historical novel—an old wives' tale worthy of little respect from serious men in their workaday hours. The second objection, he declared, is the familiar one of the sophist. It is, in effect, a denial of the possibility of all human or earthly knowledge. That the scientific historian faces great obstacles is undeniable; that he should therefore abandon his task does not at all follow. Science continually faces obstacles in observing and classifying its data. Perhaps no two things on the earth—no two leaves in a forest—are precisely alike. And all earthly things are subject to change, confusion, decay, and destruction. The situation stresses the need for great pains and precautions, and for a method which can adapt itself to changing circumstances. It does not give rise, among scientists, to sentimental lamentations over the fallibility of human knowledge. In comparison with the historian the chemist is indeed fortunate. He creates his data in the laboratory; he re-creates them as often as he wishes; he is able to dissociate his labors from his personal or social prejudices; his results are usually of readily apparent application to life. But these advantages proceed entirely from the nature of his subject matter. The historian can never be a scientist as the chemist is one. But this does not mean that history cannot be a science: it means that history is not chemistry.

For his part, the scientific historian seized upon the deep and fundamental point at issue between his method and that of his opponents. The purpose of literature, of art, is to produce a complete and finished effect. Now the historical record is never full enough to justify this aim. What the literary historian is thus forced to do is to add something to the records to complete his picture. He begins to deal with conjectures, possibilities, probabilities; to clothe the bare and insufficient framework of fact with what could, or would, or should have happened; to arrange his materials in accordance with the literary demands for important protagonists, opposition of forces, suspense, dramatic action; to create a mood and an atmosphere which are to be accepted as the spirit of the time. In doing these things he not only neglects extremely important, though less picturesque circumstances, but he departs from truth to fact, which is the proper domain of history. His finished work is an entire whole to which nothing can be added. Thus literary historical study can make no progress with the centuries. The *History* of Herodotus is fully equal to that of Macaulay, for both are complete and entire. Literary history is perfected history. The literary historian is a metaphysician—the creator of closed, unchanging entities in which it is not possible to distinguish the elements drawn from fact from those created by poetic fiction. With the issue clarified in this way, the triumph of the new methods could no longer be doubtful.[16]

The spectacle of this civil strife—but lately concluded —among historians is highly instructive to anyone desirous of setting up scientific methods for literary criticism. It was already apparent, from the very nature of science, that a scientific critic must adopt a detached and impartial attitude, and that his results must be openly arrived at. But the survey of the conflict in the field of history has disclosed further principles of scientific

---

[16] I wish it to be noted that I am here sketching the course of a certain conflict which took place within the field of historiography in the later nineteenth century. I make no pretense of detailing the methods of historical research at the present time. My account follows those given by (among others) Bernheim's *Lehrbuch der Historischen Methode und der Geschichtsphilosophie*, Langlois and Seignobos's *Introduction to the Study of History*, J. T. Shotwell's *Introduction to the History of History*, J. M. Vincent's *Historical Research*. The ''literary'' view is discussed in Frederic Harrison's *The Meaning of History, and Other Historical Pieces*, and G. M. Trevelyan's *Clio, a Muse*.

method and has indicated the nature of the opposition against which such a method will be forced to contend. One may declare that additional characteristics of a scientific criticism will clearly be these:

1. It will be empirical. It will rest entirely upon data which can be observed, measured, and tested. It will oppose itself to any system which employs materials which lie outside the ordinary experience and observation of men.[17]

2. It will have an aim—a definite and specific purpose to which to address itself. It will have a subject matter which will provide the materials by means of which its aim shall be effected. These are possessions indispensable for any legitimate and independent department of knowledge.

3. Within the confines of its subject matter it will erect a logical system whereby the materials it employs will be directed toward the aims it wishes to attain. This system will be inductive; it will proceed from observed particulars to hypotheses and conclusions based on great numbers of them. Moreover, this method will, to a great extent, be classificatory in nature. It will form the standard by which works of literature can be judged.

Already at this point a criterion has been found by means of which the disabilities of the systems of Taine, Brunetière, and Hennequin may be pointed out. They all fail to erect, within the borders of the subject matter of criticism, a method by which may be reached results pertaining distinctively and exclusively to literature. The

---

[17] I am fully aware that there are writers (including, I believe, but few scientists) who declare that science is not entirely empirical nor entirely inductive. The nature and the involvements of this argument as they concern literature and literary criticism will be discussed at length in succeeding chapters of this work.

determinants of a work of literature, for Taine, are his famous "la race, le milieu, le moment." But these influences, certainly, must determine a large number of the products of human activity; there is nothing essentially literary about them. A work of literature explained on the basis of them is still very incompletely judged, for nothing is thereby concluded about its nature as literature nor its rank in merit among other works of its time. Brunetière took over from biology the idea of evolution and applied it to literature to explain the origin and development of literary *genres*.[18] But the subject matter of biology is entirely different in character from that of literary criticism. Surely, then, in transferring a principle from one field to another there is marked danger of the fallacy of false analogy. And if the principle is not basically literary, it will not adequately explain a work of literature. The esthopsychology of Hennequin wishes to follow all the paths leading from the work to regions lying outside of it. It therefore submits the work to a threefold analysis: an aesthetic, dealing with technique; a psychological, dealing with the author himself; and a sociological. But to consider a piece of literature in the totality of its relations is a task of impossible magnitude. If it were accomplished it could arrive at no result of especial significance or validity for literature, since it has posited no distinctively literary aims and has followed no critical method.[19]

---

[18] I do not make the mistake of asserting that Brunetière's theory of "l'évolution des genres" constitutes his entire significance as a critic. Numerous writers have uttered warnings against this error. For example, in his *La critique française a. la fin du XIXe siècle* (1925), A. Belis condemns those who consider the theory "non seulement comme une pièce importante de l'apport critique de Brunetière, ce qui serait assez juste, mais comme le tout de son activité, ce qui ne laisse pas d'être aussi faux que possible."

[19] This assertion is, I believe, proved by the results of Hennequin's own analysis of Victor Hugo's works in illustration of his principles.

It is evident that a valid scientific criticism must be founded on principles formulated from the subject matter of criticism—from literature itself. It must be a native growth. Its elements cannot be gathered within another department of knowledge and be imposed on literature *ab extra*. For the result is then a standard essentially foreign to literature, and its application means a dogmatism, a closed system, abhorrent to the spirit of science.

At this point, accordingly, the genuine difficulties begin. It is one thing to gain a general idea, by observing the qualities of general scientific method and by viewing some of its principles as they have been applied in other fields, of what the characteristics of a genuinely scientific literary criticism must be. But it is quite another matter to attempt to enter the realm of literature and to begin active operations therein. Several considerations, in fact, bar the way to such a direct entrance. In the first place, it has been declared that a scientific criticism must be empirical. But what are the precise demands, not of a superficial, but of a thoroughgoing empiricism? In the face of what opposition must it be maintained? Evidently, here is a preliminary matter whose importance cannot safely be ignored. A consideration of it leads one directly into the field of philosophy. In the second place, it has been asserted that the purpose of a scientific criticism must be to erect a method by means of which the merit of a work of literature may be determined. A critic employing the method will thus make judgments concerning the beautiful in literature. But through this fact another consideration becomes involved. What relation does the beautiful in literature bear to the beautiful in all art, and, indeed, to the beautiful in general? To deal with this necessary and important question is to enter the department of general aesthetics.

That a sound and firmly based literary criticism must be erected upon a groundwork of philosophy and aesthetics is an idea not at all new. G. H. Lewes wrote in 1865:

Criticism is to aesthetics what the practice of medicine is to physiology—the application to particular cases of the fundamental knowledge of the constitution and organisation of man, aided by a mass of particular observations. . . . . The necessity for a philosophical *fundus* . . . . to criticism . . . . cannot, one would think, for an instant be doubted.[20]

And, in 1897, John Mackinnon Robertson wrote:

It is the getting behind spontaneous judgment, the ascertaining how and why we differ in our judgments, that the critics have mostly left unattempted. And as this getting behind practice is strictly a philosophical process, they are indeed not to be blamed, as critics, for not attempting it; mental philosophy being one thing and literary and humanistic judgments another. But, for one thing, the attempt must be made by somebody, and one would fain see an experienced critic do it; and for another, the study of criticism cannot be finally satisfactory to people of philosophic mind unless it be relatable to philosophy like other human activities.[21]

Yet at its junction point with aesthetics is precisely where literary criticism is weakest. There are critics who deny any connection. Professor George Saintsbury, in the first chapter of his *History of Criticism*, writes:

The Criticism which will be dealt with here is that function of the judgment which busies itself with goodness or badness, the success or ill-success, of literature from the purely literary point of view. Other offices of the critic, real or so-called, will

---

[20] *The Inner Life of Art.* Quoted by R. P. Cowl, *The Theory of Poetry in England* (1914).

[21] "The Theory and Practice of Criticism," in *New Essays Towards a Critical Method.*

occupy us slightly or not at all. We shall meddle little with the more transcendental Aesthetic, with those ambitious theories of Beauty, and of artistic Pleasure in general, which, fascinating and noble as they appear, have too often proved cloud-Junos.

It is impossible to contest the justice of Benedetto Croce's animadversions on this passage:

Thus [he writes] is produced a book instructive in many respects but wholly deficient in method and definite object. What is lofty Rhetoric and Poetic, the theory of Criticism and literary taste, if not Aesthetic pure and simple? how can the history of these be compared without due notice of metaphysical Aesthetic and other manifestations whose interaction and development are the fabric of history itself?[22]

Professor Saintsbury deceives himself in thinking that philosophical and aesthetic implications can be ignored in literary criticism. His very denial of them is an aesthetic (and a philosophical) judgment which fixes his status as a critic and gives to his volumes on the history of criticism their well defined character.

Writers on general aesthetics do not fail to include literature among the arts with which their subject is properly concerned. On the other hand, they make little pretense of a full and adequate treatment of it. They regard the question of beauty in literature as only one— and scarcely the most important—division of beauty in all the arts. And they often feel that literature stands somewhat apart from the other fine arts. Painting, sculpture, architecture (and sometimes music) show themselves amenable to treatment as a unified group. Since literature is the recalcitrant member, it is often dismissed in a brief and summary manner.[23]

---

22 *Aesthetic,* trans. Douglas Ainslie (1922), p. 477.

23 In his *The Aesthetic Attitude* (1920), Professor H. S. Langfeld, after a long discussion of the principle of empathy in painting and sculpture,

Responsibility for this situation cannot be charged against the writer on aesthetics. It is the literary critic who has been negligent. It is his business to examine the foundations, the backgrounds, the implications of literary judgments. The task must be modestly done, for the field is huge and his main interests lie elsewhere. But he must seriously address himself to it if he would erect a method which is more than superficial in nature. The true approach to literary criticism, one must conclude, lies through the avenues of philosophy and aesthetics.

---

dismisses literature as follows (p. 142): ''Perhaps its importance may seem least evident in literature, but even here much of the effect is produced by the dynamic appeal both in the form and content of literary compositions, whether it is prose or poetry.''

# CHAPTER II

# THE ISSUE IN PHILOSOPHY

The Darwinian influence in philosophy is represented by pragmatism or instrumentalism.[1] Pragmatism takes as its starting point the world of ordinary human experience in its entirety—the whole acting and interacting world of persons, living things, inanimate objects, and forces. Of this world man is a definite part; he is bound inseparably with it, interacts with it, and, like it, undergoes change. However, since we are men and can look only through human eyes, the spectacle this world presents is that of a struggle between man and the non-human environment—or rather (since each of us is an individual) between *a* man and his entire environment, human and non-human. Moreover, since we are men, the environment has no importance or meaning except in its relations with us.

In order to sustain life man must satisfy certain physiological needs, desires, or instincts, notably those of food and sex.[2] These satisfactions must be obtained within, and at the expense of, the environment. It, in its relation to man, presents various aspects—some favorable, some indifferent, and some inimical. Apparently it does not exist for the express purpose of satisfying man's

---

[1] The latter term is, of course, associated particularly with Professor John Dewey. I prefer and shall employ the term ''pragmatism'' used by William James, although I am following Professor Dewey as the chief representative of this philosophy.

[2] The term ''instinct'' is a generalization built up from the observed workings of human behavior. Instinct does not exist anterior to or apart from experience.

desires. His life, therefore, is a constant struggle to
shape his surroundings in accordance with his wishes, as
these are determined by his needs. It is a grim and complicated business. The countless, muddled, animate and
inanimate elements of the continuum of the environment
form a complex mixture tending to elude and to resist
human control. In it, new aspects continually appear, and
new connections are formed; all is subject to constant
flux. What appears at one moment to be friendly and
desirable may, at the next, prove obstinately indifferent
or inimical. Moreover, the man's powers, which direct
the attack, are not only limited in extent, but may be
fatally weakened by illness, injury, or old age. Again, a
man never fights a lone battle. One instinct has forced
him into some sort of family relation. Other instincts,
and his various activities in accord with them, have impelled him into groups of his fellow-creatures. In this
way additional complications arise. For these groups are
as genuine an influence in the man's life as are his non-
human surroundings. The demands they make frequently
conflict with his individual desires. Thus he is imperatively called upon to make difficult compromises which
shall relate himself to a group and his various groups
with one another.

Of such a nature are the rules by which the game of
life is played. They must be accepted, willingly or un-
willingly, by every living human being. Further still,
every man, if he is to survive, must play the game with a
certain minimum of success. He must procure food, protect himself against excessive heat and cold, escape accidents, conquer diseases, avoid or defeat enemies. Within
individual groups or societies certain methods of action
or behavior, in connection with these various activities,
have been found to lead, under ordinary circumstances,

to the minimum of success necessary for survival. These actions are the means, the tools, by which the members of the group satisfy, in however imperfect a manner, their human needs or instincts. As children they have learned them from their elders. As adults they must accept them with little question, for they are faced with the continual necessity of labor for survival.

The results which the group attains by the use of the tools it employs, cannot afford satisfactory gratification to the desires of its members. The discrepancy between the what is and the what might be is too easily apparent; the imperfections of the tools are too clearly indicated by experience. The desires of men, founded on their needs, are directed toward winning over the environment as complete a victory as possible, in order to gain the security of an increased margin of survival against chance mishaps, illnesses, old age. The utmost (and so fantastic) goal of such desires would be to have organized the entire environment in the service of the wishes of men, and to have done it with such finality that it would remain in that condition without change or alteration. But the environment has always obstinately refused to undergo such an enormous discipline. The individual's victories over it are merely small, fleeting episodes in the course of his retreat to old age and extinction. Nevertheless, victories *are* possible. If things cannot arrive at perfection, they can at least be made somewhat more favorable to men than they are at present.[3] And even the smallest victory is gratifying to man's instinctive desires. Consequently if no settled group belief intimidates him, a man

---

[3] In other words, pragmatism, ethically, is *meliorism*. The attitude is derived from the observation that the environment can be made to serve progressively the expanding desires of men. It postulates no ''life force'' or other extra-experiential entity existing within the environment to cooperate with or guarantee human reasonings and desires.

will adopt a new or improved tool which has demonstrated its efficacy in superior dependability, in saving time or labor, or in increasing the product of labor. For the use of the new tool will mean for him a slight but highly pleasing victory in the fight; with it he will gain the increased expression or the freer and safer satisfaction of his desires.

It is important, therefore, to examine the processes by which one of these new tools is formed. The potential creator of it has been employing the traditional and accepted methods for attaining results in some special field of activity. For some reason he becomes dissatisfied with them. Perhaps his labors seem incommensurate with their product; perhaps he chances upon materials of which the existing methods take no account; perhaps the conditions under which the labor has been carried on suffer a sudden change—so that the older methods are no longer effective. In short, the prospective creator—the experimenter—is faced, at the beginning of his labors, with a problem. It is, moreover, a specific one. It directs his efforts to definite activity within some special department of human endeavor. In most cases it clearly indicates what the nature of a satisfactory result will be—a result which, by resolving the difficulty, will permit of activities in that department under circumstances more favorable to the laborer.

The experimenter is faced, then, by the first of the three steps necessary for his investigation. His materials concern an activity which is carried on within the general environment. In order that he may devote his entire attention to them alone, he must abstract them from the surroundings of which they are a part and take them into his laboratory. There he will be able to survey them minutely, and to discover and record the individual phenomena of which they are composed. This—the observation of data—is the business of his first step. The second step of the experiment results from the properties possessed by all the data in common. Obviously they unite in some way to effect a certain result; it is for this reason that they are constituent parts of the investigation. Perhaps under certain conditions they all react in a certain way; perhaps they can be pieced together into a pattern. At any rate, since they are all relevant to a certain activity, they have an element of unity in terms of that activity. It is the experimenter's task, in his second step, to state this unity in the form of a general principle or hypothesis. When he has done so, he must clearly recognize the nature of the result he has attained. It has been arrived at by abstracting and examining only a small part of the entire environment. In itself, therefore, it is of no necessary validity within that environment, for it represents only a fraction of a heterogeneous whole. A third and final step is thus clearly necessary. The hypothesis, a product of the laboratory, must be refitted into the frame from which it was extracted by being applied to the problem in the world which occasioned the experiment. The hypothesis is true and valid in the degree in which it meets this test—according to the degree of success with which it resolves the problem.[4]

The processes just described are those by which all tool-forming judgments are formed. The knowledge thus secured is the only dependable, verifiable knowledge known to man. It is that employed notably by the physical sciences—hence it has popularly acquired the name of "sci-

---

[4] I have here followed Dewey's *How We Think* (1910), G. H. Mead's "Scientific Method and the Individual Thinker," in *Creative Intelligence* (1917), and E. A. Burtt's *Principles and Problems of Right Thinking* (1928). I have reduced Professor Dewey's five steps (pp. 72–77) to three without altering the character of the process he describes.

entific" knowledge. Thus the attitude of pragmatism is that of science; it *is* the scientific philosophy.[5] Based entirely on human experience, it is thoroughly empirical.[6] It is experimental in character and it makes no pretense of producing perfect results. The best tool is simply demonstrably better than others constructed for the same purpose; in turn it may be superseded by a still better. The system is thus an open and cumulative one, providing for man's constant desire to construct increasingly better tools. The formation of a new tool necessitates merely a repetition of the three steps required for the old one, with this difference—that the first step will include new data, or will more closely scrutinize the old, so that the hypothesis

---

[5] I am aware that many think of naturalism and realism as the philosophic bases of science. I see no difference between what is called "naturalism" and pragmatism—except that the former inclines to narrow itself to the materials furnished by the natural sciences, whereas pragmatism includes all of experience. Moreover, the term "naturalism" seems to be a product of the ancient fight between nature and religion, or empiricism and idealism. In other words, it appears to be a name given to it by its enemies to brand it as restricted to *mere* "material" reality emptied of metaphysical content. This is particularly true of its older name, materialism. I conceive pragmatism to be the heir of materialism, naturalism, positivism—superior to them because it includes them and, from its broad conception of experience, challenges effectively all metaphysical contentions. This same situation holds, it seems to me, with respect to present day realism (Holt, etc.), which narrows its propositions to a dependence on fact, whereas pragmatism bases them on attempts to reach fact by hypothesis. Realism seems also to disregard the humanistic or social significance of propositions. Finally, it appears to be fixed in some of its positions through an ancient antithesis: conscious of the idealist's declaration that objects are made by thinking, it has been forced into the polemical opposite extreme of declaring that objects are *not* made by thinking.

[6] Since pragmatism has a wide and inclusive conception of "experience," its empirical character will differ from historical empiricism as set forth by Locke. The unfruitfulness of the latter resulted from the fact that it concerned itself almost exclusively with epistemology—with inquiries into the possibility of knowledge. To deal with the problem it made artificial divisions and isolations of sense data. Thus it was not truly empirical at all. And it was conscious of the opposition of rationalistic systems. Cf. Dewey, *Reconstruction in Philosophy* (1920), p. 90 f.: "When the isolated and simple existences of Locke and Hume are seen to be not truly empirical at all but to answer to certain demands of their theory of mind, the necessity ceases for the elaborate Kantian and post-Kantian machinery of *a priori* concepts and categories to synthesize the alleged stuff of experience."

formed in the second step will be of wider scope or of more exact outline. The new thus absorbs the old; yet it adds something, perhaps but a trifle, never before employed.

If knowledge is cumulative, can we say that man, in due course of time and by mathematical progression, will extract all possible meaning from his environment by observing and measuring all of it, by framing it into one coherent pattern, and by forging this into a gigantic tool to serve his interests? Such a final goal for humanity is, one may say, ludicrously impossible in view of man's present attainments. For human knowledge is constantly attended by human error, the great obstacle to consistent and rapid progress.

An error is something which injures or destroys the validity of the steps of the judgment-forming process. Human error has two general sources: in the first place, it may be that the experimenter *cannot* adequately observe his data. Perhaps he lacks proper training, or has had little experience; perhaps his powers are weakened or made unsound by disease or old age. Moreover, errors arise from human limitation. The very fact that the experimenter is a man—an animate creature dependent on a nervous system, subject to external influences and physiological changes, and limited in space and time—restricts the range and accuracy of his observations. For these reasons it is almost always impossible for an observer to examine all the data within even a limited field; for these reasons he often misses the significance of those that do enter the range of his vision. Finally, no one doubts that many classes of data still elude the observation of man—a situation which should cause, not sentimental lamentations, but renewed efforts. For here lies the region of future conquest.

A second source of human error lies in the fact that the experimenter often *will not* observe accurately. He may wilfully suppress or ignore data which do not accord with his personal and instinctive desires, and thus find only what he wishes to find. He may project his own human nature into non-human phenomena, ascribing to them feelings and impulses like his own. Again, error may arise from the circumstance that the observer is always a member of various groups of his fellow-creatures. A man is regularly the father of a family, a toiler at a vocation, a member of a community, a political party, a tribe or society, a nation. Membership in these groups is to him a very serious and a very real thing. An experimenter feels the demands each of his groups makes on him; he may (if his labors involve them) consider these demands as of more importance than the particular evaluation of phenomena on which he is engaged, and may thus refuse, more or less consciously and deliberately, to render any judgment which runs counter to what he thinks are the interests of his groups. Or, since group interests frequently conflict, he may exalt one group over the others and have this choice reflected in whatever judgment he makes. Again, his bias may result from his position within any one group. His social rank, whether high or low, may cause him to neglect, despise, or fail to see numerous important phenomena.

It is the great merit of the experimental or scientific method that is able to a large degree to protect itself from human error arising from the sources here mentioned. But ceaseless vigilance and slow, untiring effort are the price of protection. In fact, the dominant impression to be gained from a consideration of valid, workable human knowledge is the immense difficulty of acquiring it. It must be wrested from an indifferent, fluctuating, chaotic, entangled environment by one who has the patience and perseverance to encounter its dirt, decay, and flux. In order to make any headway in his labors, the experimenter must be thoroughly trained and experienced. He must be constantly vigilant against error. He must be capable of rigid self-discipline. He must allow the data to speak to him; he must not permit his wishes as an individual or as the member of a group to speak to the data. He must be prepared, finally, to arrive at results which, though workable, are essentially tentative and temporary. He must accept the fact that nothing external to human knowledge guarantees its validity or permanence.

To conclude that man's instinctive, universal desire[7] to attain the utmost satisfaction of his wishes can be realized in the world only by a patient working with the environment which results only in relative success, is to place a strong curb upon that desire. The road is long and difficult; no prospect of a perfect consummation of one's wishes is held out as a reward; the human qualities demanded are acquired only by mature faculties capable of a candid acceptance of the actual, visible conditions of life. It need occasion little surprise, consequently, that the majority of men of all times (including the present) have refused to face the situation.

The savage endows his non-human surroundings—animals, trees, rivers, mountains—with his own personality. He makes such objects human, or considers them the possessions of creatures with human characteristics. By his prayers he entreats them to serve his wishes; by his magic he attempts to compel them to do so. The advantage of anthropomorphizing the environment is that one has then to do, not with senseless objects or blind forces,

---

[7] This desire is based on a goal set up when the individual combines the choicest bits of his experience. It has no existence apart from experience.

but with men and women—beings whose motives may be understood and whose favors may be won. The impulse to personification has thus been a constant one. Even today it colors collective nouns like "state," "church," "justice," giving the impression that such words are things—that some substance or personality lies behind them.

Even the man who acknowledges the non-human nature of the environment feels, nevertheless, a considerable impulsion toward denying it more than partial validity. For he has discovered by bitter experience that it recognizes no liability with regard to man. It is indifferent to his most cherished wishes. It is not impressed by the dignity which man affects. To gain his ends he must follow it; it will not follow him. If the environment is thus unconciliatory, why not find something apart from it and superior to it which *will* guarantee the dignity and validity of man's wishes? This something will not have the distressing qualities of the tangible, visible surroundings. It will lie outside ordinary human experience and the daily environment; thus one will be able to gain knowledge of it in some more congenial way than that necessary to gain workable knowledge in the every-day world. It will be at rest, not in constant flux; thus men will be assured a fixed goal toward which to strive. It will be a complete whole readily comprehensible by human logic, not an imperfect and seemingly disjointed part. It will never become dirty, or decayed, or altered, but will remain perfect, pure, and unchanging—for no less a state would be worthy the dignity of man. It will be favorably disposed toward man's desires, and it will furnish him the assurance that these desires are not mere animal instincts but dignified and worthy aims capable of easy and rapid fulfillment.

Numerous other considerations impel man to this non-empirical "reality." The primitive man, noting that in his dreams enemies are easily killed, dead friends live again, and events generally follow an extraordinary succession, ascribes to that dream world the "wild experience" which perplexes him in his waking hours. The fear of death, of the unknown, of disease and old age, drives man in every stage of society to seek whatever security he can find; and when he discovers little reassurance in his surroundings, he seeks for it elsewhere. Again, every man during an extended period of his life has been guided, chastised, and comforted by a parent; likewise, every man recognizes in his daily activities the power and authority of other men. It is natural for him to transfer these relations to his surroundings—to seek the chieftain or parent of the earthly phenomena he encounters. Moreover, a man's (or a youth's) very ignorance of the nature of his environment may lead him beyond experience. Lacking intimate contact with the intractable qualities of the physical world, he may not see in it any impediment to his individual wishes for a prolonged and heightened satisfaction of desires.

The search for an extra-experiential something lying anterior to physical phenomena is the moving force of every religion, and it has been the occupation of philosophy from the time of Plato to within the present age.[8]

---

8 Cf. Dewey, *Reconstruction in Philosophy*, 23: "This is the trait which, in my opinion, has affected most deeply the classic notion about the nature of philosophy. Philosophy has arrogated to itself the office of demonstrating the existence of a transcendent, absolute or inner reality and of revealing to man the nature and features of this ultimate and higher reality. It has therefore claimed that it was in possession of a higher organ of knowledge than is employed by positive science and ordinary practical experience, and that it is marked by a superior dignity and importance—a claim which is undeniable *if* philosophy leads man to proof and intuition of a Reality beyond that open to day-by-day life and the special sciences."

In philosophy the business of conducting the search has received various names: idealism, transcendentalism, spiritualism, mysticism, phenomenalism, realism (in the sense that Plato is called a realist), rationalism, vitalism. These philosophical sects differ indeed in the motives which actuate their desire to find a metaphysical reality and in the ends they wish to attain. They may wish to understand life, to establish values, to explain the character of knowledge, to defend religious beliefs, to obtain release from an uncongenial environment. Yet they all conceive philosophy to be the quest of a genuinely real which lies behind an apparent real. They are thus basically identical. We may designate them by the common name of idealism.[9]

To look at the history of philosophy is to see the character, the methods, the problems of idealism. Plato[10] observed that individual things grow, decay, die, pass from one state to another, but that the general terms or species, which are their prototypes, remain (so he thought) fixed

---

[9] I prefer the term "idealism" to "metaphysics" or "absolutism." As to the propriety of using it in the inclusive sense I give to it, cf. W. E. Hocking, *Types of Philosophy* (1929), p. 325 f.: "Idealism has at times appeared as simply another name for philosophy itself. For philosophy in seeking to understand the world must assume that the world is intelligible; that thought can penetrate the opaque screen of nature,—which is to say that the reality which explains nature is not itself opaque in turn, but as understandable by thought as thought is understandable by itself. Idealism would thus be simply the philosophical form of that fundamental belief of all human aspiration that 'the things which are seen are temporal, but the things which are unseen are eternal'." Cf. also the assertion of Windelband, *infra*, p. 44.

[10] At the present time Plato is usually (though not always) called a realist. It seems to me that this classification does violence, if not to the term "realism," at least to Platonic tradition. Plato places his reality in a transcendent realm; all idealists, I am contending, do the same in effect. It is true that Plato's "ideas" are independent of human thinking. But the basic question is not, as I see it, the relation of the absolute to the human mind, but the character of the "real." To me the term "transcendental realist" would thus be acceptable.

and immutable. He was led, therefore, to ascribe genuine reality to these general terms, existing in their own right, which he called "ideas" or "forms." The individual things of the earth thus became for him mere unreal, imperfect copies of their ideas. They are, in fact, "non-being," and deserve little consideration. Descartes allows physical objects a genuine validity; within their own bounds, he concedes, they form a complete system. But there is also a separate mental realm of far superior significance. God (a spiritual entity) guarantees both realms. The test of reality is a clear and distinct mental idea. Spinoza also recognizes two realms—one of extension and one of thought. Both of these are attributes of one substance, God, who is thus pantheistically immanent in all things. With Leibniz the mental and physical are different phases in the existence of a spiritual monad, a mirror of the universe, complete in itself because lacking any doors or windows for the ingress of outside influences. With Kant ultimate reality consists of things-in-themselves which are represented by sense data. Only the sense data, however, are known to the human mind. The mind itself has two faculties, the sensibility and the understanding. The former apprehends the sense data and, by a special power of its own, brings them within time and space. The understanding has two subfaculties. The first, judgment (*Verstand*), arranges the sensations in accordance with certain a priori concepts or categories; the second, reason (*Vernunft*), unites the judgments under the guidance of regulative ideas (like "God" or "the soul"), which are transcendent entities (noumena). In this complex process, it may be observed, numerous extra-experiential entities are involved—the human mind, the innate categories, the thing-in-itself, the absolute or universal. With Hegel the absolute mind does not remain, as with Plato, in another realm. On the contrary, it unfolds itself in the environment; it *is* the whole process of life. It is the unity of which all finite reality is a manifestation.

Opposed theoretically to the idealists has been a long line of empiricists, whose basic intentions are to allow no reality outside the world of sense experience. Yet these philosophers have been regularly drawn into the prevailing idealism of their day. Aristotle conceived physical objects as combinations of the absolutes "form" and "matter." Yet, since this combination is always realized in an actual physical object, the conception parts with empiricism only in that Aristotle includes a pure form, God, as the summit of his system. His philosophy is characterized by his insistence that earthly objects are real and that the mind knows them alone. Yet he also accepts an "active intellect," which, writes an authority in discussing the Aristotelian Thomas Aquinas, is "a special spiritual power within me which 'shines upon the sense data, and makes them capable and ready to produce a knowledge in which reality is deprived of all its concrete and individual figures'."[11] Although Francis Bacon was the avowed opponent of metaphysics, yet his own experimental method is set in a metaphysical frame. He grants fixed universals, but he wishes to arrive at them, not by innate powers, but by considering a sufficient number of particular and mundane copies of them. John Locke will have thought dependent entirely upon sensation. And yet the mind never knows the object directly

---

[11] Maurice De Wulf, *Mediaeval Philosophy, Illustrated from the System of Thomas Aquinas* (1922), p. 25. His quotation is from the *Summa Theologica.*

and immediately; it knows only the idea it has of the object. What assurance is there, then, that the idea is like the object? And what need is there, as Berkeley pointed out, for an object at all?[12] The conclusion to be drawn from such instances as these is that the empiricists of the past centuries—the philosophers who should have built up a system basically opposed to that of idealists— were very imperfectly empirical (being thus not empirical at all), and were consequently unable to make any effective challenge of idealism.

What, now, does the pragmatist say of the idealist's system, which so completely opposes his own?

He will say, in the first place, that the motives which actuate idealists are natural, universal, and essential. All men wish to bring their environment into a state which answers to man's ideas of what an environment should be—a state of complete subservience to his wishes. Upon this impulse, it has been seen, depends the progress of civilization. But before progress can actually take place, it is essential that the impulse be harnessed—that it be made to solve problems in the world through the construction of the steps by which all mundane knowledge must be achieved. This does indeed fetter the impulse, but it is of little avail to inveigh against the hard conditions of life. They are unsatisfactory, but they cannot be basically altered through human agency. Now the idealist thinks he *can* change them by digging under or soaring above our world to another realm. What he does thereby, the pragmatist says, is to construct a fiction, a myth, a dream.

The dream, the pragmatist will freely grant, is a natural and splendid one. It *should* be true. To get behind

---

12 See also *supra*, p. 27, note 6.

an environment indifferent to the affairs of men in order
to find a sympathetic mind like our own but infallible,
which pervades and animates it; to pass over change,
confusion, dirt, decay, to a realm wherein unchangeable,
absolute essences maintain unmarred their crystal purity;
to spy, through the ceaseless, disheartening toil of life,
a goal of calm and rest where all things "stay put" and
retain their benevolence toward man; to feel, after experiencing failures in earthly affairs, that there is a place of
compensation for those failures, which assures men that,
whatever their earthly fates may be, they do not live and
strive in vain—who does not feel drawn by such mighty
and instinctive human desires? The dream refreshes the
toiler and encourages him amid disappointments. It
should be part of the life of every human being. But to
classify the absolute realm as a useful and beautiful
fiction will by no means satisfy the idealist.

The idealist's first undertaking, the construction of an
other-worldly realm, is a task of little difficulty. It is
easy for a philosopher in his study to ignore this world,
and the universal desires of man clearly point the way
to another. The flight aloft is rapid and congenial. The
idealist's troubles begin, however, after he has attained
his ideal world. For he will by no means admit that this
transcendent world is a dreamland merely. He asserts
that all the essences therein are real and genuine, and
that they enter into any valid system of human knowledge
and any judgment of earthly values. He must therefore
connect his ideal world with the world in which we live;
he must explain it, that is, in terms of ordinary human
experience. In short, he is obliged, while clutching tightly
to the treasures amassed above, to attempt to descend to
the earth. It is this descent which subjects him to his
great difficulties. He finds himself facing a stubborn

dualism.[17] He must deal with and attempt to reconcile two orders of existence. The one, the ideal, contains essences which are eternal, pure, and unvarying; the other, the ordinary world, contains objects whose characteristics are the direct opposite of these. How shall the two opposing worlds be joined, since they must be made to work together? How shall one pass from the metaphysics to the physics? Under what terms shall man, the knower, be granted knowledge of both these realms?

To solve this eternal dilemma, idealists have employed various tactics. To some of them the world of ordinary reality becomes "non-being," "appearance," a mere superficial phenomenon. The pragmatist feels that such a view is guilty of rank ingratitude toward ordinary experience. For, as Professor Dewey writes:

[T]he contents as well as the form of ultimate Absolute Experience are derived from and based upon the features of actual experience, the very experience which is then relegated to unreality by the supreme reality derived from its unreality. It is "real" just long enough to afford a hint of the essential contents of the latter and then it obligingly dissolves into mere appearance.[14]

Another group attempts to provide a means for harmonious intercourse between the two realms. Descartes rather lamely points out the pineal gland as the meeting

---

13 I am committed in the present work to the assertion that all idealism is based on a dualism—on the fundamental assumption of two orders of existence. It is to be noted, however, that the particular idealistic system, founded on this bifurcation, will regularly declare itself to be monistic (or even pluralistic). Cf. Hocking, *Types of Philosophy*, 242: "Idealism appears historically as the type of philosophy to which dualism has naturally led the course of thought. For as dualism has arisen each time because of an exceptionally vivid intuition of what the mind is, the meaning of that intuition cannot be realized by resigning the mind once more to inclusion within nature,—one of its own objects; but rather by achieving a new and revolutionary monism in which the mind takes nature into itself."

14 *Experience and Nature*, 61.

place of mental and physical. Spinoza refers both of them back to God, who thus becomes a substance composed of two mutually exclusive attributes—matter (extension) and thought (inextension).[15] Leibniz asserts that a pre-established harmony introduces an order into the life of the monads. One may also postulate a neutral substance with a double aspect—or employ any other example of a *petitio principii* in attempting to explain an unknown by postulating another unknown.

But one need not keep the absolute in a realm aloof from the ordinary world. One may attempt to insert it into the "material" world at some point and so associate it directly with the act of knowing. Two *loci* present themselves: the knower and the realm of ordinary experience itself.

The "mind" of man seems to serve the idealist's purpose well. It is impossible to observe the mental processes at work in the manner in which one observes the working of the physical environment. What objection, then, can the empiricist make if the mind of the knower is made the locus of the dualism which the idealist's system carries with it? One may have a superior mind, or soul, closely related to the ideal world, and a lower mind joined to the body and to physical objects. One has then a dualism which can be expressed by the use of any number of terms or metaphors. Plato explains the dual mind by his famous metaphor, in the "Phaedrus," of the chariot driver and the two steeds. Aquinas, following Aristotle, contrasts the ordinary *intellectus possibilis* with the spiritual *intellectus agens*. In the system of Kant, the sensibility produces the sense

---

[15] I here describe Spinoza's "thought" negatively in order to point out the opposition.

data; the understanding, with its innate categories, is in touch with the universals. In other systems of this kind, knowledge a priori is ranged against knowledge a posteriori, the instinct against the intelligence, the unconscious mind against the conscious mind.

To the pragmatist (in philosophy) and the behaviorist (in psychology)[16] the dual mind postulated by certain idealistic systems constitutes an arbitrary assumption which is utterly untenable. It is based, they declare, upon antique and discredited psychology. One can no longer speak of a "mind" and localize its activities in the brain; one must deal with the entire sensori-cerebro-motor system with its ganglia in all parts of the body. The mind (if one wishes to employ the term at all) can be thought of only in connection with its activity and can be defined only in that connection—as "an instrumental method of directing natural changes."[17] By considering it (or some professed part of it) apart from experience and the environment, the idealist makes "mind" (just as the introspectionist makes "consciousness") an absolute and independent entity. And immediately a further dualism is imposed upon the world of ordinary experience—a dichotomy of knowing and being.[18]

---

16 The pragmatist is, on the psychological side, inevitably a behaviorist— the opponent of the vitalist or introspectionist. His behaviorism cannot, however, be that professed by Mr. John B. Watson. The issue between the Watsonian and the (as I think) valid behaviorism is the question whether or not a man can learn through experience. Watson's man is a robot who twitches his muscles, but who draws no lessons, apparently, from his previous activities. His system ignores the face value of experience in order to resolve it into something else—into physics. For a discussion of this question, see M. C. Otto, "Instrumentalism," in *Philosophy Today* (1928).

17 Dewey, *Experience and Nature*, 160. Since the term undoubtedly possesses a pronounced vitalistic flavor, I shall employ it only when referring to the principles of idealism.

18 Thus emerges the famous epistemological problem: Is human knowledge possible? According to the terms in which it is stated, this problem is,

With Hegel and his disciples (F. H. Bradley, Bosanquet, Croce) the absolute idea unfolds itself in the environment. On earth there is to be no dualism of spirit and matter, of subjective and objective. For the spiritual absolute, or reality, becomes the process and activity of life. Accordingly, the world of experience, which is the manifestation of the absolute, must become a logically articulated system as the absolute attains to self-consciousness. The oppositions, antagonisms, and discrepancies that exist within it may be reconciled by a theory of the identity of opposites[19]—in Hegel by a triad of thesis, antithesis, synthesis, expressing the dialectical process of the absolute idea. The function of the absolute is thus to synthesize and reconcile all earthly differences.[20] Since the absolute alone is reality, these differences must be unreal appearances. The truth is the self-consistent whole which is expressed by the absolute. Error is partial truth.[21] It follows that all thinking by man results in partial truth, since it can express only a fragment

---

the pragmatist believes, a cul de sac from which no emergence is possible. Professor Dewey writes of the situation (''Philosophy'' in Beard, *Whither Mankind*, 1928): ''There is something ironical in the very statement of the problem of the possibility of knowledge. At the time when science was advancing at an unprecedented rate, philosophers were asking whether knowledge was possible.''

[19] The resemblance of the Hegelian system to that of Spinoza has been often remarked.

[20] Cf. Bradley, *Appearance and Reality* (ed. 2, 1897), p. 455 f.: ''There is but one Reality, and its being consists in experience. In this one whole all appearances come together, and in coming together they in various degrees lose their distinctive natures. The essence of reality lies in the union and agreement of existence and content, and, on the other side, appearance consists in the discrepancy between these two aspects. And reality in the end belongs to nothing but the single Real. For take anything, no matter what it is, which is less than the Absolute, and the inner discrepancy at once proclaims itself and falls apart into two jarring factors.''

[21] *Ibid.*, 192.

of the totality of the absolute. Among the degrees of
truth and reality, that is least fragmentary which most
completely attains the coherence of the absolute system.[22]

This system frees itself from none of the characteristic idealistic difficulties. We must note, in the first
place, the complete dependence upon an absolute which
transcends finite experience. When the attempt is made
to interpret experience in terms of this absolute, experience undergoes a total inversion. It now contains none
of the stuff of ordinary experience. There is no reason
for knowledge; for all of its members are already logically related and categorized, and its oppositions all
fused and resolved. Moreover, there is no place for a
knower; he is a mere spectator. And there is no test
of truth that can be stated in terms, not of the absolute,
but of man. Finally, the dualism of spirit and matter
can *still* not be resolved except by the expedient of declaring matter to be "mere appearance" or non-being. Such
a declaration is made, for example, by Bradley:

> The physical world is an appearance; it is phenomenal
> throughout. It is the relation of two unknowns, which, because
> they are unknown, we cannot have any right to regard as really
> two, or as related at all. It is an imperfect way of apprehension,
> which gives us qualities and relations, each the condition of and
> yet presupposing the other. And we have no means of knowing
> how this confusion and perplexity is resolved in the Absolute.
> The material world is an incorrect, a one-sided, and self-contra-
> dictory appearance of the Real. It is the relation of two unknown
> things, things, which, to be related, must each be something by

---

[22] *Ibid.*, 364: "Hence to be more or less true, and to be more or less
real, is to be separated by an interval, smaller or greater, from all-inclusive-
ness or self-consistency. Of two given appearances the one more wide, or
more harmonious, is more real. It approaches nearer to a single, all-
containing individuality. To remedy its imperfections, in other words, we
should have to make a smaller alteration. The truth and fact, which to be
converted into the Absolute, would require less rearrangement and addition,
is the more real and truer."

itself, and yet, apart from their relation are nothing at all. In other words it is a diversity which, as we regard it, is not real, but which somehow, in all its fulness, enters into and perfects the life of the Universe. But, as to the manner in which it is included, we are unable to say anything.[23]

The entire program of interpreting finite experience as an absolute experience results, the pragmatist asserts, in the destruction, not only of experience, but of a knower, and consequently of a test for truth. What remains is a Neo-Platonic mysticism practically identical with that of Plotinus.

The pragmatist must conclude that the idealist's whole case rests on his assertion that there are two realms of existence. There is the ordinary world (even if it exists only to be explained away). But there is also a magical essence, a transcendental reality, an other-worldly spiritual realm. It is entirely different from the reality of every-day experience. And knowledge of it cannot be attained by observation and experiment applied to scientific problems arising in the environment. Since the absolute transcends the environment, it must be known by direct intuition, by revelation, by a feeling of wholeness. A knowledge arising in this way seems to lie completely outside the criticism of the empiricist. Obviously a knowledge which is entirely different from earthly knowledge cannot be judged directly by earthly knowledge. How, then, can the idealist be attacked on his own grounds? The empiricist cannot enter the realm of the absolute, but he can point out what he believes to be the insoluble problems and disastrous effects which are produced when idealism is accepted as a valid philosophy.

---

[23] *Ibid.*, 265 f.

The idealist conceives the entire task of philosophy to be the search for metaphysical reality. He accuses the pragmatist of begging the most fundamental questions, declaring that the latter assumes a world of beings without inquiry about their origin—without inquiring what Being is. The following words are typical:

Immanent Positivism of this kind is . . . . nothing less than a denial of the possibility of philosophy, for it rejects our essential stimulus to research. As history shows, our irrepressible impulse is to seek the metaphysical reality, and in this sense philosophy is necessarily a process of transcendental thinking. If it were true that this is only a continual aberration, a self-deception of the scientific [!!] mind, philosophy is impossible, and we might as well give up the name with the reality. If there is no absolute realm, there is no such thing as philosophy, which is supposed to deal with it. In that case we should have only the various empirical sciences; and philosophy ought to be too proud to give its name to a synthesis in which we might gather together the most important facts of these sciences.[24]

The pragmatist replies that he does not evade metaphysics but challenges it. The true evasion is to flee from the world to a dream, an *ignis fatuus* which lies in a realm of absolute perfection. He denies that the experience of men supports a division between "real" and "ideal"—a division which ascribes to each a separate realm of existence. Values grow up within human experience and are realized therein, subject always to future modification. End and means are inseparably connected, the attained end becoming material or means for the construction of a new end. Thinking arises from the observed and recorded actions and changes of objects; it is the instrument for further observation and regulation of those actions and for the determination of the rates of change.

---

[24] Wilhelm Windelband, *An Introduction to Philosophy*, trans. Joseph McCabe (New York, 1921), p. 39.

The environment, moreover, does not support perfection. As a man the idealist knows that knowledge does not have to be perfect in order that it may be called knowledge at all. He has never, as a man, encountered perfect knowledge. He knows, however, that tools which are eminently "workable" can nevertheless be produced. He himself has made many errors and has experienced many failures. But he knows that his errors have been real and valuable elements in giving direction and progress to his schemes of action. Again, the idealist, as a man, accepts the flux and change of the environment every moment of his life. Like every other person, he orders his life in accordance with it. He knows that his linen becomes soiled, that food decays, that fences break down and gutters are eaten through with rust, that his friends grow old, become ill, die. He would be dumbfounded if these changes did *not* occur. He knows, consequently, that lack of perfection does not mean lack of reality or imply non-existence. He is fully aware that iron is eminently useful despite the fact that it will rust. The process may be retarded by the use of paint, or the builder may plan to replace the rusted bar after a certain time—all of which means that whenever iron is used its corrosion is a genuine element of the situation.

When the idealist makes his absolute an integral part of the knowledge process and thus endeavors to insert it into the knower or the experience known, the result, the empiricist declares, is that an irresolvable dualism springs up. There are set up two water-tight compartments which experience does not support. One of these is an ideal or spiritual world reached only by contemplation, intuition, insight, inspiration, indefinable and magical sensation. Herein are supposed to reside all the real values which make up the social life of mankind—

truth, beauty, the good, justice, and so forth. The other is the "material" or "physical" world, which is composed, it appears, only of objects furnishing sense data, and which is blind, chaotic, unstable, and mutable. In short, it is the world of ordinary experience arbitrarily denuded of practically all the values of importance to man. The idealist's "matter" is thus a purely arbitrary conception whose content accords neither with common experience nor with scientific usage.[25] And it follows that there can be no communion between these two realms. The ideal end is eternally divorced from the earthy means. No "material" value can ever realize its perfect "ideal" prototype. Thus philosophy can have little to do with daily life, and the philosopher must deny the reality and validity of the conditions he is obliged to accept as a human being. The effect on human conduct is even worse. For, on these terms, a man's daily "earthly" activities are stripped of ethical and social values. He can thus be careless of ethics in the affairs of his daily life provided that he also pause at times to contemplate the indescribable vision of ideal morality which comes, so it is believed, from the spiritual world. In the words of Profesor Dewey:

[U]sually a compromise is worked out, by which a man for his working-hours accepts the philosophy of activity for some future result, while at odd leisure times he enters by conventionally recognized channels upon an enjoyment of "spiritual" blessings and "ideal" refinements.[26]

It may be granted that the characterization just made of the idealist's two compartments of existence is a simplification which, to some extent, constitutes a caricature

---

[25] When the idealist speaks of "materialists," he means, I believe, empiricists to whom he ascribes his own conception of "matter."
[26] *Human Nature and Conduct*, 275.

of idealism. It describes the methods of the camp followers rather than those of the leaders. Great numbers of astute thinkers have been, and are, idealists. But this fact is an added warning for the empiricist. For, if the idealist's problem were valid, these thinkers would have solved it. Since they have not, it is logical to question the terms in which they have stated it. It is the method of idealism, not the reasoning powers of idealists, that the pragmatist denounces. Moreover, the chief weakness of idealism is precisely that it cannot protect itself against caricature. Its dualism has become fixed in popular thought. That fact enables any slovenly thinker, by using counters like "soul," "body," "spiritual," "material," "mental," "physical," to set up an easy but completely fictitious duality between supplementary elements and thereby to confuse and obstruct human thought. The idealist opens the door, also, to the *Schwärmerei* of mysticism, ranging from the ecstacies of Plotinus to the visions of the epileptic and the lunatic. One has only to declare that knowledge of the absolute comes by way of mystic revelation. Then no one can be excluded if, by his own assertion, he has seen the vision. And there is no standard by which the deceptions of the fraud and the cheat may be exposed and rejected. Intelligence, training, experience go for nothing; they seem, in fact, to be hindrances to pure and simple-minded clairvoyance.

And every type of idealism is marked by the fatal weaknesses emphasized by caricature. The entire method can set up no definite tests for truth and error. If truth is absolute, error vanishes—as do also all relative truths. If reality lies in some manner apart from what is empirically given, then ordinary reality can have no reputable status in its own right. Some idealists may attempt to

honor the facts of "material" experience; others may
dismiss them as unreal appearance. The issue is one of
individual taste alone. No idealist can grant validity to
the things and forces of the environment; it was his conviction of their incompleteness or unreality which led him
to become an idealist. This means, the pragmatist declares, that every idealist is an opponent of scientific
knowledge. It is not only that such knowledge is to him
an inferior and helpless affair—but he also needs a mystery in order to insert his absolute into the knowledge
process. This necessity causes him to seek out some
phenomenon, like the "mind," which has resisted empirical description. But the advance of scientific definition
and analysis of such phenomena leads to the inevitable
retreat of the idealist.

There are many indications at the present time, the
pragmatist believes, that the issue in the field of philosophy has thrown the idealist on the defensive. This is
not to say, however, that idealism will quickly vanish
from the field. The motives which actuate many of its
adherents are those natural for mankind to possess: the
desire to support religious beliefs, to seek a better world
to relieve the miseries of this, to gain immediate knowledge of reality in a manner unburdened by necessities of
long training and watchful labor. Idealism owns all of
the attractions which literary fictions have for men.
Indeed, the pragmatist declares that idealism is a *literary*
philosophy. The idealist's principles produce results
parallel in many respects to those of the literary or
romantic historian (who may be called the idealist of
history). He is animated by the literary aim of attaining artistic perfection. Nothing can be added or subtracted from his philosophy, and it makes no provision
for error. Consequently, one idealistic system is fully

equal to another. Like the literary historian, the idealist in philosophy takes a number of empirically established data and fills out their interstices with "spirit"—with the aim, in some cases, of showing what a world should or could or would be if human desires were granted their ultimate satisfactions. Under these circumstances, it clearly appears that any compromise between empiricist and idealist is impossible. One cannot have an empirical philosophy which contains even the slightest tinge of idealism. For the embarrassing thing about idealism is that it proves too much. Allow but one absolute essence behind or above the environment and you have proved everything at one stroke. You no longer have a real need for the environment.

The twentieth century has witnessed thus far, in philosophical circles generally, a definite revolt against dualism.[27] Idealism has felt this reaction. The most popular present day idealism seems to be that of Hegel—the very system which attempts to hide its basic dualism by denying distinct realms of subjective and objective, and by interpreting the environment as a manifestation of the absolute. The fact that idealism has veered toward a form in which it appears least like itself and least ostensibly antagonistic toward empiricism, seems to the pragmatist a definite indication of its present defensive status.

---

[27] Cf. A. O. Lovejoy, *The Revolt Against Dualism* (1930), p. 3: "The cleavage of the universe into two realms having almost no attributes in common, the divorce between experience and nature, the isolation of the mental from the physical order, has seemed to not a few representative and influential thinkers to be unendurable in itself and the source of numerous artificial problems and gratuitous difficulties which can be solved only by denying their presupposition. Thus the thing above all others needful for philosophy in our time has appeared to many acute intelligences to be to get rid of this 'bifurcation of nature'—without falling into the idealism or phenomenalism which had hitherto seemed the only alternatives, and which, in fact, were in their historic genesis mainly consequences of the same fundamental preconceptions."

The efforts of idealism to approach empirical methods sometimes result in a confusion of the issue at stake. The system of Henri Bergson furnishes a case in point. Bergson is an idealist (or vitalist) who has, in usual fashion, used a phenomenon difficult to examine empirically as the cover under which to introduce his metaphysical system. The pragmatist observes that a man's actions can to a large extent be classified around certain desires universally felt and acknowledged. He calls these desires "instincts." That he may differ with another pragmatist in his enumeration of them is a matter of little importance. What *is* important is that he always uses the term empirically. It is this term into which Bergson reads the familiar spiritual content. He ranges "instinct" with what he calls "intuition," and he opposes it to what he calls "intelligence." In the words of H. M. Kallen:

By "intuition" Bergson designates "that kind of intellectual sympathy by which one sets oneself in the interior of an object in order to coincide with the very reality of that object, with its uniqueness, with that in it, consequently, which cannot be expressed." The knowledge so attained is absolute, inasmuch as mind and object coincide. In this coincidence the "point of view" disappears. The whole object is apprehended at once in its innermost reality, its perfection, its infinity, its simplicity. Symbolize, analyze, and you shatter this simple intuition; absolute knowledge gives way to relative knowledge; "points of view" become important. All you attain with your symbols and analyses, however, is merely the bringing to terms of the unknown with the known, the generation of an infinite collection of predicates that are intended to bring back a unique and simple subject, and can never, never attain their original unique unity of interpenetrating qualities in which each is all and all are each.[28]

---

[28] *William James and Henri Bergson* (1914), p. 70 f.

The idealism of Bergson's system stands clear and self-confessed. His terms "intuition" "intelligence" express the same dualism as the "mental," "physical," "soul," "body," "reality," "appearance," of other idealists. It is therefore with a feeling of surprise that one contemplates the fact that Mr. Bertrand Russell, in his *Mysticism and Logic,* classes together as "evolutionism" the principles of Nietzsche (an undoubted romanticist), of Bergson, and of pragmatism![29]

Another possible source of confusion arises from the very success which scientific methods have achieved. The spectacle of the idealist trimming his sails in the direction of pragmatism is a frequent one. One has thus to be exceedingly wary of metaphysical systems which loudly proclaim that they are thoroughly empirical or scientific. S. Alexander, for example, conceives of existence as consisting of various *empirical* levels brought about by the *nisus* generated from the matrix of Space-Time, which contains the stuff of reality. Along these levels are generated matter, life, mind, and God. Thus:

Within the all-embracing stuff of Space-Time, the universe exhibits an emergence in Time of successive levels of finite existences, each with its characteristic empirical quality. The highest of these empirical qualities known to us is mind or consciousness. Deity is the next higher empirical quality to the highest we know; and . . . . at any level of existence there is a next higher empirical quality which stands towards the lower quality as deity stands towards mind. . . . . There is an empirical quality which is to succeed the distinctive empirical quality of our level; and that new empirical quality is deity.[30]

---

[29] In *Mysticism and Logic, and Other Essays* (1921). The essay first appeared in the *Hibbert Journal* of July, 1914. Professor R. B. Perry follows Russell's classification in his *Philosophy of the Recent Past* (1926), p. 168 ff.

[30] *Space, Time, and Deity* (1927), 2:345.

When one asks what is the quality of the energy which causes the various "empirical" levels to emerge, one discovers a self-sufficient energizer—that is, the familiar absolute. The hierarchy of levels mysteriously related has no right to the term "empirical."

The situation is further illustrated by the methods of Sigmund Freud. It is probably unnecessary at the present time to undertake seriously to combat Freudian psycho-analysis. It was never generally accepted by psychologists, and a large number even of its supporters have abandoned it. Significantly enough, psycho-analysis was accorded its most enthusiastic reception by journalists, who popularized several of its catchwords, such as "complex." What is noteworthy about Freud's methods is their "scientific" pretensions—their loudly heralded "scientific" nature. Behind these proclamations lies the familiar business of insinuating a psychic realm by a metaphysical interpretation of an empirically negative phenomenon—in this instance the "unconscious." The pragmatist and the behaviorist make use of the term, for obviously one is not actively aware at any specific time of all that one knows and has experienced.[31] With them it has a strictly negative, not a positive content; it means literally *un*conscious. For Freud the "unconscious" is a mind force, a psychic realm. He speaks of "unconscious ideas," and his entire system is grounded on a dualism of conscious and unconscious ideas.

---

31 Cf. Dewey, *Experience and Nature*, 7: "Because intellectual crimes have been committed in the name of the subconscious is no reason for refusing to admit that what is not explicitly present makes up a vastly greater part of experience than does the conscious field to which thinkers have so devoted themselves."

With the psycho-analysts, writes A. Wohlgemuth:[32]
"The 'Unconscious' is not a scientific conception; it is
mysticism and mythology.[33] And Wohlgemuth continues:

Freud, however, *does* talk about "unconscious ideas," and
although he and his followers repeatedly protest that their doctrine does not violate any conceptions of modern psychology,
yet their whole nomenclature and speech do so. On perusing the
literature of the subject one cannot help conceiving the "unconscious" as a vast region, a Hades into which ideas and thoughts,
desires and affects, etc., are relegated, and from which they try
to escape.

They may indeed *try* to escape, but they cannot pass that
good and ever vigilant little sprite, the Endopsychic
Censor, who immediately pounces upon any ruffianly
unconscious idea and either flings him to the bottom of
the pit to welter once more among his foul associates, or
at least forces him to put on Manifest Content, the silken
outer cloak of respectability, before allowing him to flit
off to the conscious world. All this is genuinely entertaining. But as a picture of Hades it does not measure
up to the standard set by Dante and Milton, and as a
description of a "House of Fame" it will probably not
be preferred by the student of literature to the equally
authentic and vastly more poetic account set down by Dan
Geoffrey Chaucer.

---

[32] *A Critical Examination of Psycho-Analysis* (1923), p. 21.

[33] Cf. John B. Watson, "The Unconscious of the Behaviorist," *The
Unconscious: A Symposium* (1927): "Freud was particularly well versed in
the Old Testament and was widely read in folk-lore. One cannot help but
accuse him of having been much influenced in his youth by the fable of the
devils who resided in the Galilean swine and who were cast out by the great
master therapeutist with a few mystic words. Is it any wonder that Freud
with the background he had gave us the idea he did of the unconscious?"

# CHAPTER III

# THE ISSUE IN AESTHETICS: THE BEAUTIFUL

The essential elements of the idealist's conception of Beauty are set forth in the dialogues of Plato. In the "Phaedo," for example, Socrates speaks as follows:

. . . . I shall have to go back to the familiar words which are in the mouth of everyone, and first of all assume that there is an absolute beauty and goodness and greatness, and the like; grant me this, and I hope to be able to show you the nature of the cause, and to prove the immortality of the soul. . . . . Well . . . . then I should like to know whether you agree with me in the next step; for I cannot help thinking that if there be anything beautiful other than absolute beauty, that can only be beautiful in as far as it partakes of absolute beauty—and this I should say of everything.[1]

To expand and complete this conception one may turn to the famous discussion of beauty in the "Enneads" of the Neo-Platonist, Plotinus:[2]

Beauty is something which is evident at the first glance—something which the soul recognizes as intimate and sympathetic to its own essence, and which it gathers in and assimilates. . . . . This is why the soul, being what it is—that is, of a nature superior to that of all other beings, when it perceives an object which has an affinity with its own nature or which possesses only some trace of it, rejoices, is transported, draws near the object possessing its own nature, thinks of itself and of its inmost essence.

---

[1] Jowett's translation. The "Apology," the "Phaedrus," and the "Ion" contain passages of similar import. Plato's treatment of poets in the "Republic" is considered *infra*, p. 274.

[2] First Ennead, book six. The excerpts I quote are my own translations of the French of Bouillet's *Les Ennéades de Plotin* (1857).

And again:

The soul knows beauty by an entirely separate faculty whose function it is to recognize all that involves beauty, even when the other faculties are concerned in the judgment.

These conceptions of beauty are logical corollaries of the idealistic philosophical system, for in them are displayed the notion of two realms of existence and a plan by which a knower may gain experience of both. The entire plan or attitude may be comprehended within the following three articles:

I. The Beautiful, like the Good and the True, is an absolute—an unchanging reality behind earthly appearances.

II. An earthly object is beautiful if it partakes of the essence of the eternal beauty—if a spark of that divinity is within it.

III. The observer is able to recognize earthly beauty by means of a special faculty within him which is in intimate touch with absolute beauty.[3]

This idealistic schema went into Christianity with the remainder of the Platonic system. There the Beautiful was somewhat overawed by its more austere companions, the True and the Good. Yet in their company it attained an intimate connection with the idea of God—an association which became fixed in the popular mind and formed an excellent basis for the speculations of later idealists. Nor was it pulled from its medieval setting by early modern philosophers like Descartes and Locke, for the subject of beauty largely escaped their attention. But

---

[3] I have indicated, in dealing with philosophy itself, that idealists may be classed under the following heads: (1) those who keep the absolute entirely apart from the earth; (2) those who attempt to introduce it into experience (objects, etc.); and (3) those who try to insert it into the "mind" of man. The three articles set down in the text above may thus be said to include all idealistic aesthetic systems, united by the absolute but differing over the question of its place in experience.

after Baumgarten, in 1750, first used the term "aesthetic" in its modern sense, and after the German romantic movement (that backwash of medieval mysticism) had fairly begun, the idealistic scheme of beauty entered upon a career of great prominence. It was accepted, embellished, embodied in idealistic philosophical systems, by Kant, Lessing, Schelling, Schiller, Goethe, Hegel, Fichte, Schopenhauer, Nietzsche, and great numbers of lesser known writers. It has extended in an unbroken line to the present day in the "l'art pour l'art" school, in Guyau, Bosanquet, Croce, and in the *Einfühlung* group. Superficially viewed, these writers may seem to differ markedly. Fundamentally, however, they agree in their adhesion to the three principles (just enunciated) of the idealistic conception of beauty. Their disagreements are only family quarrels.

It is scarcely questionable that idealism has been and still is in a position of dominance in aesthetics—that the idea of beauty carries with it pronounced idealistic implications. There is more than one reason for this situation. Yet an important circumstance which has encouraged the idealist to consider the field of general aesthetics as peculiarly his own is the fact that his natural opponent, the empiricist, has failed to establish a tenable base from which to conduct a satisfactory opposition. When one surveys the speculations of professing empiricists in aesthetics, this failure is soon apparent.

An empirical aesthetic[4] must deny all three particulars of the idealist's position—that beauty is an absolute,

---

4 The system of aesthetics and of literary criticism that I am setting forth in these pages may be designated as empirical, as pragmatic, or as scientific. I shall prefer the first of these designations. "Scientific," as I have shown, has become as a term blurred, popularized—and thus somewhat distasteful to discriminating students. The term "pragmatic," it seems to me, belongs rather to philosophy proper. By using the term "empirical" one is able to establish valuable historical connections, and to

that it spiritually inhabits a beautiful object, that a special sort of knowledge or a special faculty of the mind is employed in discovering it.

If beauty is not an absolute, then what is it and where is it to be found? Two obvious *loci* immediately suggest themselves: first, the beautiful object itself, and, secondly, the subject or observer.

Does beauty reside in the beautiful object? Assuredly, popular phraseology would lead one to think so. The common expression is: this scene *is* one of great beauty; or, that object *has* much beauty. And the ordinary religious opinion is that God created a universe beautiful in His sight. But the genuine empiricist must completely dissent from the popular view. If beauty dwells within the object, it must be either a visible (empirical) or an invisible (ideal) quality of that object. If it is invisible, then it is the mysterious essence, the absolute, of the idealist. To describe it one will be obliged to use the many terms or metaphors which the idealist employs to express mysteriousness—inherent, intrinsic, innate, indwelling, and so forth. And in order to recognize it the observer must possess a special mental faculty, for the ordinary processes of knowledge, based on empirical evidence, are here quite useless. When a professed empiricist fails to comprehend this situation, he fatally embarrasses his speculations. Lord Kames, for instance, wrote in 1762:

> Considering attentively the beauty of visible objects, we discover two kinds. The first may be termed intrinsic beauty, because it is discovered in a single object viewed apart without relation to any other. . . . . The other may be termed relative

---

point more directly the basic opposition to idealism. As for other possible designations: "realistic" has unfortunate philosophical and popular implications; "inductive" is too vague; "experimental" seems superficial and is open to grave misunderstanding.

beauty. Intrinsic beauty is an object of sense merely: to perceive the beauty of a spreading oak, or of a flowing river, no more is required but singly an act of vision.[5]

However much one may approve Lord Kames's observations in connection with his empirical principle (relative beauty), one must be continually aware that they rest upon a purely idealistic foundation (intrinsic beauty), and that the author cannot be granted the name of consistent empiricist.

Is it possible, then, for the empiricist to discover some visible and observable quality present in all beautiful objects? Obviously it is not. A play, a symphony, a building, a tree, and a woman, may all be beautiful. Yet what visible quality have they in common? Edmund Burke declared that beautiful objects must be small and smooth. William Hogarth thought that beauty resides in the serpentine line. Sir Joshua Reynolds, following the Père Buffier, looked upon beauty as the golden mean between extremes of oddity and deformity—as the norm toward which nature seems to strive. The spectacle presented by these definitions is that of an empiricist looking at general aesthetics from the limited confines of some special artistic interest of his own. It is impossible to believe that their authors intended these definitions to have universal validity in aesthetics. For, even granting their soundness in certain limited respects,[6] they are surely meaningless when applied to fine arts like literature and music, as well as to many other classes of beautiful objects.

---

[5] *Elements of Criticism*, Chap. III.

[6] This is a concession that almost no one would make. Sir Joshua's theory seems particularly untenable to the reader of the *Origin of Species*—who knows that great numbers of (for instance) domestic animals, like pigeons, are not the norms of nature, but her ''sports'' or monstrosities which have been fostered and developed by human agency.

This empirically unprofitable subject is worth pursuing further. Theories of beauty based on some visible quality of the object are not only too narrow; they have also a pronounced idealistic flavor. To say that a serpentine line is beautiful to all observers at all times can only mean, the idealist will assert, that it has an intrinsic beauty. This beauty consists, he will add, in the simplicity and purity of the figure—which means that it is a direct expression of the absolute idea of beauty unclogged by the complexities and disharmonies of earthly non-being. Thus Socrates declares, in the "Philebus":

I do not mean by the beauty of form such beauty as that of animals or pictures, which the many would suppose to be my meaning; but, says the argument, understand me to mean straight lines and circles, and the plane or solid figures which are formed out of them by turning-lathes and rulers and measures of angles; for these I affirm to be not only relatively beautiful, like other things, but they are eternally and absolutely beautiful, and they have peculiar pleasures. . . . . And there are colours which are of the same character. When sounds are smooth and clear, and utter a single pure tone, then I mean to say that they are not relatively but absolutely beautful and have a natural pleasure associated with them.[7]

It must be concluded that under no circumstances may one place beauty in the object and remain an empiricist. The charge of idealism is one which certain groups of experimental psychologists of recent days must face when they determine by the questionnaire method that one object is beautiful and that another is not. Fechner's "golden section," the supremely beautiful rectangle, was determined by counting the votes of numerous people who viewed rectangles of various dimensions under orders to

---

[7] Jowett's translation.

choose the most beautiful of them. However empirical the intentions of the experimenter, his result clearly implies that the "golden section" is intrinsically beautiful. And the entire experiment is based on the assumption that the recognition of beauty is effected through a mental faculty identical in essence in observers of all ranks and ages, and of so simple a nature that only a slight introspection is necessary to determine the object which calls it into play.

The search for a tenable empirical position leads thus to the subject or observer. Here the empiricist is faced by the contention of the idealist that beauty is apprehended by a special sense in the mind of man. Until he can reject this conception entirely he can set up no effective opposition to idealism. Unfortunately, almost all professed empiricists have here been impeded by two fatal obstacles. In the first place, they have regularly considered the "mind" of man to be an entity existing anterior to experience and to a certain degree outside of it. Worse than this—they have, in the second place, regularly relied upon the ancient and now thoroughly discredited "faculty" psychology, which divides this "mind" into a number of apparently independent compartments: the sensibility, the imagination, the emotions, judgment, reason, and so on.[8]

Edmund Burke nobly denounces the position of the idealist, who speaks "as if the Taste were a separate faculty of the mind, distinct from the judgment and

---

[8] Professor Charles Lalo, in his *Les Sentiments Esthétiques* (1910), sets forth and condemns the error of: ". . . . la séparation artificielle des facultés de l'esprit, que l'ancienne psychologie représentait volontiers comme des fonctions séparées, collaborant d'ordinaire, à moins qu' elles ne se combattent, comme autant de 'petits êtres' doués de personnalités distinctes, et parfaitement capables d'agir en nous l'un sans l'autre, en s'ignorant mutuellement."

imagination; a species of instinct by which we are struck
naturally, and at the first glance, without any previous
reasoning, with the excellencies, or the defects of a composition."⁹  Yet he himself allows the human mind three
separate faculties: "All the natural powers in man, which
I know, that are conversant about external objects, are
the Senses, the Imagination, and the Judgment."  Addison had postulated the same threefold division many
years previously.¹⁰  Both agree that the imagination is
the faculty eminently concerned with the beautiful.  And
the aesthetic process is this: sense data come into the
mind from the object; there they are seized upon by the
imagination, which has the power of combining them with
each other as well as with memory images of data from
former occasions, to build up a composite and beautiful
whole.

There is something lacking here, however.  One may
say properly to Addison and to Burke that *every* object—
beautiful or otherwise—must deposit its sense data in the
mind, if that organ is to be sensible of it.  Does the imagination, then, choose only those data which are already
beautiful?  That view would be an acceptance of the
idealist's intrinsic beauty.  Or does the imagination
accept sense data indiscriminately and make its combinations of them beautiful through some power of its own
which it imparts to them?  No; Burke and Addison will
not grant it that ability.  "This power of the imagination," writes Burke, "is incapable of producing anything
absolutely new; it can only vary the disposition of those

---

⁹ "Introduction on Taste," in *A Philosophical Enquiry into the Origin
of Our Ideas of the Sublime and Beautiful* (1756).

¹⁰ *Spectator*, no. 411 (1712): "The pleasures of the imagination .... are
not so gross as those of sense, nor so refined as those of the understanding."

ideas which it has received from the senses."[11]   Here
again, it would seem, the only solution of the problem is
the one which can readily be supplied by the idealist.
One does wrong, he will assert, to restrict the imagination in this manner.  It possesses a genuine and unique
creative power.  It adds to the sense data a spiritual
essence of its own to form a composite which is not a mere
lifeless mosaic of sense impressions, but a fused and
organic unity of beauty.  Thus the idealist circumvents
Burke by merely changing the name of the special faculty
of the mind (whose existence Burke denies) from "soul"
or some such word, to "imagination."  And the result
is the "creative imagination" of Coleridge and other
romanticists.

The ascription of beauty to a faculty of the mind leads
to difficulties from which release is gained only by surrender to the idealist.  No empirical solution is offered,
for instance, by the "associationist," Archibald Alison,
who, however, feels the difficulty which Burke ignored.
For Alison the aesthetic process involves: "first, the
production of some simple emotion; and secondly, the
consequent excitement of a peculiar exercise of the imagination."[12]   This is to say that non-aesthetic objects
merely enter the mind as sense data; aesthetic objects
do the same *and also* release a simple emotion.  But
surely, then, those objects whose sense data strike some
simple emotion must themselves be intrinsically beautiful.  Dugald Stewart, writing twenty years after Alison,
is brought to this very conclusion.  "If," he writes,

---

[11] This is the well-known eighteenth-century "neo-classic" conception of
the "imagination."  Cf. Sir Joshua Reynolds, *Discourses*, no. 7:".... the
imagination is incapable of producing anything originally of itself, and can
only vary and combine those ideas with which it is furnished by means of
the senses. . . . ."

[12] *Essay on the Nature and Principles of Taste* (1790).

"there was nothing originally and intrinsically pleasing or beautiful, the associative principle would have no materials on which it could operate."[13]

The position of the stalwart empiricist, David Hume, marks a decided advance toward tenable empirical principles. "Beauty," he writes in his essay "Of the Standard of Taste,"[14] "is no quality of things themselves: It exists merely in the mind which contemplates them; and each mind perceives a different beauty." These words constitute an attempt to deny all the articles of the idealist's credo. Beauty is not an absolute. It does not mysteriously inhabit an object. Finally, it is not apprehended by a special faculty of the mind. On the contrary —of the rules of taste Hume writes: "Their foundation is the same with that of all the practical sciences, experience." He then declares that the one who judges of beauty must not be diseased in mind or body, not be lacking in experience, not be subject to prejudices. In fact, the large combination of qualities demanded means that excellent judges rarely appear: "But where are such critics to be found? By what marks are they to be known? How distinguish them from pretenders?" And even among the best judges, it is doubtful whether two "sources of variation" can ever disappear—the first, "the different humours of particular men"; the second, "the particular manners and opinions of our age and country."

All this, no doubt, is sound empirical doctrine. If one refuses to rest within the shelter of an absolute, then one must enter the strife, the uncertainties, the difficulties of the every-day world. To judge of beauty will be as difficult as to gain workable knowledge. An important

---

13 *On the Beautiful*, Part I, Chap. VI.
14 *Philosophical Essays*, No. 23.

consideration will surely be the training and impartiality
of the judge. Personal abilities are as important in
aesthetics as they are in any of the sciences. And the
data of aesthetics can scarcely be less difficult to determine and observe than those, for example, of the
historian.

Hume's essay is, nevertheless, onesided, and it may
easily be misleading. It is true that, if the foundation
of aesthetics is human experience, then each "mind"
must perceive a different beauty, since no two people,
presumably, have precisely identical experiences. But
is this situation fatal to further empirical investigation?
On the contrary, the assertion of it is a commonplace.
All sciences are based on experience with the environment, and are carried on by individual "minds." All
social phenomena—laws, education, customs—have the
same foundation. Yet legal enactments are not thought
of as impossible because "justice" is a term interpreted
differently by each individual "mind."

The fact which Hume does not make clear is that a
"mind" is not a monad existing in complete isolation
from the environment and thus sharing no experiences
with other "minds." *That* is, essentially, the idealist's
position. The true empiricist will ask: just how great
is the difference between the beauty perceived by one
"mind" and that perceived by another? How many
elements are common to the perceptions of both? And
if these elements held in common are many, do they not
provide a basis upon which a positive method, a scientific
classification, may be reared? To conclude—it is evident
that Hume exaggerates the negative side, the difficulties,
of the empirical position, and that, furthermore, he does
not point the way to a positive method. Thus he plays
directly into the hands of the idealist who—in order to

prepare the way for the triumphant entry of his absolute
—loses no opportunity to attempt to show that the many
disagreements and differences among individuals prove
the futility of all "earthly" knowledge.

Numerous writers of more recent days have followed
Herbert Spencer in approaching aesthetics through
physiology or physiological psychology. For Spencer,
"the highest aesthetic feeling is one having the greatest
volume, produced by due exercise of the greatest number
of powers without undue exercise of any."[15] For his
disciple, Grant Allen, aesthetic pleasure is "the subjective concomitant of the normal amount of activity . . . .
in the peripheral end organs of the cerebro-spinal
nervous system."[16] Miss Ethel Puffer holds that: "The
beautiful object possesses those qualities which bring
the personality into a state of unity and self-complete-
ness";[17] and she speaks of the loss of marginal states of
consciousness and of repose arising from balance of impulses. Professor H. R. Marshall bases his theory on the
physiological sensations of pleasure and pain: "Beauty
is relatively stable, or real, pleasure. Any pleasant
element may become part of a field that is relatively
stable. We call an object beautiful which seems always
to yield pleasure in impression, or contemplative re-
vival."[18] Mr. I. A. Richards founds aesthetics on the
following psychological situation:

Most behavior is a reconciliation between the various acts
which would satisfy the different impulses which combine to
produce it; and the richness and interest of the feel of it in

---

[15] *Principles of Psychology*, Part IX, Chap. IX.

[16] *Physiological Aesthetics* (1877), p. 34.

[17] *The Psychology of Beauty* (1905), p. 49. The third chapter of Professor Langfeld's *Aesthetic Attitude* contains a sound criticism of Miss
Puffer's theory.

[18] *The Beautiful* (1924), p. 78.

consciousness depends upon the variety of the impulses engaged. Any familiar activity, when set in different conditions so that the impulses which make it up have to adjust themselves to fresh streams of impulses due to new conditions, is likely to take on increased richness and fullness in consciousness.[19]

It is true that these explanations ascribe beauty, not to a "mind" or to a special faculty of it, but to the entire mental-physical organism. Yet they are of little value for an empirical aesthetic. They may approach, but they do not seriously enter the field of aesthetics. They define its subject matter only in terms of another department of knowledge—physiology. Thus their definitions are liable to misinterpretation when applied to the question of the beautiful. A good tennis player does indeed bring his muscles into vigorous action; but to set forth the physiological processes involved in the activity of muscles would not be an adequate description of the game of tennis, and it would be neither illuminating nor sound to declare that excellence in the game is in direct proportion to the vigor with which the muscles are agitated. And since these explanations scarcely enter aesthetics, they cannot establish therein bases for methods of further classification, analysis, and comparison. Surely one must possess a means of discriminating between the reactions resulting from the reading of "Hamlet," from a good meal, from a pleasant odor, or from a general sense of well-being proceeding from a state of good health.

One has the impression that these writers, in deference to, or in fear of, the idealist, have allowed their investigations to be governed by his insistence that a definition of beauty must set forth *one* universally valid phenomenon adequate to explain without further analysis

---

[19] *Principles of Literary Criticism* (1925), p. 109 f.

all possible individual manifestations of beauty. As a result the definitions, in order to remain empirical, must point out a phenomenon so broad and inclusive as to be only distantly related to a restricted field like aesthetics. What Professor Langfeld writes of Marshall's hedonistic theory is true of all these systems:

> It does not, however, enable us to decide the aesthetic values of various forms of the drama, the effect of violent emotions in the appreciation of art, the function of realism, the relation of content and form, and a multitude of similar questions which are involved in the fundamental problem of the nature of beauty.[20]

If these writers do nevertheless discuss such specific questions, it is on the basis of a new set of postulates which have little or no organic relation to the physiological speculations with which they begin.

It appears, then, that empiricists in aesthetics have had little success in discovering and setting forth the principles of a beauty which can be successfully opposed to the absolute beauty of the idealist. Yet the demand is a fair one. One must know whether it is possible to define empirically the qualities an object is held to possess when it is called beautiful by anyone. It is clear that the term is one of wide application. A definition, to be adequate, must be grounded on broad, elementary principles; yet it must be of a character sufficiently distinctive to mark out without ambiguity the boundaries of general aesthetics. Under these circumstances, the radical empiricist—the pragmatist and the scientist—will begin with his basic materials, the general spectacle of a man living within an environment.

It has been declared in earlier pages that a man's life may be envisaged as a contest between him and his

---

[20] *The Aesthetic Attitude*, 36 f.

environment. There is a contest or struggle because he makes demands on it that it will not allow—or will allow only on conditions imposed by itself. Thus an opposition between the man's desires, which are the expression of his instincts, and the results of his actual experiences, is always apparent to him. This feeling of discrepancy, although it causes in him an active dissatisfaction, is nevertheless of the greatest personal benefit, for it provides him with the impulsion to seek out those elements in his surroundings which promise some measure of support for his designs. By possessing himself of these, he gains some assurance of controlling the future in his favor. In accordance with this universal human endeavor, practically synonymous with survival itself, a definition of the beautiful is possible. *"Beautiful" is a term applied by a man to an object (or situation) to indicate that the object (or situation) is in the state in which he wishes it to be—a state of readiness for immediate assimilation to his individual ends.*

But this is idealism. To say that the beautiful is not that which *is* but that which·*should be* (as judged by the experience of the individual) is to call it the ideal as distinct from the real or actual. Yet the empirical ideal is the direct antithesis of that of idealism. The idealist does, indeed, the empiricist contends, arrive at his perfect world by observing a certain number, few or many, of earthly phenomena and filling out the framework they form in accordance with the dictates of his instinctive human desires so that the result becomes a complete and static whole. He constructs a dream world on the basis of a certain number of carefully selected data; since it meets his wishes, it is beautiful to him. But this is the empirical view of idealism; it is by no means the idealist's view of his own system. A fundamental principle of idealism is that its ideal and absolute beauty is a real and genuine existence, that it is independent of earthly phenomena, which are mere imperfect copies of it, and that experience of it is the only valid aesthetic datum.

Thus the definition of beauty which has just been given sets up a thoroughly empirical idealism entirely opposed to that of the idealist. Its ideal is not a metaphysical essence; it is represented or guaranteed by no absolute existing in a realm of essences like itself. Such a beauty does not magically inhabit an object, and no special faculty is required for its recognition. Instead, it is based empirically upon phenomena universally evident and practically synonymous with life itself—that all men strive to win the greatest possible advantage over the environment in order to secure existence on the best possible terms; that, on the basis of their previous experiences and at the instigation of their instinctive desires, they lay plans unceasingly for the accomplishment of such an aim; and that they seek out and turn to their purposes those elements of the environment which give promise of furthering the progress of it.

If the beautiful is firmly grounded in human experience, and if it is not an absolute inhabiting another realm, then it must follow, for the empiricist, that there is only one standard by which its quality and degree may be estimated—the standard, namely, of human experience itself. It may readily be anticipated that such a standard will be attacked by the idealist through the use of the same tactics he employs against empiricism in general.

The idealist will declare that if no absolute guarantees the permanency of the beautiful, then beauty must base itself on the flux and confusion of mere "earthly" experience. No two men can have exactly the same experiences with a constantly shifting environment. Consequently, if a man's conception of beauty is determined by his aims, as they have been qualified and directed by his experiences, his estimates of beautiful objects will differ from those of every other man. And there can be no arguing about tastes. Each individual is his own measure of beauty, since he knows, better than any other person, what his desires are. Thus, the idealist will assert, the logical result of any system built upon flux is the establishment of the chaos and anarchy of pure personal whim.

This argument has by now a familiar ring; its source, moreover, stands well revealed. Basically, it means simply that beauty, since it is not an absolute, must be considered relatively to human experience. This, surely, lies basic to the empirical position. But to the idealist it is the perfect alone which has reality; the imperfect or relative is, by definition, unreal or non-existent. He attempts, therefore, to give an *aut Caesar aut nullus* character to his argument. A thing must be *either* perfect *or* non-existent. Either beauty is an absolute, or it can be nothing whatever—*non tertium quid*. To the empiricist this is merely the idealist's usual strategy of contemning or ignoring the materials upon which all sciences must be reared.

It is to be presumed (since the question of individual variation through heredity remains practically a sealed book) that no two men are born with precisely identical sensory-motor systems. It is obvious that no two men ever acquire precisely identical funds of experience. But it is equally obvious that a man is not a thoroughly unique entity existing in monad-like isolation. In common with all other human beings he possesses a number of instinctive desires centering around food and sex. With others of his kind he lives under certain climatic conditions and within a certain geographical radius. The members of the many groups to which he belongs share the distinctive interests of those groups. Such groups—his family, his friends, his community, profession or industry, state, and so forth—have been of direct concern to him during all of his life. From them he, together with other men, has received his education. He has adopted their customs, and he lives in accordance with their laws and traditions. All these social phenomena, since they are readily evident elements of human experience, will properly form the materials with which a consideration of the beautiful may concern itself.

Thus the empiricist will openly recognize that every man is to a degree unique in that he possesses certain inexplicable individual differences. But he will add that this degree is, relatively, very small, being far outshadowed by qualities which the man shares with others. Again, the fact of apperception is an integral part of the empiricist's position. Observers will see in an object only what their respective funds of experiences permit them to see; and, if their experiences have markedly differed, they will not, for all practical purposes,[21] see the same object. But it is also the empiricist's contention that their disagreements concerning, for example, the beauty of the object will vary about certain norms, and that they will decrease in the proportion in which the observers' common membership in groups increases—so that the empirically undeterminable differences arising purely from individual variation, although they must be estimated and allowed for, cannot work injury to a system which places its emphasis elsewhere.

---

[21] That is—with regard to the plans of action or conduct which any of them may construct upon evidence which includes the observation of this object.

An object is beautiful if it is in the state in which an observer wishes it to be—if it is in readiness for immediate assimilation to his purposes. A second effort of the idealist will surely be to point out that it is, not the beautiful, but the useful which is here being defined.

The conception of the beautiful (*dulce*) as opposed to the useful (*utile*) has had a long life, flourishing most vigorously whenever idealism has most markedly prevailed. Such a dualism is, the empiricist believes, a necessary corollary of the idealist's position. For the idealist, the "useful" is equivalent to the practical, the "earthly." The reference of a useful object is always to another object on the earth—or to mundane human behavior generally. Since beauty, for him, is an absolute, a beautiful object, on the contrary, can have no earthly reference. The spirit of eternal beauty is within it, and it can point, if it is pure, only to the realm of the absolute. Thus a direct opposition is brought about; the useful and the beautiful occupy different realms. But more follows. Whatever has significance for ordinary human life is *de facto* useful. And it must be that the beautiful, since its reference is to the absolute alone, is never realizable within mundane human experience. For such a beauty, since it would be one related directly to human conduct and other earthly objects, would lose its immediate reference to the absolute—and would thereby be transformed into the merely useful. Thus the idealist's inevitable dualism stands once more revealed. For him, the beautiful (spirit) can never be useful; the useful (material) can never be beautiful. And it can be seen that most of his efforts in the field of aesthetics must be devoted to attempts to reconcile these two orders of existence—to unite them in conformity with the undeniable facts of human experience.

If one refuses to do violence to experience in the interests of a dualism, what can be said then about the useful as distinguished from the beautiful? "Useful" is clearly the more inclusive term. It is, in fact, as broad in scope as human activity itself.[22] Nothing which enters the circumference of human interests can have its utility denied. The beautiful, therefore, is a subdivision of the useful—which means that anything which is beautiful must also be useful. Yet two distinctive characteristics separate the subdivision from the major division of the classification.

In the first place, the beautiful contains a clear reference to the future. The useful refers to what a man possesses and finds employment for in his present activities. The beautiful represents a goal at least one step in advance of the actual; it stands for what the man could use if he possessed it. The actual tools he employs to arrive at the goal thus determined are useful. When the goal is attained, the beautiful is realized; it is added to and absorbed into the general fund of the individual's experiences. And, on the basis of the now augmented body of experience, a new goal, a new beautiful, is set up and becomes the object of endeavor. The attained beautiful thus no longer occupies its former status. It is no longer beautiful, since a new goal has superseded it. It is now an actuality, an object of utility for future activities. In this respect the idealist's contention that the beautiful can never be realized finds empirical support, but only in the sense entirely opposed to that in which he conceives the situation. It is indeed the function of the beautiful to translate itself into the useful. But the change involves no flight to another realm of existence. Both beautiful and useful exist on the same plane and within a closely woven nexus. The distinction between them is based

---

2 It is, in other words, synonymous with "value."

empirically upon their differing relations to human experience. And within individual experience it is not possible to draw a clean-cut distinction between the two. The transposition of an attained beautiful into the useful is qualified and conditioned by the possessor himself, by the nature of the goal he has realized, by the length and the degree of completeness of the possession—so that the individual is frequently unable to say of any object whether its status is that of beauty or utility.

If one disregards the matter of temporal reference, there is still another distinction between the useful and the beautiful. There is a difference of degree. The beautiful has been defined as that which is in a state of readiness for *immediate* assimilation to an individual's wishes. It must be apparent that beautiful objects or situations will only rarely be encountered in life. The material of human experience regularly comes to a man with its elements intertwined and commingled. Even when a situation is, on the whole, favorably disposed toward him, it usually leaves a number of things to be desired. Judged even by liberal standards, its state is rarely one of pure benignity or of entire fitness for his individual desires. Yet such a state is one which must be closely approached (since complete attainment is perhaps impossible) by a beautiful object. The useful, on the other hand, makes no such stringent demands upon earthly phenomena. A thing may be only mildly benevolent, even neutral or somewhat inimical, toward a man, and yet play a definite part in his activities. Utility does not turn from incompleteness or limited adaptability; it is always willing to work with phenomena of this character. Perhaps they can be partially employed; perhaps they can be combined with other phenomena in a composite more completely amenable to human wishes. But the beautiful demands the elimination of elements inimical to man's wishes so as to render the object immediately assimilable. Consequently, the beautiful, a subclass of the useful, may be further characterized as the *supremely* useful.

The position of the empiricist on the question of the beautiful and the useful is thus the direct antithesis of that of the idealist. Instead of divorcing the two by ascribing them to separate worlds, the empiricist points out that they differ only in degree and in temporal reference. And he goes much further than merely denying the idealist's contention that beauty is unrealizable in experience. *The empiricist declares that it is precisely the function of the beautiful to transpose itself into the useful. Further still—since beauty is supreme utility, its ability so to translate itself constitutes the standard by which the quality of its beauty is tested.*

Is such a contention vulnerable? Suppose the idealist sets forth the obvious truth that a man's desires continually impel him to set up a desired goal which cannot possibly be realized within the environment. A man, that is, may easily construct a beauty which can never be attained on earth. Is such a conception, according to the empirical attitude, to be denied the name of beauty since it is not capable of direct translation into utility? The empiricist will reply that such a beauty is a legitimate type of the beautiful. Nevertheless, its value depends upon its utility—upon the relation it bears to human experience. In every case it does bear such a relation. Thus the example sets forth a very common situation which by no means does violence to the empirical position. The beautiful may be non-potential and still be useful. The quality and nature of its utility are, however, subjects whose consideration must be postponed until sufficient data are at hand for adequate treatment.

And this last matter, that of specific data, concerns directly the great disadvantage under which the empiricist labors in a field as general as that of abstract beauty. He cannot, on the basis of his definition of the beautiful, adequately describe any specific beautiful object. The idealist, on the contrary, can readily do so. This difference reflects the inexpugnably opposed points of view of idealism and empiricism in aesthetics.

For the idealist the field of aesthetics contains only two elements—absolute beauty and the individual earthly phenomenon or specimen under consideration. Of this specimen there is only one question to be asked: does beauty dwell within it? The answer is provided by the special faculty in the mind of the observer. The idealist's system is thus adequate to determine (as he believes), without any addition or alteration, the presence of beauty in any object whatever. It matters not whether the object be a tree, a goblet, a play, or a painting—whether it be, that is, an example of natural beauty, of artistic beauty, or of beauty in what are called the fine arts.

With the empiricist the situation is entirely different. He is concerned with the matter of scientific classification —a question which faces scientific research in every department of knowledge. The entomologist, beginning with the branch *hexapoda* or *insecta,* proceeds to the order *coleoptera,* the family *Lucanidae,* the genus *passalus,* the species *cornutus,* and thus arrives at the individual stag beetle he has before him. Furthermore, since his observations are based entirely upon empirical evidence, his primary interest lies in the specimen he is examining. It is an object; it may be observed, measured, dissected, described in detail. But the branch *insecta* is not an object—not a Platonic "idea" of an insect of which all known individuals of its kind are mere unreal, imperfect copies. It is a convenient empirical division made to include all six-legged invertebrates. It is built up from the examination of individuals, and its sole reason for existence lies in its relation to them. It demands that all its subdivisions be concerned with six-legged creatures; otherwise it does not describe any individual insect. It would be absurd to say that there is no difference between insects in general and stag beetles since all have six legs. The difference lies in those characteristics which distinguish stag beetles from all other insects, and it is precisely those characteristics which concern the entomologist when he examines and classifies his specimen.

For the empiricist in aesthetics, "the beautiful" is an empirical classification covering his entire subject. To define it will be to point out some elements which it has in common with all its subdivisions. But it is no absolute, and it has no adequate descriptive force. He cannot, on the basis of a definition of it, pretend to give a satisfactory account of the beauty of, for example, an individual poem. For a poem belongs to the subclass poetry, which is contained within the larger division, literature, which is one of the fine arts included within art in general. And the characteristics of each one of these divisions are of primary importance in describing the beauty of the poem. Finally, it is the poem itself which is the focus of the empiricist's attention, for it may be empirically examined. And the more closely his classification approaches the individual specimen, the more specific and complete his descriptive analysis will become.

This is why professed empiricists have shown to best advantage when they have dealt with the specific field in which each is a specialist. In such a field they can discuss technique with a skilled craftsman's knowledge—as when William Hogarth and Sir Joshua Reynolds discourse on

the art of painting; or they can deduce from specific works
empirical principles valid within the limits of a subclass.
But about the beautiful in general they have either manifested no interest, or they have been guilty of the error
of ascribing to it by way of definition the results attained
in the narrow department of their own interests—as when
Hogarth declares that the serpentine line is characteristic
of *all* beauty.

The faces of the idealist and the empiricist are turned,
accordingly, in opposite directions. The former finds his
absolute and his special mental faculty adequate to determine beauty in any object. For him aesthetics contains
individuals but no species. And his starting point is
always the absolute itself. The empiricist, on the contrary, begins with individual specimens of the beautiful.
Upon these he rears inductively a series of classifications
of ever increasing scope but of ever decreasing characteristics. Abstract beauty is simply the most inclusive
division of his classification. He can proceed from it to
the individual object only through the successive subclasses, for each of these adds characteristics essential
for adequate analysis.

This fundamental distinction explains why the idealist has flourished most successfully in general aesthetics.
He has infected almost every worker in the field with the
idea that it is necessary to discover *one* principle of
beauty which shall fully explain all individual manifestations of the beautiful. This necessity being accepted,
there is only one road to a solution—an absolute. To the
empiricist such a search seems absurd. This basic disagreement means that the issue between idealist and
empiricist cannot be fully exhibited within the field of
general aesthetics. Therein the latter vigorously combats
the system of the former. But his tactics must be mainly

defensive. To follow the positive implications of an empirical attitude means the study of specific objects. But judgment within a specified field—like painting, music, or literature—is regularly termed "criticism." Consequently — whereas the idealist considers aesthetics to mean the search for absolute beauty, the empiricist regards it as a subject of little interest since its very general characteristics are merely a part of a classification built up from criticism within a special field. Accordingly, it is in criticism, not in general aesthetics, that the issue between idealist and empiricist can be directly joined.

# CHAPTER IV

## THE ISSUE IN AESTHETICS: ART

The idealist's principles remain the same whether they are applied to beauty in general or to the beautiful within any of its departments or subdivisions. To examine artistic beauty is thus for him merely to reconsider in a different setting the three elements of his system— the absolute, its spiritual presence within the object, and its affinity with a special faculty in the mind of man.

The idealist's view, according to the first of these contentions is, then, that the beautiful in art is represented by a Platonic idea, a perfect prototype, an absolute. What is the result of the application of this assumption? It will be well to arrive at an answer through an examination of the assertions of a number of idealists.

All one wants to know is whether the mere representation of the object is to my liking, no matter how indifferent I may be to the real existence of the object of this representation. It is quite plain that in order to say that the object *is beautiful,* and to show that I have taste, everything turns on the meaning which I can give to this representation, and not on any factor which makes me dependent on the real existence of the object. Every one must allow that a judgement on the beautiful which is tinged with the slightest interest, is very partial and not a pure judgement of taste. One must not be in the least prepossessed in favor of the real existence of the thing, but must preserve complete indifference in this respect, in order to play the part of judge in matters of taste.—Kant.[1]

---

[1] Kant's *Critique of Aesthetic Judgement,* trans. J. C. Meredith (Clarendon Press, 1911), book 1, § 2.

For art has to leave reality, it has to raise itself boldly above necessity and neediness; for art is the daughter of freedom, and it requires its prescriptions and rules to be furnished by the necessity of spirit and not by that of matter.—Schiller.[2]

It is only by being frank or disclaiming all reality, and by being independent or doing without reality, that the appearance is aesthetical. Directly it apes reality or needs reality for effect, it is nothing more than a vile instrument for material ends, and can prove nothing for the freedom of the mind. Moreover, the object in which we find beauty need not be unreal if our judgment disregards this reality; for if it regards this the judgment is no longer aesthetical. A beautiful woman, if living, would no doubt please us as much and rather more than an equally beautiful woman seen in a painting; but what makes the former please men is not her being an independent appearance; she no longer pleases the pure aesthetic feeling. In the painting, life must only attract as an appearance, and reality as an idea. But it is certain that to feel in a living object only the pure appearance requires a greatly higher aesthetic culture than to do without life in the appearance.—Schiller.[3]

Art cannot, without forfeiting the nobility of its nature, direct itself to any outward end.—Schelling.[4]

To require moral ends of the artist is to destroy his profession.—Goethe.[5]

---

[2] *Works* (Boston, 1884), vol. 8: *Letters on the Aesthetical Education of Man.* The quotation is from the second letter.

[3] *Ibid.*, letter 26.

[4] From his *Über das Verhältniss der bildenden Künste zu der Natur.* I quote the excerpt from Miss Rose Frances Egan's ''Genesis of the Theory of 'Art for Art's Sake' in Germany and in England,'' part II, p. 15. Miss Egan's work, in the *Smith College Studies in Modern Languages*, is in two parts: part I in vol. 2, no. 4 (July, 1921); part II in vol. 5, no. 3 (April, 1924). Her purpose is to show that the principles of the ''l'art pour l'art'' movement cannot be distinguished from the German romantic theories which preceded it. Her material is extensive and her thesis is sound. She does not, I believe, extract the full significance of the former, nor give adequate expression to the latter. As I acknowledge in footnotes on each occasion, I have drawn upon her quotations and translations.

[5] From *Dichtung und Wahrheit.* Quoted by Miss Egan, Part II, p. 16.

It is no doubt the case that art can be utilized as a mere pastime in the service of pleasure and entertainment, either in the embellishment of our surroundings, the imprinting of a delight-giving surface to the external conditions of life, or the emphasis placed by decoration on other objects. In these respects it is unquestionably no independent or free art, but an art subservient to certain objects. The kind of art, however, which *we* ourselves propose to examine is one which is *free* in its aim and its means. . . . . Fine art is not art in the true sense of the term until it is also thus free, and its *highest* function is only then satisfied when it has established itself in a sphere which it shares with religion and philosophy, becoming thereby one mode and form through which the *Divine,* the profoundest interests of mankind, and spiritual truths of widest range, are brought home to consciousness and expressed.—Hegel.[6]

Thereby the false position to which we have already directed attention vanishes, namely, that art has to serve as a means for moral ends and the moral end of the world generally by means of its didactive and ameliorating influence, and by doing so has its essential aim not in itself, but in something else. . . . . A work of art would in that case be merely a useful instrument in the realization of an end which possessed real and independent importance outside the realm of art. As opposed to this we must maintain that it is art's function to reveal *truth* under the mode of art's sensuous or material configuration, to display the reconciled antithesis previously described, and by this means to prove that it possesses its final aim in itself, in this representation in short and self-revelation. For other ends such as instruction, purification, improvement, procuring of wealth, struggle after fame and honour have nothing whatever to do with this work of art as such; still less do they determine the fundamental idea of it.—Hegel.[7]

The work of genius is music, or philosophy, or paintings, or poetry; it is nothing to use. To be of no use belongs to the char-

---

6 *The Philosophy of Fine Art,* trans. F. P. B. Osmaston (1920), 1:8 f.
7 *Ibid.,* 76 f.

acter of the works of genius; it is their patent of nobility. All other works of men are for the maintenance or easing of our existence; only those we are speaking of are not; they alone exist for their own sake, and are in this sense to be regarded as the flower or the net profit of existence. Therefore our heart swells at the enjoyment of them, for we rise out of the heavy earthly atmosphere of want. Analogous to this, we see the beautiful, even apart from these, rarely combined with the useful. Lofty and beautiful trees bear no fruit; the fruit-trees are small, ugly cripples. The full garden rose is not fruitful, but the small, wild, almost scentless roses are. The most beautiful buildings are not the useful ones; a temple is no dwelling-house. A man of high, rare mental endowments compelled to apply himself to a merely useful business, for which the ordinary man would be fitted, is like a costly vase decorated with the most beautiful painting which is used as a kitchen pot; and to compare useful people with men of genius is like comparing building-stone with diamonds.—Schopenhauer.[8]

These distinctions established, we must condemn as erroneous every theory which annexes the aesthetic activity to the practical, or introduces the laws of the second into the first.—Croce.[9]

"Aesthetic" in the sense here meant indicates an attitude toward life, an art of living, which is, opposed to everything non-aesthetic in that it contains its value in itself, does not point beyond itself, and serves no end lying outside itself. When I call all non-aesthetic things—that is, all things pointing beyond themselves; activities of life not serving ends in themselves— "practical," I thus assert the existence of two great spheres of life: the world of the aesthetic on one side, and the world of the practical on the other.—Müller-Freienfels.[10]

---

[8] *The World as Will and Idea*, trans. R. B. Haldane and J. Kemp (1886), 3:154 (book 3, chap. 31).

[9] *Aesthetic*, 50.

[10] *Psychologie der Kunst* (1922), 1:4 (my translation).

These quotations[11] present a situation which has already been encountered in connection with the question of the beautiful *versus* the useful. The complete separation of these two is, it was seen, a position made imperative by the idealist's two realms of existence. In the realm of art, the artistic object, which is basically a material thing, must partake of the absolute's spiritual qualities. This means that all of its "material" elements must point directly toward their metaphysical goal. If there are any earthly references or complications, these cannot represent the beautiful, for *their* status would be determined not by spirit but by the relations in which they stand to men, to other earthly objects, or to some other independent absolute (like morality, which represents the Good). Here, then, are the two familiar realms, the never-failing dualism. One realm, that of the artistically beautiful, is free, independent, complete, self-centered and self-engrossed. The other, that of the useful, contains some base material intermixture—some reference to the existence of the object among other objects or some value outside itself relating to utility for human activity or behavior.

Now if, as the empiricist declares, this dualism does violence to the basic texture of human experience, then its absurdity should be more apparent within the realm of art than when it is applied to such an abstraction as beauty in general. For, in the narrower realm, the

---

11 Testimony from idealists of the kind provided by these excerpts is of primary importance for my contention as to the basic identity of all idealistic systems of aesthetic. But to extend the list further would, I fear, be pure pedantry. It may be observed that I have centered the evidence around the important figures of Kant, Schiller, and Hegel. To include earlier writers would be to quote, for example, the words of Augustine (*Confessions,* IV, 15): "Pulchrum esse, quod per se ipsum; aptum [the useful] quod ad aliquid accomodatum deceret."

demands and implications it makes can be given more definite and specific application.

Let it be supposed, then, that a consistent idealist wishes to render a judgment about the beauty of (to borrow Schiller's example) the portrait of a woman. What elements of the portrait and what references and implications associated with it must be discarded as non-aesthetic? In the first place, the spectator must not desire to possess the portrait, nor speculate upon its value in the market. He cannot consider how effective it would be if it were hanging above the mantelpiece in his drawing room. Again, his reflections must contain no reference to the bodily existence of women. He must not compare the portrait with its original, or with any living woman of which it may remind him. The qualities of the figure in the portrait must not arouse his sexual desire or his social feelings to thoughts of the general uses to which woman may be put—her desirability as inamorata, as wife, as companion, as citizen. Moreover, he must avoid any reflections upon the national, historical, or social type of beauty exhibited by the woman of the portrait, and also any consideration of her headdress, her attire, her jewels, or other ornaments. He must have no reactions of an ethical nature—no thought of whether the features, facial expression, or dress of the woman show her to lack moral character, or whether the portrait itself might encourage what in his day and among his groups would be called vice or immorality. Finally, he cannot be interested in considering any influence on the portrait of the painter's life, his position in society, his historical period, and so forth. Neither can the painter's materials and technique concern him if they involve a reference to something outside the portrait. Thus he cannot compare the subject matter or the technique of this portrait with

those of any other portrait either by the same painter or
by another. He cannot, that is, judge the portrait by any
standard external to it.[12]

What, it may well be asked, remains for the idealist
to consider when he surveys the portrait? He may properly concern himself with the materials this one artist has
selected for this one picture and the technique he has
employed, provided that he ask only one question of them.
Do they so arrange, combine, and harmonize themselves
that the result is something which adequately represents
absolute beauty? If they (as he thinks) do, then they are
a worthy earthly receptacle for the spiritual indwelling
of that beauty. Here, accordingly, is the second article of
the idealist's system: that a beautiful work of art partakes of the nature of eternal beauty—that a spark of
the divine essence is within it. It is well to note, however,
before proceeding to consider it, that it comprises within
itself the *entire* task of an idealist's aesthetic judgment.

---

12 Professor D. W. Prall, in his *Aesthetic Judgment* (1929) writes
(p. 19) that the experience of beauty is "delight in the object as directly
apprehended, with no reference beyond this apprehended form or appearance." Again (p. 20): "For it is characteristic of aesthetic apprehension
that the surface fully present to sense is the total object of apprehension.
We do not so much perceive an object as intuit its appearance, and as we
leave this surface in our attention, to go deeper into meanings or more
broadly into connections and relations, we depart from the typically aesthetic
attitude." Consequently (p. 320 f.): "A scholar may tell us when a picture
was painted, and where, and by whom, and even what materials the artist
used. He may say what the subject is and what the position and shape and
size and color of every detail in it; he may even trace its design and indicate
the excellence of its technique. But he is not a safe guide to its aesthetic
value unless that value has been felt by him in really delightful aesthetic
contemplation of the picture, so that its point as art and its beauty as
aesthetic surface, the one the soul of the other, and hence manifest only in
the sensuous content which is its actual aesthetic body, are plain to him.
This feeling of delight, the point of the picture as art, is the focus of a
perspective, from which alone its details of quality and character and structure appear as the constituent aspects of its beauty. This is its unique
beauty and its unique value, and criticism that has not viewed it as in this
perspective of delighted grasp of it as a whole, can never be trusted to be
relevant, much less authoritative."

And one must not forget the price that is paid—the dualism imposed upon human experience—for making it the sole problem, nor the number and nature of the "non-aesthetic" elements which the observer is forced to reject at that dualism's command.

When one approaches the idealist's second principle, one expects to find that he considers the work of art to be a fusion of his two orders of existence. On the one hand there will be certain material qualities, necessary to the work, but in themselves inert, dead, and helpless. On the other hand there will be the spirit or soul of the work—the superior, dominating, and life-giving principle, the affinity of the absolute. The assertions of idealists conclusively bear out this expectation:

It is not amiss, however, to remind the reader of this: that in all free arts something of a compulsory nature is still required, or, as it is called, a *mechanism,* without which the *soul,* which in art must be *free,* and which alone gives life to the work, would be bodyless and evanescent (e.g. in the poetic art there must be correctness and wealth of language, likewise prosody and metre). —Kant.[13]

Thus art on its sensuous side brings before us deliberately merely a shadow-world of shapes, tones, and imaged conceptions, and it is quite beside the point to maintain that it is simply a proof of the impotence and limitations of man that he can only present us with the surface of the physical world, mere *schemata,* when he calls into being his creative works. In art these sensuous shapes are not offered as exclusively for themselves and their form to our direct vision. They are presented with the intent to secure in such shape satisfaction for higher and more spiritual interests, inasmuch as they are mighty to summon an echo and response in the human spirit evoked from all the depths of its conscious life. In this way the sensuous is *spiritualized* in art,

---

[13] *Critique of Aesthetic Judgement,* Part I, book 2, § 43.

or, in other words, the life of *spirit* comes to dwell in it under sensuous guise.—Hegel.[14]

The end or object of art must therefore consist in something other than the purely formal imitation of what is given to objective sense, which invariably can merely call into being technical *legerdemain* and not *works* of art. It is no doubt an essential element of a work of art that it should have natural forms as a foundation, because the mode of its representation is in external form, and thereby along with it in that of natural phenomena.—Hegel.[15]

Form is only the body in which it [spiritual substance] clothes itself, and in which it becomes objective.—Schelling.[16]

If, however, he [the artist] wishes consciously to subordinate himself to actuality and to copy existing objects with slavish fidelity, he will produce larvae indeed, but not works of art.—Schelling.[17]

The genuine, lawgiving artist strives after artistic truth; the lawless, following a blind instinct, after an appearance of naturalness. The former leads to the highest pinnacle of art; the latter to its lowest step.—Goethe.[18]

The elements of this inevitable and familiar dualism are surely clear. Artistic beauty, the idealist is convinced, is an absolute transcending earthly experience. Yet he sees that art has certain "earthly" ties. First, a work of art *does* imitate the human environment. It may copy it more or less exactly—may follow it at a greater or lesser distance. Yet it never breaks free of imitation even (as Lucretius well demonstrated) through its centaurs and gryphons. Secondly, art obviously employs an earthly medium—language, the canvas and pigments,

---

14 *The Philosophy of Fine Art*, 1:53.
15 *Ibid.*, 62.
16 From his *Philosophie der Kunst*, quoted by Miss Egan, Part I, p. 56.
17 From his *Über das Verhältniss der bildenden Künste zu der Natur*, quoted by Miss Egan, Part II, p. 14.
18 From *Einleitung in die Propyläen*. Quoted from J. E. Spingarn's *Goethe's Literary Essays* (1921), p. 15.

musical notation and musical instruments. Thirdly, there exist, it seems clear, certain rules or customs in connection with various arts—certain methods of technique which impart a fairly definite pattern or character to the work. The idealist cannot deny the mundane associations of these three elements. The question arises: What validity do they possess in determining the beauty of any work of art? The solution here is a matter of the individual taste of the idealist making the judgment. The question really amounts to very little. For the integrity of the absolute must in no way be impugned—so that the "earthly" elements can never be more than shadows. And, by accepting the "disinterestedness"—the non-useful character—of art, the idealist has already confined strictly within the limits of the individual work whatever validity it pleases him to grant. The process of ascribing such validity thus becomes a generous and graceful, but meaningless and supererogatory gesture.

But a far more serious question impends. The work of art is a unity, not a duality. How, then, shall the two entirely opposite elements of its nature be fused? An occasional idealist can be found who wisely fears to encounter this classic nemesis of idealism. Thus Benedetto Croce asserts that: "When the intuition has been distinguished from the expression, and the one has been made different from the other, no ingenuity of middle terms can reunite them. . . . ."[19] It is safer and simpler to declare that there is no psycho-physical problem at all—which Croce does:

In reality, we know nothing but expressed intuitions: a thought is not a thought for us, unless it be possible to formulate

---

[19] It is highly unusual for an idealist to commit himself to this extent. The empiricist can only retort that, since this is certainly the case, the conclusion definitely implied is: then one must not make such an arbitrary separation.

it in words; a musical image exists for us only when it becomes concrete in sounds; a pictorial image only when it is coloured. . . . . Thought, musical fancy, pictorial image did not indeed exist without expression; they did not exist at all previous to the formation of this expressive state of the spirit. . . . . Poetry is born as those words, that rhythm, and that metre.[20]

There is thus, according to this view, no problem at all, since there is only one element in art—namely, spirit. Matter is merely the spirit appearing on earth.

But the great majority of idealists in aesthetics are reluctant to rule out the sensuous side of art by a simple fiat. To them the question presents the problem of encountering and reconciling a genuine dualism. One anticipates, accordingly, that their solutions (like those of many of their brothers in the realm of philosophy proper) will be effected either through poetic metaphor, or (to use Croce's phrase) through some "ingenuity of middle terms"—that is, through the positing of another mystery to explain the mystery which confronts them.

For Goethe it is the task of the spirit to seize upon the material elements in the work of art and to weld them into a whole which is not a mere assemblage of parts, but a living, spiritual unity ("nicht blosz etwas leicht und oberflächlich Wirkendes, sondern wetteifernd mit der Natur, etwas Geistig-Organisches . . . .").[21] The artist must copy, not nature, but nature's creative methods; for "in the practice of art we can only emulate nature when we have learnt, to some extent at least, the art by which she proceeds in creating her own works."[22] Thus a beautiful poem must be a poetic whole ("der Begriff eines dichterischen Ganzen") in which the spirit has succeeded

---

20 From pp. 42–44 of his *Essence of Aesthetic.*
21 *Einleitung in die Propyläen.*
22 *Ibid.* (my translation).

in imparting life to all the sensuous elements ("die Bele-
bung des Ganzen").

Concerning this problem, Schiller writes:

In a really beautiful work of art, the substance ought to be
inoperative, the form should do everything; for by form the
whole man is acted on; the substance acts on nothing but isolated
forces. Thus, however vast and sublime it may be, the substance
always exercises a restrictive action on the mind, and true aesthetic liberty can only be expected from the form. Consequently
the true search of the matter . . . . consists in *destroying matter by the form;* and the triumph of art is great in proportion
as it overcomes matter and maintains its sway over those who
enjoy its work.[23]

For Hegel the work of art is the objectification of the
divine Idea:

It has already been stated that the content of art is the Idea
and the form of its display the configuration of the sensuous or
plastic image. It is further the function of art to mediate these
two aspects under the reconciled mode of free totality. The first
determinant implied by this is the demand that the content,
which has to secure artistic representation, shall disclose an essential capacity for such display. If this is not so, all that we possess
is a defective combination.[24]

It is a good statement of the idealist's case, therefore,
to say that the work of art presents (to employ a metaphor) the spectacle of spirit filling the interstices of matter and binding all the sensuous elements into a unified,
living, and spiritual whole. Every particle of matter is

---

[23] Letter 22 of his *Letters on the Aesthetical Education of Man.* It may
be observed that by "form" Schiller means a Platonic form or "idea."
Hegel and Schelling, on the contrary, interpret the term as meaning *material*
form. For the empiricist "form" means the framework, shape, or pattern
of the work—not by any means the inert, lifeless, arbitrarily manufactured,
and empirically non-existent abstraction which the idealist's "material"
essences are imagined to be. The futility of using this classic term at the
present time is obvious.

[24] *Philosophy of Fine Art,* 1:95.

(to use another metaphor) invaded and conquered by spirit. The entire work of art is then an essence as unique and original as (a simile) a living person, for it has a body ruled by a soul. It takes on, too, the purity and simplicity demanded by the absolute of its earthly representatives; for, since the matter has been spiritualized, there is no obstruction, resistance, or complexity. Accordingly, when the properly qualified spectator surveys the work, his eye cannot linger or come to rest on the material aspects. For these have become merely (metaphorically speaking) signposts pointing beyond to the inner and spiritual essence of the work. Since this inner spark has descended from, and is of identical nature with, the other-worldly absolute, to know the one is also to know the other. To see a beautiful work of art truly is to see the absolute shining through it. The spiritually gifted observer has this power. Schopenhauer writes:

Thus, although the kind of knowledge which is peculiar and essential to genius is knowledge of *perception*, yet the special object of this knowledge by no means consists of the particular things, but of the Platonic ideas which manifest themselves in these. . . . . Always to see the universal in the particular is just the fundamental characteristic of genius, while the normal man knows in the particular only the particular as such, for only as such does it belong to the actual, which alone has interests for him, i.e., relations to his *will*. The degree in which every one not merely thinks, but actually perceives, in the particular thing, only the particular, or a more or less universal up to the most universal of the species, is the measure of his approach to genius. And corresponding to this, only the nature of things generally, the universal in them, the whole, is the special object of genius.[25]

The words of Schopenhauer may properly introduce the third major contention of the idealist: that beauty in

---

[25] *The World as Will and Idea*, 3:142.

art is recognized by a special faculty in the mind of man. One must first comprehend clearly, however, the conclusion to which the idealist's belief in a mystical union of matter and spirit within the work of art commits him. What makes a work of art beautiful is the residence within it of the spark of eternal beauty. The fact of this spiritual presence means always that the "material" elements in the work have undergone *complete* spiritual subjugation. If there existed only one fragment of unsubdued "matter," the spirit could not be present, for its presence under such circumstances would be a denial of its omnipotence. Consequently, there are only two possible judgments concerning any work of art. If the spark is present, the work is perfect in beauty. If the spark is not present, the work has no aesthetic significance whatever. The absolute can know nothing of degrees of beauty —of a more or a less beautiful, nor of kinds or types of beauty. To deal with works in which beauty does not reside is not to engage in the study of aesthetics at all, for such merely "useful" works can be of no significance for an independent, free, and disinterested beauty. To say that a work is beautiful *in its kind* would be to go outside the work to an external standard, and it would also involve the granting of final validity to classifications built up from "material" characteristics. And to venture to fix the relative grades of two *absolutely* beautiful works is to attempt as great an absurdity as if one should proclaim one corpse "more dead" than another.

One comes now to the idealist's final principle—that man is made aware of the presence of eternal beauty in an object by means of a special faculty of his mind. In the realm of art there is, at this place, an important complication. Before artistic beauty can be recognized by an observer, it must be created by an artist. Here are, then, two distinct questions: the creation of the work of art by an artist, and the recognition of its beauty by an observer —in other words, the questions of creation and of criticism.

It is upon the first of these—upon the phenomena of artistic creation—that the idealist in aesthetics places his emphasis. The actual descent of the spark from the absolute into the special mental faculty of the artist—where its presence reveals to him how to create a work of art which shall be a worthy dwelling place for it—is known by the term "inspiration." It is a spiritual experience of maximum intensity; consequently, it cannot be described in terms used to set forth the details of ordinary mundane occurrences. The closest one can approach a description is through the use of metaphor:

Wir können nichts tun, als den Holzstosz erbauen und recht trocknen; er fängt alsdann Feuer zur rechten Zeit, und wir verwundern uns selbst darüber.—Goethe.[26]

Le bonheur de l'inspiration, délire qui surpasse le délire physique correspondant qui nous enivre dans les bras d'une femme. La volupté de l'âme est plus longue.—Alfred de Vigny.[27]

The true artist, in fact, finds himself big with his theme, he knows not how; he feels the moment of birth drawing near, but he cannot will it or not will it.—Croce.[28]

There is a painful pregnancy in genius, a long incubation and waiting for the spirit, a thousand rejections and futile birth-pangs, before the wonderful child appears, a gift of the gods, utterly undeserved and inexplicably perfect.—Santayana.[29]

---

[26] Letter to Schiller of Feb. 28, 1795. Quoted by Müller-Freienfels, 2:143.

[27] Quoted by H. Delacroix, *Psychologie de l'art* (1927), p. 185 note.

[28] *Aesthetic*, 51.

[29] *Reason in Art* (1922), p. 8. Excerpts such as those given above could be indefinitely increased in number.

The one who experiences inspiration is, in the language of the idealist, termed a "genius."[30] He is a man set apart from other men. Other artists may be talented. They may have a knowledge of the material elements of their arts—a knowledge acquired empirically from experience within the environment. Now the genius himself *may* possess this ordinary sort of artistic knowledge. But he is also the recipient of a direct vision of the beautiful —an absolute and infallible knowledge which they do not and cannot possess. Under these circumstances the ancient and inveterate enemy of idealism again stalks upon the scene. The inevitable dualism must be encountered. Does the spark from the absolute strike *anyone* in accordance with inscrutable laws of its own? Or must the genius endeavor to attract the bolt by diligently acquiring a mastery of the material elements of his art? Must the musical genius have labored through a long apprenticeship during which he has practiced scales, studied harmony and orchestration, analyzed and interpreted the works of other composers, and made many attempts at composition himself? In short, must a genius have talent?

Evidently, the situation provides much opportunity for family quarrels between idealists. In fact, a fairly distinct line of cleavage separates their numbers. On the one wing are those who practically ignore the artist's training to place all their emphasis upon the magical properties of inspiration. Such an idealist is Socrates in the "Ion":

For all good poets, epic as well as lyric, compose their beautiful poems not as works of art, but because they are inspired and possessed. And as the Corybantian revellers when they dance are

---

30 For an interesting article on this word, see Society for Pure English, *Tract* 17 (Clarendon Press, 1924).

not in their right mind, so the lyric poets are not in their right mind when they are composing their beautiful strains: but when falling under the power of music and metre they are inspired and possessed; like Bacchic maidens who draw milk and honey from the rivers when they are under the influence of Dionysus, but not when they are in their right mind. And the soul of the lyric poet does the same, as they themselves tell us; for they tell us that they bring songs from honied fountains, culling them out of the gardens and dells of the Muses; whither like the bees they wing their way. And this is true. For the poet is a light and winged and holy thing, and there is no invention in him until he has been inspired and is out of his senses, and the mind is no longer in him: when he has not attained to this state, he is powerless and is unable to utter his oracles. . . . . and therefore God takes away the minds of poets, and uses them as his ministers, as he also uses diviners and holy prophets, in order that we who hear them may know that they speak not of themselves who utter these priceless words in a state of unconsciousness, but that God is the speaker, and that through them he is conversing with us.[31]

For Schelling, genius is "ein Stück aus der Absolutheit Gottes." The genius himself "can only follow that law which God and nature have written in his heart—no other."[32] For Schopenhauer, genius is the power of releasing the intellect from earthly servitude to the will to live:

It also follows from the fact that the kind of knowledge peculiar to genius is essentially that which is purified from all will and its relations, that the works of genius do not proceed from intention or choice, but is guided in them by a kind of instinctive necessity. What is called the awakening of genius, the hour of initiation, the moment of inspiration, is nothing but the attainment of freedom by the intellect, when, delivered for a

---

[31] Jowett's translation. The idea of a peculiar affinity between genius and insanity has been a recurrent one from Plato to Lombroso.

[32] Miss Egan, Part II, pp. 21 and 23 f.

while from its service under the will, it does not now sink into inactivity or lassitude, but is active for a short time entirely alone and spontaneously. Then it is of the greatest purity, and becomes the clear mirror of the world; for, completely severed from its origin, the will, it is now the world as idea itself, concentrated in one consciousness. In such moments, as it were, the souls of immortal works are begotten. On the other hand, in all intentional reflection the intellect is not free, for indeed the will guides it and prescribes its theme.[33]

Croce, like Bergson, opposes intuition to intellect. Art springs from intuition. Now:

. . . . intuitive knowledge is expressive knowledge. Independent and autonomous in respect to intellectual function; indifferent to later empirical discriminations, to reality and to unreality, to formations and apperceptions of space and time, which are also later: intuition or representation is distinguished as form from what is felt and suffered, from the flux or wave of sensation, or from psychic matter; and this form, this taking possession, is expression. To intuite is to express; and nothing else (nothing more, but nothing less) than *to express*.[34]

But expression—what is that? "Expression is free inspiration."[35] The work of art, therefore, is the "free inspiration" of the genius.

To the idealists on the opposite wing, the problem of the genius is not altogether so simple. Kant is very decided in his opposition to the notion of untalented or untrained genius:

Now seeing that originality of talent is one (though not the sole) essential factor that goes to make up the character of genius, shallow minds fancy that the best evidence they can give of their being full-blown geniuses is by emancipating themselves from all academic constraint of rules, in the belief that one cuts

---

[33] *The World as Will and Idea*, 3:143.
[34] *Aesthetic*, 11.
[35] *Ibid.*, 51.

a finer figure on the back of an ill-tempered than of a trained horse. Genius can do no more than furnish rich *material* for products of fine art; its elaboration and its *form* require a talent academically trained, so that it may be employed in such a way as to stand the test of judgement.

Coming at the question more directly, Kant continues:

So far as beauty is concerned, to be fertile and original in ideas is not such an imperative requirement as it is that the imagination in its freedom should be in accordance with the understanding's conformity to law. For in lawless freedom imagination, with all its wealth, produces nothing but nonsense; the power of judgement, on the other hand, is the faculty that makes it consonant with understanding. . . . . And so, where the interests of both these qualities clash in a product, and there has to be a sacrifice of something, then it should rather be on the side of genius; and judgement, which in matters of fine art bases its decision on its own proper principles, will more readily endure an abatement of the freedom and wealth of the imagination, than that the understanding should be compromised.[36]

In his later career, Goethe uttered numerous warnings against a blind belief in "original genius." He vigorously condemned the excesses of the younger "Sturm und Drang" writers. Art requires more than letting oneself go, in ignorance or in contempt of the rules. When art has risen to perfection, it has been accompanied by knowledge, regularity, sincerity, and force ("Kenntnis, Regelmäszigkeit, Ernst und Strenge").[37] Pure genius itself will not suffice. For: "Nature is separated from art by an enormous chasm which genius of itself is unable to bridge without external assistance."[38] Hegel is equally firm in this matter:

---

[36] *Critique of Aesthetic Judgement*, Part I, book 2 §§ 47 and 50.
[37] *Einleitung in die Propyläen.*
[38] *Ibid.* I use Miss Egan's translation (Part II, p. 7).

The real and indeed the sole point to maintain as essential is the thesis that although artistic talent and genius essentially implies an element of natural power, yet it is equally indispensable that it should be thoughtfully cultivated, that reflection should be brought to bear on the particular way it is exercised, and that it should be also kept alive with use and practice in actual work. The fact is that an important aspect of the creating process is merely facility in the use of a medium ["eine äusserliche Arbeit]; that is to say, a work of art possesses a purely technical side, which extends to the borders of mere handicraft.[39]

It is clear that there exists a distinct division among idealists over the question of the importance and validity of talent as an aid to the inspiration of genius. For the members of one group—one may call them the "easy" idealists—the only fact which matters is the mystical communion of the absolute with the special mental faculty of the artist—so that it is sufficient to call the work of art the product of the unconscious, the will to live, the intuition, the soul, or whatever other term the special faculty may be known as. The "difficult" idealists, like Kant, Hegel, and the mature Goethe, feel that the spectacle of an untrained "original genius" following the free wanderings of his instinct (or otherwise named special faculty) is uncomfortably close to that of the drunken man or the idiot mumbling his gibberish. This feeling, it is to be observed, is based directly upon empirical observation. They consequently declare that inspiration is not enough—that it must be supplemented by patiently developed talent.

Since this is a family quarrel among idealists, it may be thought that the empiricist can well avoid entering it. It is impossible, however, for him to remain aloof. He is

---

[39] *The Philosophy of Fine Art*, 1:40.

directly concerned with the pretensions of the "difficult" idealists. These writers are idealists; yet they wish to palliate what they observe to be the absurdities of the idealist's position by appropriating the materials of the empiricist. They have eaten their cake; yet they wish to have it, too. They assume, naïvely or knowingly, that idealism and empiricism can be reconciled by picturing them as copartners striving harmoniously for one goal. The entire history of philosophic thought starkly belies this assumption. It is the empiricist's duty, therefore, to demonstrate its false and untenable nature by pointing out the contradictions and fallacies inherent in it.

The "difficult" idealist declares that inspiration—the communion of the spirit of eternal beauty with the special mental faculty of the mind—is not sufficient to explain the artistic productions of the genius. Since inspiration is independent and perfect aesthetic knowledge, he declares, in effect, that perfection is not enough. This seems an absurdity. A perfect, one would think, must either be a sufficient explanation of the phenomenon it deals with or it is not a perfect at all. Now the agent which is to assist and supplement the absolute is the kind of aesthetic knowledge arising from talent. Its source is entirely "earthly." It is acquired by observation of elements of the environment, by continual trials in imitation of models, by muscular agility, by constant practice, by patient progression toward a clearly defined goal. It is the ordinary, mundane sort of artistic knowledge; consequently, it is always incomplete and ever capable of being improved. Thus it is precisely opposite in character to inspired knowledge.

One is to assume, then, that the perfect absolute must have the assistance of the ever imperfect and earthly if it is to accomplish its ends. How can two implacably opposed sorts of knowledge afford each other mutual aid? Furthermore, there has now been erected from empirical materials an external standard or law to which the absolute—which is supposed to lie completely outside all mundane laws—*must* bind itself. Artistic inspiration *cannot* visit anyone who is not talented.

Now the empirical term "talented" can be applied only to a man who is exhibiting the capacity of his talent by actual construction of works of art. Consequently inspiration can strike only the artist who is already producing works through the sole agency of talent. But there are many degrees of talented accomplishment. Is the idealist not obliged to agree that the highest talent affords the most fitting aid to the absolute? Is it not true, then, that the chances of the artist in the matter of receiving inspiration are increased in direct proportion to the increase of his talent? The absolute must thus feel a special affinity with the most highly talented artist. This is to say that it always fights on the side of the heaviest artillery. The spark from the absolute strikes most frequently (if not exclusively) those artists whose works of artistic beauty are capable of the most satisfactory explanation merely in terms of the talent they have acquired. Is it, then, not sufficient to say that talent by itself produces beautiful works of art? What part can be ascribed to the absolute? Does it merely add its blessing? If it does more, then what empirically inexplicable gap lies between a work produced by an artist of the highest talent and one created by another artist of equal talent who has also been inspired by a vision of absolute beauty?

The question, it can be seen, is now entirely reversed. The "difficult" idealist generously grants that the materials of the empiricist are a necessary adjunct to the idealistic explanation of a work of artistic beauty. The empiricist ungenerously retorts that, if empirical materials or means are employed at all, they must be fully employed. None of them can be allowed to remain inoperative. And when this is done, he adds, it is discovered that the absolute is *not* a necessary adjunct to the empirical explanation of a beautiful work of art.

According to the "easy" idealist, the genius follows the gleam of the absolute and ignores the earthly demands and exactions of talent. Surely this is, for the idealist, the only tenable position. Inspiration is independent, perfect, and complete aesthetic knowledge. It comes from the absolute, whose ways, for man, are mysterious and inscrutable. He who experiences the visitation has received a free gift which he has done nothing to merit. The recipient has no personal influence over the situation. He is simply the passive agent through which the absolute speaks. When the spark of beauty strikes him it takes complete possession of him; the beautiful work of art it causes him to create is thereby fully accounted for.

Certainly, absolute knowledge cannot be aided or influenced by the merely "useful" knowledge which serves a man's purposes in his ordinary, uninspired, daily activities. These two kinds of knowledge are mutually abhorrent to each other; the presence of the one involves the entire absence of the other. And to cultivate the earthly knowledge which is the concern of talent means for the genius to incur the danger of a clouding, a short-circuiting of his pure conducting qualities as a medium. It is only when he loses his right mind (Plato), when he follows the laws God has written in his heart (Schelling), when he denies his will (Schopenhauer), when he abjures intelligence (Croce)—that he is in the pure state which is the necessary preliminary for inspiration.

Opposed in all particulars to the idealistic view of beauty in art stands the aesthetic whose principles are developed in strict accordance with the dictates of .. radical empiricism and of scientific classification. A definition of the beautiful in obedience to these dictates has already been presented. This has now to be followed with an empirical definition of art.

*The spectacle presented by art is that of a man (the artist) expressing his desires on his environment through a medium. The successful result of this expression is a product (the beautiful work of art) which represents a portion of the environment in the state in which the artist (and, it may be, a spectator) wishes it to be—a state of complete subservience to those desires.*

If this definition is scientific, then it has shown the beautiful in art to be a subdivision of the beautiful. A scientific subdivision has two properties. It unites itself with the larger division by the possession of the characteristics which identify that division. Secondly, to justify its existence as a genuine subclass, it owns, in addition, certain distinctive characteristics of its own. The definition ascribes both these properties to the subdivision of the beautiful in art.

The kinship of artistic beauty with general beauty is readily apparent. The background in both is that of a man living in the midst of a heterogeneous environment, and endeavoring to stamp upon it the impress of the human desires which he is incapable of satisfying with the fund of experience at that moment in his possession. In both divisions, also, the man applies the term "beautiful" to the object (or situation) which has those qualities toward which his desires point—which is in the state in which he wishes it to be. Such an object gives direction to his present activities. By possessing it he can win what is for him a highly pleasurable victory over the environment, for he can immediately assimilate it to his purposes. And by adding his experience of it to his general fund of experience, he can formulate plans for a new goal of desire.

Thus general beauty and artistic beauty are both an expression of the ideal—the what *should be*—as distinguished from the actual—the what *is*. But they are purely empirical "ideals." They are set up by men within the environment. The human desires which frame them arise within and as a result of experience. The goal which these ideals express may be, for the individual, capable or incapable of realization within the ordinary environment. The standard, the sole standard, must be human experience itself. It follows that the most desirable—that is, the most beautiful—ideal is the one which has the most direct and the fullest relations with the standard by which it is judged. Such an ideal will have the qualities of complete potentiality—the ability to translate itself, in the life of some individual, fully and directly into the actual.

But the beautiful in art distinguishes itself from the beautiful in general by possessing characteristics of its own. These are three in number:

1. The man expressing his desires upon the environment is called an *artist*.

2. The expression of these desires is contained within a *medium*.

3. The result or product of the labor of expression is known as a *work of art*.

It is these three distinctive differences which justify the existence of the subclass. Consequently, it is with them that a discussion of the beautiful in art is primarily concerned.

In the world of ordinary activities a man will apply the term "beautiful" to any object or situation which meets his wishes. He will do this regardless of the influence he has exercised in bringing about the status of the object or situation. Some of the things he calls beautiful have been fashioned entirely by his own exertions. Others have been under his control only to a limited degree. Perhaps the greatest number exist in complete independence of his personal efforts; he has not in any way been instrumental in fashioning them. They have been created by others; they have resulted from a collocation of circumstances in which, not the situation, but only its component members have been subject to control; or they may be portions of the environment entirely free from human direction.

But when the man is called an artist, two specific implications are imported into this general state of affairs. In the first place, an artist is engaged in creating a beautiful through the agency of his own efforts by laboring in some well defined activity. Secondly, these efforts are of a character so consciously directed, deliberate, and aggressive that their product is an object which has been brought under the complete control of the artist's desires.

The artist is not thereby different from other men. In life every man labors to control the future in his favor. But his difficulty is that his attempts are always partly frustrated by the innumerable intractable phenomena of a heterogeneous environment. No matter how laborious his present efforts, a man is seldom able to attain the precise future result he desires. Discordant elements, evading control, regularly intermingle with the products of human efforts—so that the result attained is less satisfactory than the result aimed at. It is to overcome this situation to some degree that the scientist removes from the environment to his laboratory certain more or less homologous phenomena. Faced with the same situation, the artist turns from the general environment to a medium in which it may be represented.

His advantages thereby become pronounced. For the medium he employs will have two characteristics. It will be of such a nature that perhaps a considerable portion of the human environment can be represented within it. And it will to an advanced degree be amenable to his personal control. The aims which the artist, as a man, wishes to see gratified within the world, he can, as artist, impress upon his medium. Therein he can attain them, if not more easily (for the medium imposes demands of its own), at least more readily and successfully than in life. For he can omit from his representation those uncongenial, inimical, or discordant elements which, in life, would fight against the occurrence of the end he strives for. And he can manipulate the elements he does not omit—so that the result attained within the medium can be in complete harmony with his human desires. In this way the work of art gains a completeness, a perfection, which is not usual (perhaps not possible) with objects and situations in life. It can set up an ideal which represents certain aims of men carried, under certain circumstances, to logical and desirable completion. The result is as entire as the correct answer to a problem in mathematics. Nothing can be added to it. It has employed all the potentialities which the circumstances afford.

The work of art has another advantage as well. It not only forces the elements of the environment it represents to accept the deep impression of human aims; it also compels them to "stay put" and retain that impress—thus gratifying a universal human desire which seldom attains gratification. In life a beautiful object or situation fades or otherwise dissipates itself in a comparatively brief space of time. The continuous flux of the environment will not permit it to remain stationary. The work of art, because of the usual nature of its medium, is a less temporary beautiful. This is not to say that it is permanent or eternal. For neither artist nor medium can exist apart from the universal flow of things. The desires of the artist may, in the future, change so radically that he no longer considers his artistic product beautiful. And the material of which the medium is composed is itself subject to the vicissitudes, fluctuations, and calamities to which all phenomena must submit. But absolute permanency is not required. Any stability of greater duration than that ordinarily afforded by the shifting circumstances of life will emphasize the beauty of the work of art.

It has now been shown that the beautiful in art, a subclass of the beautiful, may be identified by three distinctive terms associated with it—artist, medium, work of art. The next step in an empirical description will obviously be to examine the nature of artistic expression within a specific medium. To do this, however, will be to leave the subject of artistic beauty in general and to enter the restricted confines of a new subdivision. Since literature is the particular art which is here being approached, this next step will be to pass beyond the field of aesthetics into that of literature and literary criticism.

There must likewise be a postponement of any serious effort to force an issue with the idealist on the basis merely of an empirical definition of the beautiful in art. It is evident that the specific data which the empiricist requires for such a contest have not yet been encountered. On the question of the beautiful in art, just as on that of abstract beauty, the position of the empiricist must be mainly defensive. It is essential, however, even for a defensive position, that he make a complete denial of the spirit-matter dualism which the dictates of the idealist's system require him to introduce into aesthetics.

It has been seen, in connection with the subject of abstract beauty, that the idealist, in obedience to his principles, must assume a complete divorce between the beautiful and the useful. This cleavage is reflected in art as an opposition between art and life. It is the idealist's duty to emphasize such a division. To the empiricist, no attempt to assert a fundamental distinction between art and life can be successful. For both are grounded on human experience itself. A society which possesses any margin above that of mere existence will employ itself in endeavoring to increase its margin. Its members, on the basis of the experiences they are undergoing, will formulate plans for achieving the fuller expression of their instinctive human desires. Such plans lead them to definite vocations—to labors by means of which new tools may be fashioned to gain victories over a reluctant environment. Art is one of these vocations. The artist is a laborer among other laborers.

It is undeniable that there is a commonly accepted, even if superficial, distinction between labor in an art and labor in an ordinary vocation. It was asserted (in the preceding chapter) that the beautiful may be distinguished from the useful by the fact that it contains a distinctly strong reference to the future, and that it is regularly applied as a term to designate the highest degree of the useful. These same two distinctions are applicable to the question of art and life.

In any vocation the object of the laborer is to control the future in his favor. Actually, of course, the future *cannot* be made certain; there are in it chance contingencies largely beyond the power of man to anticipate. Success in present pursuits, however, brings a favorable future within the range of the probable or possible. If the objects which the man's vocation concerns show themselves tractable to his manipulation of them in accordance with his wishes, then the augury of future benefit is bright. Now the medium of the artist is always one upon which the desires of men may be markedly impressed. This is particularly the case in what are called the fine, or final, arts—literature, painting, music, sculpture, and architecture. Each of these has a distinctly representative medium—a medium, that is, which is capable of reflecting comparatively large portions of the environment within itself. Consequently, in each work of fine art the future reference is strong. For in it the artist can, on the basis of his present experiences, depict through labor upon its medium a future state conforming to his desires.

In the ordinary occupations of men such a comprehensive forecast is rarely possible. The objects or situations in these occupations resist the stamp of man's desires. Hence they cannot be employed to project or prefigure a markedly favorable future. To be of use in this respect they must usually be taken in conjunction with other objects or situations. If the latter lie outside the field of the individual's activities, he will possess little guaranty. The future reference of the objects of concern to him in his specific vocation will be weak; they will refer rather to other objects in the present upon which they are contingent. Under these circumstances the laborer's vocation may indeed enable him to procure present subsistence—to earn his living; and it may to a certain indefinite degree assure his future by enabling him, through his labors within it, to save against sickness and old age. But it is always true that, in the measure in which the vocation fails to grant the laborer the strong guaranties he desires in order that his margin of survival may be increased to its utmost possible extent—in that degree the vocation becomes unsatisfactory to him.

And if the strong future reference of art—particularly of fine art—encourages and invigorates human effort, the present satisfactions it affords are equally satisfying. An art can be mastered; it can to a marked degree be made to subserve the purposes of men. Art may, indeed, be defined as a vocation within which the desires of man may be expressed with a gratifying fulness. It is a supremely useful labor. And the fact that it combines present utility with a strong future guaranty makes it a satisfactory labor. But it thereby differs from other satisfactory labors only in degree. For the standard of satisfaction in all labors depends upon the degree to which they meet the two universal human demands just enunciated.

To the idealist, however, beautiful art occupies another sphere of existence. It represents solely the spiritual absolute; hence it is free, disinterested, and independent. It is entirely removed from earthly vocations. These are merely "useful," since activity in them always has reference to other earthly interests—such as earning a living. In order to set up the dualism thus made imperative, the idealist once again forces human experience into two arbitrary and artificial categories. On the one hand, he relegates to the fine arts all satisfactions for present expression and future well-being demanded by men in their activities. On the other hand he displays what he calls "useful" labor—labor from which most human gratifications have been deliberately eliminated.

Now it is certainly true that, in a machine age in a highly complex society, great numbers of workers are unfortunately obliged to engage in labor which is of such a nature that no appreciable progress toward the satisfaction of even the most moderate expression of human desires is possible within it. Such workers usually have little knowledge of the processes necessary to create the whole of the product with which their labor is associated; their efforts are confined to mechanical acts which involve only a fraction of the entire creation. Thus they have no control over the product of their labors and no opportunity of impressing their personal aims upon it. Labor of this sort is indeed sharply separated from art. But it is likewise sharply separated from healthy and normal human labor. Since it means the starvation of any human impulses above those of bare survival, it is a maddening business for any normal man: "I screwed on nut 22," said the factory laborer, "till I got to be nut 22 myself."[40]

One readily sees that the starvation of impulses which mechanical labor imposes will force the laborer to seek relief in outside recreations. He may enter the fine arts in search of such relief. In this case it is important to inquire the character of the type of art which affords

---

[40] Cf. Ruskin (*Lectures on Art*, delivered at Oxford in 1870): "..... life without industry is guilt, and industry without art is brutality." In these same lectures Ruskin gives his well-known solution: "Agriculture by the hand, then, and absolute refusal or banishment of unnecessary igneous force, are the first conditions of a school of art in any country." In Erewhon such a solution could indeed be carried into effect. To banish machines from the present industrial society would be as calamitous as it would be impossible. And it would not provide an effectual solution. "But a people," writes Mr. Santayana (*Reason in Art*, 21), "once having become industrial will hardly be happy if sent back to Arcadia; it will have formed busy habits which it cannot relax without tedium; it will have developed a restlessness and avidity which will crave matter like any other kind of hunger." One must, nevertheless, admit than an industrial system brings evils in its train. And one may contend that any genuine improvement in the situation must come about by alterations in the character of industrial labor itself, and not through increased provision for outside amusements and recreations —which are drugs merely.

him compensatory gratification—an inquiry which must receive attention at some future stage of the present discussion.

It has already been observed in what further implications the idealist's basic spirit-matter dichotomy involves him. If the beautiful in art is an absolute, then all the elements of which art is composed must also be spiritual —holding in abhorrence the thought of any connection or association with the material. The artist retires from the world to a communion with his special faculty; the material elements of a work of art are overpowered and sublimated by spirit; the work itself, being the perfect representation of something in another realm, is not affected by the desires of men nor subject to the flux of the environment.

But if art is a labor not differing in kind from other human labors, then these three elements—artist, medium, work of art—have as full and firm a connection with the experiences and the surroundings of men as have the elements of any other vocation of man.

The artist is a man with human impulses living amid earthly surroundings. When he expresses himself within an artistic medium, it is his personal experiences, prejudices, aims, idiosyncrasies, which will be reflected therein. He seeks from his labor the human gratifications sought by all laborers—existence for the present, the opportunity of expression, and some encouraging guarantee for the future. If he would procure these returns from his art, he must seek a market for his product. He must shape his work to meet the needs and wishes of his fellow men, so that, in return for his labor, they will grant him the personal satisfactions he desires. This consideration—the economic aspect of art—has always been of the greatest importance in determining the character of the artist's

labors. Artists have always obeyed its demands. Painters of the Renaissance used religious themes (often
with donors' portraits included) ; the seventeenth-century
Dutch painters drew portraits of rich burghers and mer-
chant companies. The composer of music has written love
songs, dance tunes, and military marches. Literary artists have earned a livelihood from royal whim, political
influence, priestly countenance, tribe approval, and the
general favor of the public. Their productions have reflected almost every individual and group interest known
to man. They have written stories and poems of love,
paeans of praise to royalty and to military or civil leaders, political pamphlets, tales of adventure and heroism,
of utopian realms, of religious practices and benefits, of
achievement in daily life, of past glories of chief and tribe.

The medium employed by the artist is part of the
environment, and develops, changes, and fades in the
manner normal to earthly things. The work of art is
directly conditioned by these changes. The use of steel
in building affects architecture. The changes in the living
language and the discovery of new forms of expression
(the sonnet, the essay, the novel) cause changes in literature. Improvements in musical instruments as well as
new forms of expression (counterpoint, the whole tone
scale, symphonies, tone poems) influence music. And a
mastery of the medium must be gained in the manner in
which all human knowledge is acquired—by observation,
practice, elimination of error.

The work of art itself exists within the environment
in no less degree than does the medium. Calamity, decay,
or Warburton's cook may effect its total disruption. It is
dependent, too, upon the favor of men. Should it no
longer reflect their desires, it is forgotten, for then it is
no longer beautiful.

To say that an artist is a man, that he must procure enough food to support life, that he must have an eye to his market, that he must master his medium by constant practice, that his work may fall to pieces—what are these but ponderous truisms? They are granted without question by everyone. The idealist, when not directly confronted or cornered, admits them himself and is willing to lead the unwary to believe that he grants them a certain amount of genuine validity. Now since they *are* commonplaces, it is most important to note that the aesthetic of the idealist *is based upon* the denial or the calm ignoring of them. In place of an art which grows out of, belongs to, and is in constant intercourse with, the environment, the idealist has an art essentially separate from all earthly things. Instead of an art which expresses the experiences and desires of men, he has an art which expresses the will of the absolute. Idealist art is an ivory tower. To gain admission there, one must, like the neophyte in the ancient mysteries, cast off all earthly garments and, naked, pass through the portals. Within the walls there is one power, and no other—the absolute, whose ways are past finding out.[41]

---

41 Two writers on aesthetics at the present day have attempted to govern their labors by strictly empirical principles. One of these is Mr. Laurence Buermeyer, author of *The Aesthetic Experience* (1924). The other is Professor Charles Lalo, whose many volumes are not so well known in America as they deserve to be. My discussion of art is indebted to the works of both these writers—particularly to M. Lalo's *L'art et la vie sociale* (1921). Both of them combat with vigor and effect the idealistic principles of aesthetics. Unfortunately, however, the importance of both for an empirical aesthetic must remain largely negative. On the positive side, they both fail to erect a working method. Mr. Buermeyer contents himself with theory unsupported by consistent empirical data. M. Lalo is willing to accept all individual opinions of whatever sort about a work of art; he conceives criticism to consist of an attempted synthesis of these. Their main difficulty, it seems to me, arises from the situation which I have pointed out in the chapter above: an empiricist must formulate his critical method by observation within a specified field—like literature. Within the department of general aesthetics he cannot force an issue with the idealist, for he cannot therein disclose the origin and the full strength of his own method.

# CHAPTER V

# LITERATURE

*The spectacle presented by literature is that of an artist (a literary artist, or author) expressing his desires on his environment through the medium of language, so as to arrive, when successful, at a result (the beautiful work of literature) which shows a portion of the environment in the state in which the artist (and presumably a reader) desires it to be—a state of entire submission to those desires.*

The beautiful in literature is thus a genuine subdivision of the beautiful in art. Both of them show their kinship to the beautiful in general, since both deal with the what should be. They are united, furthermore, in that they set forth this ideal through an artist working in a medium to attain, as a product, a work of art. The smaller division, however, differs from the larger, and justifies its existence as a subclass, through the facts that the artist is a literary artist or author, that his medium is the specific one of language, and that his product is a work of literature. It follows that these three special characteristics must be the subject of any discussion of the beautiful in literature.

There can be no more important medium than that employed by literature. Man is eminently a tool-using animal; but he is almost equally a language-using animal. Were it not for his second characteristic ability, his first would be of little general benefit. Language is the agency employed by men to transmit to other men the sum of their experiences with the environment. It is thus one of his most effective weapons in the eternal fight which must

be waged with that environment. It reports human desires, thus giving meaning and direction to human effort;
it makes possible the existence of groups united for common purposes. By transmitting the results of personal
efforts, language causes the experiences of a few to be
added to the fund of those of all; and it gives to human
knowledge a cumulative and relatively permanent character. In brief, language is vicarious experience. It is
experience *verbalized*. From his earliest days a man
depends on language for the development of interests of
major importance to his existence. It follows that language, since it must serve to report all human experience,
is man's most expressive and inclusive medium. And if
language can be made to a considerable degree a substitute for experience, it must follow, likewise, that men
have learned to feel an association peculiarly close
between words and things.[1]

It is this universal medium of spoken or written language that the literary artist employs in order to create,
through his labors with it, a product which shall express
his conception of the beautiful. It is important, therefore,
to note the basic qualities of this medium—to see how
adequately it can represent the complex phenomena which
compose the environment upon which the author has personal desires to express. Certain weaknesses of the
medium are at once apparent. Spoken language has a
certain pitch and rhythm. But it cannot reproduce sounds
in the way that music does. Nor can language present
objects directly to the eye of the observer—so that it is
inferior here to the media of the painter and the sculptor.
But these two limitations detract little from the general
effectiveness of literature as a medium. Men, it has been

---

[1] Indeed, from this point of view, one may hold that the idealist's error
is that he confounds the two.

noted, feel the closest association between words and things. If objects or sounds, consequently, are verbalized with sufficient fidelity, language can suffer no great disability from the fact that it is not itself an object or a medium directly expressive of sound.[2]

If the limitations of language as a medium do not materially detract from its effectiveness, its basic and characteristic ability gives it, on the other hand, a position of eminence among the representative media employed by the fine arts. The literary medium can accurately reproduce the most salient and universal property of the environment—its flux, change, motion in time. It can represent men in continuous and progressive contact with this environment, attempting to impose their aims upon it. It can thus penetrate to the heart of human life and deal with its most complicated relations. For the spectacle presented by life itself may, it has been seen, be envisaged as that of a combat between man and his surroundings.

The fact that literature employs language as its agency of expression means, consequently, that its characteristic ability is that of portraying men in action amid the unceasing flux or continuum of the enviroment. Other fine arts can merely suggest action of this sort; they cannot adequately portray it. Thus it is by the unique ability it possesses that the essential worth and position of literature as a fine art must be measured.[3]

But literature will employ this medium for its own purpose—that of expressing the beautiful within it. More-

---

[2] The poet and the dramatist employ measures which further counteract these disabilities. See *infra*, p. 201 f.

[3] Cf. Lessing's *Laokoön* (trans. E. C. Beasley, 1879): "I maintain that succession of time is the department of the poet, as space is that of the painter." The contention that the office of literature is to represent action is basic to the entire essay. But Lessing himself is here following the familiar opening passages of Aristotle's *Poetics*.

over, a work of literature is created by an artist. Both these facts make necessary important qualifications with respect to the use to which language is put by literature.

The author is a man living within the environment and harboring designs against it. It is these designs (together with the fund of personal experiences on which they are based) that he will necessarily express through his labors within the literary medium. And the finished artistic product will, in the author's eyes, be beautiful. It will represent his environment in the state in which he wishes it to be. Now the finished product in nearly all the arts sets forth only the final result of this personal expression. But literature, because of the nature of its medium, is able to depict the successive stages of progression toward that result,[4] and to adopt in so doing the same point of view as that from which the author, like every man, beholds the situation—that of a struggle of a man against his surroundings. The author thus directly depicts this struggle. But over his representation he possesses artistic control. Accordingly, he can state the conflict he depicts in such terms that the result he desires may be attained in the completed product. These facts considered, a more specific definition of the function of literature becomes possible. *It is the office of literature to represent ideal (i.e., fictional) action—action depicting a struggle between a character (or group of characters) and his environment which leads toward and culminates in the imposition of his desires upon it, so that the finished artistic product portrays that environment as it exists subsequent to its subjection to those desires.*[5]

---

[4] Cf. *Laokoön:* "And thus . . . . in the poet we see the making of that which, in the artist, we see only as made."

[5] It is worth noting, perhaps, at this point that the terms of this definition do not require the result of this imposition of desires to be successful. The environment may reject the pattern. In other words, tragedy is not excluded.

Three separate elements are involved in the situation just described. There is the author himself, with his experiences and his aims based on them. There is the general earthly environment in which he lives with other men. There is, finally, the conflict of human desires and environment as it is artistically worked out within the literary medium. The third element here is the product of the reactions of the first two with each other; its character varies, consequently, in accordance with the results of those reactions. It is apparent also that the aims of the author will be determined by the circumstances of his individual and personal experiences; accordingly, the author himself is the second variable among the three components of the situation. But the general earthly environment may here be regarded as a constant—as the standard which determines the character both of the author's experiences and of his work of literature which reflects them. Because of these circumstances, the situation may be more significantly stated as follows: *The character of a work of literature is a variable resulting from the interaction of the author (a variable) and the environment (a constant).*

Materials are now available for a further classification of a work of literature. For the personal wishes of an author upon his environment group themselves into three large categories.

I. The aims of the author may be so inordinate that there exists no possibility of their fulfillment within the earthly environment.

It has been remarked that all human beings seek to experience as much satisfaction of their instinctive desires as can possibly be attained. To a greater or lesser extent, therefore, their ambitions outrun the existing circumstances in which they are placed. But there is an outer limit beyond which these ambitions may not pass if they would retain a potentiality. This limit is imposed by the general environment itself. Within its stream there exist numerous forces, great numbers of concatenations of object with object, many regular and readily observable stages of progression and change. These are constant and unvarying manifestations. A man has no chance of escaping them. The very fact that he is alive means that he recognizes and assumes them as the basis and framework of all his discoveries and achievements. They are continually being forced upon his attention, and they recur with a persistence and uniformity which show them to be of the basic texture of the environment. Such phenomena are thus indubitably present within whatever section of the surroundings the author selects as the material upon which to impose his desires as man and artist.

When the desires of the author transgress the limits set up by the environment, the realization of them becomes impossible within whatever part of it he chances to live. But within a work of literature they may be exhibited as gratified. Since the author has control over the literary medium, he may set forth the conflict he depicts in such a manner that the extravagant aims he cherishes are attained. But such a result can be forthcoming only if the environment depicted within the medium breaks radically with the reality after which it is modelled. There must exist within the former some rupture of the basic texture of the latter—some ignoring of major phenomena, some break in the temporal or causal nexus. And works of literature which depict an environment thus basically distorted may be collectively characterized as literature which violates possibility.

II. The aims of the author may run counter to the normal workings of the environment, so that they can be achieved therein only by a breach of probability.

Any human desire whose realization does not demand the sacrifice of the fundamental internal connections of the environment bears within itself the possibility of fulfillment. This means that it has been gratified or may be gratified in certain geographical localities, on certain occasions, under certain circumstances, and within the experience of certain individuals. It does not mean that there is any likelihood of realization if these special conditions are absent. But the determinant of the work of literature posited as a constant was not a portion of the environment subjected to special conditions; it was the general environment taken in all its manifestations. And when viewed as a whole, the workings of this environment are seen to group themselves about certain norms. Certain results are observed to proceed from certain causes when no exceptional conditions are present. To determine these norms is a matter of great importance to all men. To foresee the special circumstances is beyond human power; to foresee the normal expectation is not. If a man bases his ambitions upon future events which are likely, the chances of success are in his favor; whereas they become markedly inferior when his aims require the operation of circumstances which are possible but not normal. Consequently, every man seeks to build upon probability—a forecast of the workings of the environment reasonably free from the chance variations of time and place.[6]

---

[6] *Webster's New International Dictionary* defines "probability" as follows: "In the doctrine of chance, the likelihood of the occurrence of any particular form of an event; the ratio of the frequency of that form of the event to the entire frequency of the event in all forms."

The aims of the author upon his surroundings may thus remain within the bounds of possibility; yet they may, nevertheless, violate probability. They will then be aims which *have been* gratified, and again under special conditions *may be* gratified—but aims which, taking the environment in all its manifestations, *should not* be gratified. The author may, assuredly, arrange the elements of the conflict he chooses to reproduce within his medium so that the fulfillment of his desires is effected. But the result will be attained only by representing an environment which, compared with its model, is acting at variance with the norms of probability. Works which reflect such a result constitute literature which violates probability.

III. The aims of the author may be of such a nature that their realization within his environment appears probable and likely.

Let it be supposed that the author, as a result of his experiences, entertains plans which the environment appears to support. His labors within the literary medium will not, in that event, be animated by the desire to illustrate how an environment radically different from the existing one would justify the wishes of man—nor how the environment when subjected to unusual, temporary, and exceptional conditions would afford a like result. His purpose will be to discover to what extent the normal and probable flow of things appears to favor the desires which he, an individual, entertains against a certain number of these things. This purpose will be assisted in every way if he can depict within his medium a conflict of man and environment which most nearly and accurately reproduces the conflict in which he and all other men are engaged within the earthly environment. His task as an author will be to apply the standards of probability, as they manifest themselves within the environment as a whole, to the particular portion of it he wishes to represent in his medium. The more fully and accurately he portrays his specific phenomena, the more clearly will be revealed the normal and likely reaction to them of the standards according to which that constant, the entire human environment, can be observed to operate. Naturally, his medium will not allow him to reproduce reality in every minute particular. But it will permit a fair and equitable reproduction in which no violence is done to the normal operations of the basic concatenations of earthly experience.

The works of literature which authors with such aims will produce may be classed as literature which obeys probability. Works of this type—and only those of this type—represent the potential aspects of human experience. They do so by employing the fullest resources of the medium to discover and report the workings of any portion of the environment as forecast by the workings of the whole of it. Their subject matter is characterized by life-like fidelity of reproduction. Every attempt is made to substitute the medium of language for the actual experiences of men. In short, literature which deals with the probable has the closest and most extensive affiliations with human life.

The value of the threefold division just made becomes apparent when the question is raised as to the purpose and importance of literature itself. What is the value of literature for human knowledge? What relation do the results it attains bear to those attained in other departments of human knowledge? What, in short, is the difference between literature and science—between the author and the scientific experimenter? It is clear that the most effective answers to such questions can be arrived at by using the materials supplied by the last of the three types demarcated, the type which is faithful to probability. This is not to declare that the two remaining types—that which violates possibility and that which violates probability—are not also to be classed as genuine literature; and it is not to deny that they have purposes and attain results of their own. But it *is* to assert that, if one is to compare literature with other departments of knowledge in respect to its influence on the lives of men, one must turn to that type of literature which, it has been shown, has the fullest, the closest, and the most significant relations with human experience.

The author and the scientist both face the same general human environment. Both, as men, lay plans continually to impress upon it the pattern of their desires in order that they may attain the present satisfaction of instinctive impulses and the guarantee of future well-being that attends an increased margin of survival. Both, accordingly, enter upon and engage in labors which may accomplish their purposes. They are aware that their respective labors must be carried on within the general environment and must thus be inevitably subject to its laws.

The fundamental difference between author and scientific experimenter appears when the materials with which they labor are given consideration. The scientist, a specialist, concentrates his attention upon phenomena which form but a small portion of the entire environment. They are not representative of it; they are only a fragment of a heterogeneous whole. Yet these phenomena are homologous; it can be observed that they act together in a definite and more or less uniform manner. It is the scientist's business to discover the precise nature of this coherence, this homology. The validity of his final step is conditioned directly upon his ability to effect this discovery in terms of an hypothesis. If his observations and his groupings are essentially sound, then the section of the environment with which he has been concerned will, in its hypothesized state, fit without violence into the general frame from which it was drawn and into which it must be reinserted.

Under these circumstances, it is clearly impossible for the scientist, in his first two steps, to impose his personal desires upon his phenomena. They will not admit this imposition; it will clash with the very definite reactions they themselves are constrained to follow. If the scientist *does* allow his desires to influence his labors within these steps, there can be only one result. His third step will be an evident failure; his phenomena, bound within his hypothesis, cannot, then, be replaced within the general frame of things. He will, consequently, by invalidating the results of all his labors, have entirely defeated his own purposes.

It is his fear of the third step that forces the scientist to employ every effort to banish from his labors, so far as is humanly possible, all influences emanating from his personal desires. He concerns himself with *fact*—with the specific phenomena he has before him. He wishes them to speak to him; he seeks the groupings which they themselves indicate and favor. It is this meticulous care in avoiding the distortion inevitably attendant upon the indulgence of human desires which imparts to all scientific effort the distinctive flavor it possesses.

The author, like every artist, exerts his efforts upon a medium. Language, it is true, is a phenomenon belonging to the contest of man and his surroundings. Yet it differs significantly from the scientist's phenomena. Language is a representative medium. Because of this fact, the author, after observing and selecting the elements of those particular surroundings with which he has had experience, can recombine these elements within his medium with the result that there is reflected therein the picture of a heterogeneous whole which is essentially as full and complete as is any human environment. Must this recombination follow any specific plan? No; for the phenomena which compose it are not homologous, and thus possess no definite and imperative coherence. The author recognizes and obeys the demands of one criterion only. He governs his treatment of the specific environment he depicts to accord with the laws of probability based upon the normal manifestations of the human environment at all times and on all occasions. This constrains him, in the first place, to select for representation within the medium such elements of his particular environment which, collectively, shall be genuinely representative of the entire environment. It follows that he must not suppress those manifestations which are inimical to the aims he is harboring, nor emphasize unduly those which favor them. In the second place, he must combine those specific elements in accordance with probability— with what he has observed to be the normal, probable, and likely reactions of the general environment at all times and places.

Having done these things, the author discovers that the exigency of the demands of probability is not severe enough to force him to relinquish the desires he entertains as a human being. They can still be impressed upon the environment he is arranging and creating within the medium, and over which he possesses an artist's control. The result is that the author's finished product sets forth the environment depicted in a state of subjection to disciplined human desires. It represents the what could be or what should be. From the point of view of the scientist, the author has created a work of *fiction;* he has judged specific phenomena, not by their own activities (not being homologous phenomena, they have no clearly defined coherence) but by his own desires disciplined merely by the far less exigent standards of the environment as a whole. From the author's point of view, however, the result has been the creation of a (to him) *beautiful* work of literature.

*The difference between science and literature may, accordingly, be summed up as the difference between fact and fiction.*[7] And this distinction characterizes the application of each to human life and knowledge.

The successful result of the scientist's labors means the setting up in the environment of a group of phenomena whose mutual interactions are known to man. There is thus created a tool whose employment in the activities of men gives promise of affording a greater margin of survival. But it is evident that this tool cannot by itself provide present satisfaction of desire for expression and future guaranties of welfare. For it is not adequately representative of the entire environment; it involves only a part of a heterogeneous whole. If man's full desires are to be asserted, this tool must be taken together with other tools involving other aspects of reality. The result of a scientific experimentation, that is to say, is useful rather than beautiful; it cannot by itself adapt the general environment to plans more favorable to the aims of men. Consequently, it does not to any considerable degree possess the two requisites of the beautiful—supreme utility for present activity, and a strong reference to the future.

---

[7] One recalls, in this connection, Francis Bacon's distinction between the *lumen siccum* and the *lumen humidum.*

The subject matter of literature is fiction. The result attained by the author within his medium is thus fictional. What application has that result? Its relation to the real environment is not clear. Certainly it does not fit into it as do the hypothesized phenomena of the scientist. For it is not the part of a whole; on the contrary, it mirrors a certain environment in its multifarious detail with no essential lack of fulness. The only evident reference of the work of literature is to the author himself. Clearly, the production of it is a labor which enables him to satisfy his instinctive desire for personal expression. He can select from his experience the elements which compose his surroundings; he can set these within the medium; he can represent a man like himself in conflict with them; he can set forth that conflict as it proceeds through successive temporal stages; and he can depict, at the conclusion, an environment in the state in which his character (and so he himself) desires it. He can, in short, transfer to his medium a faithful representation of his own struggle against his environment. And he can realize in the medium the desires he entertains as a man.

But further—his result is a disciplined result. His fictional environment is genuinely representative of his actual surroundings. The action he depicts is governed by the laws of probability manifested by the environment generally. His completed work thus presents the surroundings not only as they *should be* but as they *can be,* and *will be* if the norms of probability are operative. For the author this result is beautiful because it is immediately assimilable to his desires. But it is also potentially realizable within his own experience. It may be made a goal for his future efforts. It subjects his own future to the test of probability. The result of the test constitutes a favorable prognosis of his future personal welfare. It can give him no infallible guaranty. This is neither humanly possible nor necessary. The author is fully aware that his best laid plans may be upset by non-normal and exceptional circumstances beyond his control. Yet he is also aware that his chances are brightest if his plans are in accord with probability—and this fact becomes his surest dependence in the at best perplexed and uncertain business of conducting his life.

If science is fact, and literature, fiction—then the circumstance that both employ the medium of language has little significance. Literature can surely not allocate to itself entire possession of a universal medium such as language. Science regularly employs language to set forth and communicate the processes and results of its undertakings. But the works in which these experimental findings are given exposition are certainly not to be classed as literature.[8]

There lurks in this situation the possibility of a grave confusion. There is need, accordingly, for a clear treatment of its elements—even at the risk of an extensive discursus which may interrupt the course of the present discussion.

"Fact" and "fiction" are terms purely relative in character. When a scientist ascertains fact experimentally, he has constructed a tool which is demonstrably better than the existing ones, but which may in turn be superseded by a tool of a still more superior (i.e., more "workable") character. He has not, through his experiment, attained a realm of fact or truth ideally perfect,

---

[8] I may say here, also, that I deprecate the undiscriminating employment of the term "literature" to designate (Webster) "the body of writings having to do with a given subject, as.physics." There have been objections to its use in this capacity—and certainly an entire condemnation of its application to advertising matter, circulars, etc.

absolute, and immutable. Consequently, the standards of fact are those imposed by the present day and by men possessing both wide experience in experimentation and the most acute scientific intelligence. Now fiction consists of judgments which are rejected by the standards of fact. Fiction, judged by fact, is human error. Today the criteria of fact are so definitely formulated within the various fields of scientific endeavor that the cleavage between fact and fiction is pronounced. It seems probable that every age recognized at least some distinction between the two. It seems apparent, also, that almost every human judgment now admittedly erroneous was, at some time in human history, believed to be fact and relied on under that assumption. The progress of fact or science has meant the steady enlargement of the realm of fiction. It follows that a great portion of the material now openly admitted to be fiction and consciously used as such by the literary artist was once seriously regarded and set forth by writers anxious to ascertain fact by the standards it then possessed.

From this situation emerges a third category of judgments which employ the medium of language: a class which, intended as fact and once so accepted, has by the present day scientist been discarded as fiction. And fictitious its members obviously are. They number among them the myths and legends which once possessed every department of knowledge—history, philosophy, the natural sciences. Their judgments were superseded and rejected precisely because they were seen to involve an anthropomorphizing of the environment—an open reading into the surroundings of the desires instinctively entertained by men, and thus a finding therein of the results men wished to find. Their explanations endeavored to place the environment in the state in which it should be in order that it might be immediately assimilated by the purposes of men. They spoke to the environment instead of allowing it to speak to them. Their results, in short, are artistically beautiful.

Works of this character were produced and accepted as fact until almost within the present age.[9] It has been declared (in the first chapter of this work) that the romantic historians of the first half of the nineteenth century were the *literary* historians. They wished to recall the events of the past as they should have or could have happened, by building upon the imperfect skeleton of fact the superstructure of probable fiction. It was also declared (at the close of the second chapter) that idealists in philosophy are, in the opinion of the pragmatist, *literary* philosophers. They discover behind the environment a realm in which the desires of men are met and permanently guaranteed. The judgments of both these schools have been attacked as fictional by the exacting criteria of scientific fact of the present day. In the opinion of the attackers, they must today be judged by the standards of fiction, the subject matter of literature.[10]

---

[9] Naturally, as the criteria of fact were advanced, the fictions which still posed as fact were forced to turn from the impossible and improbable to the probable—to purge themselves of *declared* and *recognized* fictions. With Geoffrey of Monmouth, history (stories about the past) included what are now called myths and legends. The work of Polydore Vergil (early sixteenth century) attempted to eliminate the impossible fictions of Geoffrey. The skepticism of Hume barred out the improbable fictions of Vergil and the Elizabethan chroniclers. The methods of Freeman and Stubbs endeavored to eject all fiction—even the probable fictions of the romantic historians.

[10] And those interested in fact have frequently proclaimed that they must be so judged. Note—to consider only a single example in the field of history—the way in which Macaulay's *History of England* is now being written about: D. H. Macgregor, *Lord Macaulay* (1901), p. 94: "He made history a moving drama; plot and underplot are fitted together. Indeed, if Carlyle's 'French Revolution' has been well styled an epic, drama is the only term for Macaulay's 'History of England' and for his presentment of William." J. A. Morison, *Macaulay* (*English Men of Letters*), 148: "The sprightly vivacity of the scene is worthy of any novel, yet it is all a mosaic of actual fact. We may call it Richardson grafted on Hume." Charles

Literature, accordingly, must find room within its ranks for works whose creators employed the medium of language for the non-literary purpose of imparting knowledge of fact, but whose contents stand at the present time rejected by fact. Literature accepts these works without question. It has no interest in the circumstance that the writers of them *intended* them, not as fiction, but as fact. For all fiction, it has been noted, may be regarded as once accepted, but later rejected, fact. And it is true that the materials which compose great numbers of the proudest monuments of literature—the "Iliad," the "Aeneid," the sagas of the Nibelungs, Charlemagne, Arthur—were founded on circumstances which their creators or redactors imagined to be at least basically historical. And even if the author, in telling a story about the past, does *not* believe that what he relates is factual truth—even then it is obviously to his advantage to avoid the *incredulus odi* of his hearers by attaching his tale to facts about the past of which they are generally cognizant.

Since literature, to repeat, takes no account of the author's intention to follow fact as fact, it experiences no difficulty in accepting as literature all works which are

---

Francis Adams, *History and Historical Societies*, 21: "Let us regard his history as a literary monument, a work designed for the reading public. As such it was a great historical novel." As for idealistic philosophy—note Professor Dewey's pronouncement upon the sources and methods of Platonism (*Experience and Nature*, 88): "Philosophy was a telling of the story of nature after the style of all congenial stories, a story with a plot and climax, given such coherent properties as would render it congenial to minds demanding that objects satisfy logical canons. Objects are certainly none the worse for having wonder and admiration for their inspiration and art for their medium. But these objects are distorted when their affiliation with the epic, temple and drama is denied, and there is claimed for them a rational and cosmic status independent of piety, drama and story. In the classic philosophy of Greece the picture of the world that was constructed on an artistic model proferred itself as being the result of intellectual study. A story composed in the interests of a refined type of enjoyment, ordered by the needs of consistency in discourse, or dialectic, became cosmogony and metaphysics."

discarded as fiction by the criteria of science. But once having accepted them, it subjects them to its own laws. Their success or failure must be decided solely by the standards of fiction. Accordingly, the qualities of imper sonality and particularity, which would make them significant for science, will render them unsatisfactory as literature. If, instead of speaking to the environment with the emphasis of artistic control, they allow the environment to utter its own accents, they have failed to subject it as a whole to the desires of men. If they consider particular circumstances and specific phenomena rather to judge them by their own workings than by the norms of probability, they have failed—in the event that exceptional circumstances have operated—to achieve probability. And, in this case, it is no defense for them that they relate much that is true to fact. For the answer on the part of literature is properly that an event may very well *have* happened at some time and in some place —but that, nevertheless, by the standard of probability, it *should not* have happened.

A return may now be made to the main current of the discussion. It has been seen that the most readily evident value of that type of literature which is composed of probable fiction consists in the fact that it affords the author the gratification of expressing his desires upon his environment, and that it guaranties his future to a certain degree by testing the probable outcome of attempts to gratify those desires. But these qualities are not in themselves sufficient to constitute a satisfactory human labor. The reference to the present must include the satisfaction of the earning of a livelihood, a means of present subsistence. The fact that literature, during the ages, has exhibited this necessary characteristic of a satisfactory labor means that it has possessed a value not merely to authors but also to mankind generally. For human society will grant a livelihood to a laborer only on condition that the product of his labors is of genuine concern to its members. In brief, like all labors, literature has an economic and social status.

It is essential, consequently, to determine the nature of the gratification afforded by literature to society—the social reference which justifies its existence as a labor among other human labors. To whom, beside the author, is literature of concern? What are the human needs which demand its ministrations? In what ways and with what degree of completeness does it meet those needs? The answers to these questions must obviously involve all types of literature—those founded on impossible or improbable fiction as well as that based on probability.[11]

The most promising avenue of approach at this juncture may be discovered from the circumstance that a work of literature contains a human judgment upon the environment. Now it has been asserted that judgments are attainable by a single method only. The author, like the scientist, must face the three necessary steps of the judgment-forming process — observation, combination, and application. That a work of literature is composed in accordance with these processes is a fact which has already been implied or indicated, but which has not yet been emphasized. It must now be viewed in detail.

At the outset of his labors the author faces a problem. He must address himself to the expression within the medium of language of his desires upon his environment constructed upon the basis of his fund of experience. From the complex mixture which composes his experi-

---

11 Literature dealing with impossibilities and improbabilities was temporarily excluded on p. 124 *supra*. From the present point onward, however, it is included again in the general discussion.

ences he will choose for representation within the medium various aspects of the environment of which he has knowledge. As a whole they may or may not be genuinely representative of the general environment. These materials form the data of his first step. It is through them that the problem he faces must be solved. Consequently, he will endeavor to choose those elements of his experience which are most concerned with and most congenial toward the result he desires. He will, moreover, observe them accurately, so that they will, when expressed in language, mirror as faithfully as possible the models from which they are copied.

The author's second step will consist of recombining his data within the medium into a pattern which will resemble the complex whole from which they were extracted. The form which this pattern will assume is determined largely by the potentialities of the medium. It will represent a struggle between man and his surroundings—for language has the ability to represent this basic aspect of human life. The pattern will be constituted by action—will have the combination of its elements depicted as extending over a period of time; for the ability of representing action is fundamental to this medium. The standard according to which the data will be combined may or may not be that of probability based on the normal workings of the environment as a whole. But the completed pattern which results from the author's second step will always differ from the pattern in which the data which compose it existed within the earthly frame in one significant respect. The environment in the medium is shot through with human meaning and purpose. There are in it no meaningless, no recalcitrant, no aberrant elements—for none of this character were selected as data or included in the pattern. Accordingly, the result

—the completed work—will set forth an environment on which human desires are so firmly imprinted that the problem encountered at the outset has been solved. A particular environment is exhibited in the state in which it should be if the human desires which animate the work are to be gratified. This is to say that, in the author's eyes, the work is beautiful.

The completion of the author's second step finds the hypothesis which solves the problem he has posed, expressed within the medium of language. In short, it sees the work of literature itself. The author's labors terminate, apparently, with the second step. But the literary judgment itself cannot terminate with that step. It is impossible that any human judgment, scientific or literary, should be complete without a third and final step. For the scientist, the third step is all important. It is the controlling element of his labors. To fail with it is to fail utterly. The problem to which he has addressed himself originated *within* the environment; the results of his labors must be applicable *to* the environment. Moreover, the knowledge that its rigors await him, forces the scientist to submit his actions to the discipline it demands of him. One expects of the literary judgment that it, too, require a final step making similar demands.

It is obvious that the final step of the literary judgment will not be an application of the kind the scientist makes. The hypothesis or pattern contained within the work of literature is not applicable directly to the environment. From the point of view of fact—and the environment upholds only facts—the author's judgment is fictional or erroneous. The scientist is well aware that he will invalidate his entire experiment if he attempts to read his personal desires and prejudices directly into the workings of physical phenomena. Yet this is precisely what the literary hypothesis does: it subjects the environment to human ambitions, and it does so directly—without the mediation of a tool formed from a portion of it.

But this very characteristic of literature points out its proper and necessary applicability. The hypothesis of the scientist is composed of data comprising a portion of the environment; it has application to the whole of the environment, and it must be fitted within that frame. The pattern of the work of literature is composed of data drawn from the spectacle of a man concerting aims against his surroundings based on his experiences within them. The results it arrives at are applicable to the spectacle of all men entertaining desires upon their respective surroundings. *The third step of the literary judgment consists of applying the results attained within the work of literature to the experiences of men who possess desires which seek gratification through those experiences.* The scientific hypothesis, which views the environment as it is, has direct significance for the environment; the literary pattern, which views the environment through the eyes of men, has direct significance for men within the environment.

The men to whom the literary judgment is of concern are called readers or listeners.[12] They are men having experiences with their surroundings, and attempting, on the basis of their experiences, to plan measures for increasing their margins of personal safety and well-being. Under these circumstances they gain experience (visual or auditory) of the work of literature. In the measure in which it represents an environment such as theirs in the state in which men such as they desire it to assume—in that measure it is immediately applicable to their experiences: that is, it becomes to that degree

---

[12] For convenience, I shall, hereafter, call them merely ''readers.''

beautiful to them. In their eyes literature gains a value; they desire and demand experience of it. It is this desire expressed by readers which renders possible the existence of literature as a labor providing, as do other labors, the means of subsistence for the laborer. By demanding its products, readers provide the market which gives to literature a valid economic and social status.

In order to be a reader a man must possess three qualifications. In the first place, he must not be living at the bare level of existence. His life must contain a margin superior to mere survival—a margin which grants him some respite from his immediate needs and which enables him to plan further conquests looking toward its increase. A reader, in other words, is a man who is in search of the beautiful, and who feels his existence to be unsatisfactory and incomplete if this search is in any way denied him—if the labors in which he is engaged fail to allow him a certain degree of expression for his personal aims and some guaranty for the future.

In the second place, it is essential that the reader possess a familiarity with the medium of language. His previous experiences or education must have rendered him capable of comprehending words and the larger syntactical groups and orders in which they habitually appear. He must, moreover, comprehend intelligently the purpose for which the medium of language exists: the accurate reporting of human experience. Thus he will feel a connection between words and things, between the medium and life itself. Properly arranged and properly discriminative verbalization will bring before him the objects or actions thereby represented as they have presented themselves to him in life.

The third qualification of the reader—perhaps the most important of all—springs from a conjunction of the preceding two. The reader must feel so close an association between words which report human experience, on the one hand, and his own experiences, on the other, that he is able in some degree to substitute the first for the second. As a man he attains intense gratification through absorbing into his total fund of experience the objects or situations which are beautiful to him. As a reader he must attain a certain amount of the same satisfaction from experiencing, through the medium of language, objects or actions which are represented in that state which, in the world, he calls beautiful. Experience with the medium is experience vicariously received but to a considerable degree as assimilable to the reader's life as are experiences directly undergone, and in a measure equally productive of the satisfactions arising from supreme utility and strong future reference.

The three qualifications possessed by the reader bring about a basic identity between his point of view and that of the author. Reader and author are men within an environment; they have acquaintance with the medium of language; they are able in a degree to substitute expression through language for expression through actual experience. Both, moreover, are in search of the beautiful. A work of literature will appear beautiful to both in the measure in which it gratifies their desires at the expense of the surroundings in which they live. That the work will gratify the aims of the author is apparent—for he has been in control of it. How far can it go, however, toward satisfying the aims of the reader? To what degree can the basic *entente* between author and reader be extended to more particular and specific matters? How closely can the author's idea of the beautiful match that of the reader—considering how varied and divergent may be their respective funds of experience and how unlike the characteristics of their immediate surroundings?

It is obvious that means or materials exist which may be employed to lessen the distance between the two. But it is impossible for the author to make an inelligent disposal of these means unless he comprehends the nature of the reader's demands. It is both natural and imperative for the author to obey these demands. It is natural because he and the reader, sharing the same point of view, are travelling in the same general direction. And it may be surmised that the further and more specific demands of readers will not actively oppose the desires of the author, but will, on the contrary, guide, direct, supplement, and strengthen his purposes. Moreover, obedience to the demands of readers is imperative for the reason that the application to readers of the results expressed within the work of literature constitutes the third step of the literary judgment. Its importance cannot be overestimated; it is the supreme and final test of the author's work. From the clash of man and environment the author's problem arose; to that struggle his finished labors must be reapplied. The demands which emanate from this step must direct and discipline all his artistic efforts. For upon it depends the consideration which involves the very existence of the author's vocation —the possibility of procuring the means of subsistence through its agency.

Materials for a classification of the demands of readers lie ready at hand. It is obvious that the reader comes to literature from his labors in the world. The general nature of those labors will determine the complexion of his demands upon literature—for this is merely to repeat that his conception of the beautiful is based on his fund of experience. Now the reader may be engaged in what he considers to be a satisfactory labor. If so, he is assured of a livelihood, of the present expression of his human desires, and of a strong guaranty for the future. On the other hand, his occupation may be in varying degrees unsatisfactory. It will necessarily enable him to exist and to possess the margin above this minimum which is necessary if he is to be a reader at all. But it may starve the instinctive human impulses which seek expression, and it may refuse to hold out future promise.

If such a standard is adopted, the following divisions will emerge:

I. The reader's occupation is satisfactory. His constant preoccupation with it, however, occasions him a certain amount of fatigue. He desires, consequently, a temporary escape from it and from the surroundings in which it is carried on. He is in search of an intelligent and refined play. It will grant him a recuperation of his powers not greatly dissimilar from that afforded by sleep.

II. The reader's occupation is markedly unsatisfactory. He follows it of necessity. But he loathes it to such a degree that he seeks every opportunity to escape as completely as possible from every suggestion or reminder of it.

III. The reader is willing to believe—perhaps because of his limited experiences and capacities—that his activities are satisfactory—or at least as satisfactory as those of other workers. Accordingly, he seeks every assurance of this. He demands a recognition of the importance of his labor to his community and of his own dignity as laborer.

IV. The reader realizes that his experiences are unsatisfactory. But he wishes to be told that, by a simple

and regular turn of events, they may become highly gratifying and satisfactory.

V. The reader's occupation relates itself harmoniously to his life, affording him in due measure the gratifications of a satisfactory labor.  But this reader is never
content with the margin of survival he possesses; his
instinctive human desires always seek more than the aims
founded on his fund of experience can realize.  As a
result, this reader constantly seeks new experiences, for
they, added to those he already possesses, will enable him
to frame new objects of ambition, new goals of desire.
Since he is a reader, he can to a considerable extent attain
his purpose through literature.  Accordingly, he demands
of it that, through the amount and variety of its data, it
make additions to his fund of experience.  Moreover, he
requires that it demonstrate how the multiformity of
material which composes that fund, may be rendered
liable to the imposition of comprehensive plans formed
from the conjunction of exacting and ever further
encroaching human ambitions.

In order to meet demands thus variously motivated,
literature must employ all of the three categories into
which its subject matter has been declared to fall.  Literature, it has been seen, may employ impossible, improbable, or probable fiction.  The means possessed by each
of these types for meeting the demands of readers can
now be examined.

One may begin with the type of literature which feels
little hesitation in violating possibility, the very texture
of the continuum of the environment.  It may frankly
spread over the objects it represents the mist of the mar-
vellous and the incredible.  For the earthly desires of
men, it may substitute the whims of sprites.  For the
sequences of the earthly environment there may be the

marvels of myth. Or, this type of literature may seek somewhat to conceal its transcendence of ordinary experience by seeking out some far off land or some distant period of time—a place and time in which marvels may be supposed to have occurred. Here it has a free hand in molding the surroundings as it pleases.

Whichever it does, this class of fiction meets the needs of readers who belong to the first two divisions of the classification. To the man who is fatigued, it provides relief from his steady application to everyday affairs by bringing before him a milieu in which none of the observed laws of the environment have any necessary validity. After partaking of the refreshment offered by this adult play, such a reader may with renewed energy apply himself again to the problems, totally different in character, with which his life is joined. To the man who has failed to conduct his life satisfactorily, impossible fiction offers consolation for failure. It leads him to believe that the laws of the environment, against which he is conducting a losing struggle, are not final. It exhibits to him a congenial realm from which these laws are absent—a realm in which people and things are not judged by, nor harassed by, earthly standards and requirements. By experiencing the creations of this kind of literature, the reader of this class gains a drug with which to deaden the sharp misery of his dissatisfaction.

A second type of literature is that which does not exclude the improbable. It does indeed recognize the ordinary involvements and sequences of life in the world. But it does not choose data which, in combination, can set forth a balanced and representative portion of this life. Its results, consequently, are those proceeding from biased and weighted evidence. But improbable fiction thereby satisfies the desires of the third and fourth categories of the classification. It possesses a means of comforting the reader who desires to be told that his activities and accomplishments are satisfactory and important. For, if it suppresses contrary evidence, it can—by depicting a man like him in contact with an improbably represented environment—invest his labors, his abilities, and his groups with dignity and consequence. It can magnify and glorify his patriotism, his family sentiments, his business principles, his personal reactions.

Improbable fiction has the power, likewise, to comfort and enhearten the man whose experiences in the world are to a considerable degree unsatisfactory to him. It can represent to him that his labors may become abundantly gratifying through a mere external change of circumstances. It conceals the fact that the chances are against him; it does not let him know that, were these changes to come about, probability must first be distinctly violated. In practice such fiction tends to follow certain well tested themes—all of which are fashioned for the purpose of persuading the reader that circumstances may, by a regular and easy transition, cause the full satisfaction of his desires to follow hard upon the relative failure he has been facing in an unpromising vocation. A number of such tested themes may here be listed:

1. The Cinderella theme. A man or woman, imposed on by others and forced to engage in uncongenial labor, encounters circumstances which cause him to experience an entire reversal of fortune, including a triumph over the former taskmasters.

2. The maltreated youngest brother or sister. The broader experience and the imperious, malicious cunning of elders is defeated by the humble, naïve, sympathetic directness of youth and inexperience.

3. The slothful hero. As a youth the hero has shown no signs of future greatness; instead, he has been dull, inactive, and recreant. Suddenly the situation arises which stirs his latent energies, and he emerges at once as a champion without peer.

4. The ugly duckling motif. The person is ridiculed, mistreated, and shunned by those in whose company he lives. It is suddenly revealed that the fault lies, not with the person, but with the group which surrounds him— that he belongs, in fact, to a better and more distingished group, within which his merits are recognized and rewarded.

5. The theme of exile and return. Unsuccessful in his native surroundings and at the mercy of a combination of adverse circumstances, the hero decides to go, or is forced to flee, to other lands. There, however, he quickly achieves success. He returns home with great honor, carrying all before him, overwhelming his former opponents, and achieving all the aims toward which he was striving before his exile.

The type of fiction which includes the improbable thus serves as a therapeutic agent. It gratifies the man who is content with his experiences by magnifying the importance of his potentialities. It is a soothing syrup to the dissatisfied man when it represents to him that great success is possible in life on the basis merely of the future promise held out by his present labors.

There remains the type of literature which endeavors to carry out the prescriptions of both possibility and probability. In so doing, it adheres as closely as possible to the actual state of things on earth. It more nearly reflects the general character of the human environment than does either of the other two types. Consequently, it alone can meet the needs of the last group of readers in

the classification. These readers are not at odds with
their vocations in life. They are seeking neither a haven
of refuge nor a soothing syrup. For their activities as a
whole, judged relatively with those of other men, are
satisfactory human labors. They are aware, however,
that within the field of these labors further progress, increased expression, additional gratification, are possible.
Accordingly, they come to literature in search of aid and
guidance for their endeavors to increase their intra-
vocational margin of well-being.

This last group, in short, is composed of experienced
and capable men with serious and exacting demands.
They do not wish the author to lead them apart from the
every-day involvements of life; on the contrary, they
wish to be conducted farther within their bounds so that
they, as readers, may encounter new experiences to serve
as data for further personal conquests over the environment. They can obtain what they seek from literature
only if the author directs his labors within the medium
in conformity with the extensive demands which their
purposes voice. These requirements are so express that
the author's obedience to them exacts more from him
than a mere willingness to follow probability. They
require him to act in obedience to certain more specific
principles. They involve, that is, the author's technique
—the methods he employs in the selection and arrangement of the data used for composing the pattern which
constitutes the finished work of literature. To examine
the demands of this group of readers is thus to outline
the basic principles of literary technique.

A reader of the type just classified demands, in the
first place, that the author present his fictional environment from the same point of view as that which the
reader holds toward the actual environment. This

means that the author must see it as the scene of the reactions of a man with his surroundings. And since the character depicted will wish to impress his own desires upon the surroundings, which are not wholly disposed to receive it, the author must view his material in terms of a conflict between the two. On the one side will be the character with needs and desires to be gratified. On the other will be the whole complex environment itself—containing objects, situations, forces, groups, and other men. The clashes or issues of the struggle will be determined by the problems which the needs and aims of the character force him to encounter. He may be obliged to seek out objects favorable to his designs, or to defeat those unfavorable; to employ beneficial forces, or to neutralize those which are disruptive of his purposes. He may be compelled to defeat or avert the designs of other men. He may feel obliged to ally himself with certain groups, and to oppose himself to others; he may wish to define his position within his groups. In all these contests he will be able to discover allies; but he will inevitably, also, encounter obstacles and enemies.

To comply with this demand of the reader will, it has already been seen, fall in with the designs of the author. He is himself a man—so that life will hold the same basic significance for him that it does for his reader. And the medium which literature employs is the only artistic medium which can adequately portray the conflict of man and surroundings. Consequently, the very fact that he *is* an author—that he labors within the medium of language—demonstrates his interest in the conflict.

A second requirement of the serious reader forms a logical extension of the first. He demands that the conflict depicted have as many points of contact as possible with his own life, activities, and aims. The fictional character should resemble as nearly as may be a man like the reader; the fictional environment should approach a duplication of the reader's own. To a reader of this type a work of literature becomes increasingly acceptable and significant in the measure in which it approaches his narrower and more personal interests—as it deals with the things, forces, problems, and interests of his immediate surroudings and of his various intimate groups. For then its pattern will be more readily applicable to the activities of his daily life, concerning which he wishes to acquire new aims.

The more general aspects of the reader's expectations in this respect are indeed easily to be met. Author and reader naturally share the instinctive desires common to all men. Furthermore, the barrier of language—English, French, German—points the existence of certain other contacts. Author and reader will probably live under the same national government. They will have received educations perhaps strikingly similar in character. They will both be living in obedience to the same, or similar, laws. They will recognize common traditions, common social customs and usages. They will be inclined to laud the same human aims and to disparage the same prejudices and irregularities. They will have read the same literature. They will be joint members of numerous groups—religious and secular, vocational and recreational; and they will agree in some measure concerning the value and importance of them.

To extend the contact between author and reader to more specific interests is, however, a task calling for the most strenuous efforts of the former. Author and reader may, for instance, both be city dwellers, and they may both move in the same stratum of society. In such a case the author's task becomes severe mainly in one respect.

When he touches upon the more immediate surroundings and the more personal activities of the reader, he must observe them with accuracy and reproduce them with fidelity. For these are things with which the reader has most contact and knows most thoroughly; these pass daily before his eyes. For the author to fail to observe them properly means for him to lose contact at this point with his reader.

But if the author's immediate surroundings do *not* coincide with those of the reader with whom he wishes to have most points in common, then his task becomes one of the utmost difficulty. In such a case, the author, in leaving his own milieu and attempting to pass to that of the reader, abandons what is familiar to him for which is at the same time unfamiliar to him and exceedingly well-known to the reader. The difficulty becomes particularly formidable when the author attempts to reproduce accurately the reader's vocation—almost certain to be one with which the reader has a thorough acquaintance, whereas the author can scarcely have. That the latter, nevertheless, can, by experience and close observation, enter even such intimate activities of the reader, has been proved many times by example. Obviously the means exist whereby the interests of author and reader can approach identity—can become a union extending even to small particulars. The question is thus merely whether the author possesses the ability to employ the means.

In the third place, the author's data, considered as a whole, must constitute a fairly complete representation of a particular earthly environment. The resources of the medium must be fully utilized. Literature will naturally reproduce the action and change of the environment. But there must also be a serious effort to represent sights and sounds, to build up a pictorial background—to represent depth as well as surface action. If an environment is reproduced with some approach to completeness, the reader will experience little difficulty in transferring his entire attention from his worldly surroundings and fully associating himself with the surroundings depicted in the medium. He will be able to a marked degree to substitute experience through the medium for experience in life. For there will be no large gaps in the represented environment to remind him continually that he is in contact with life only at second hand—through a medium whose incompleteness and imperfection are constantly obtruding a strained and faulty mechanism upon his attention.

A fourth expectation of the reader is that the environment be *fairly* represented within the medium. Every environment contains elements which are congenial, which are indifferent, which are inimical to any design formulated by men. The materials employed by the literary artist must maintain a fair balance among these characteristics if the product of their interaction is to be representative of reality. If this balance is upset, if the author withholds or alters important evidence on either side—then his result will inevitably violate probability, and his work will thus fall into a category which is of little interest to the type of reader whose demands are being examined. But if the unfavorable is given due attention along with the favorable, then probability will have been respected. Then the result will be a portrayal, not of an incomplete and unrepresentative portion of the environment nor of certain chance configurations of it, but of the entire environment as it normally exhibits itself when an average which takes all occasions into account is struck.

Finally, the serious reader demands that the struggle between a character and his environment be depicted by the employment of the distinctive abilities of the medium, and that its elements converge toward a unified and finished result. The forte of literature is the representation of action. The conflict must thus be conducted through a period of time, during which its elements will fluctuate and its aspects undergo alteration and recombination. The process of this action may be narrative or dramatic, or it may be a combination of the two. The author, that is, may himself relate the chronological progress of his materials; or he may allow his character or characters to react directly with their surroundings without any apparent interposition of himself.[13] The required result of the action is plainly indicated by the nature of the conflict. The completed pattern must exhibit the represented environment as it exists after the imposition upon it of the aims and desires of the principal character. This imposition must take place, and its success or failure in solving the conflict must be clearly apparent. For only on these terms can a work of literature attain a finished result.

The fact that its works can be brought to a state of completion is a quality of literature which marks it as an

---

[13] This very distinction, necessarily based on empirical observation is present in the third book of the "Republic"—where it stands strangely aloof from the idealistic framework in which it is placed. Socrates observes that (Jowett's translation) "narration may be either simple narration, or imitation, or a union of the two." He cites a passage from the "Iliad," and then continues: "And a narrative it remains both in the speeches which the poet recites from time to time and in the intermediate passages? . . . . But when the poet speaks in the person of another, may we not say that he assimilates his style to that of the person who, as he informs you, is going to speak? . . . . And the assimilation of himself to another . . . . is the imitation of the person whose character he assumes? . . . . Then, in this case the narrative of the poet may be said to proceed by way of imitation? . . . . Or, if the poet everywhere appears and never conceals himself, then again the imitation is dropped, and his poetry becomes simple narration."

art—for art produces finished wholes. In a work of literature which obeys the demands of serious readers, such a
state is attained not without difficulty. For the world does
not support finished results. The environment knows no
staying put; the living man cannot reach the end of the
incessant conflict he must wage. How, then, can the
author who wishes to follow reality as closely as possible
reach the terminus required by art? Clearly, he must
define at the outset the terms upon which his pattern will
be constituted. He must concentrate the action upon certain issues; he must concern himself almost exclusively
with one unified and concerted propulsion of desire on
the part of his character. The author's work, accordingly,
takes on something of the aspect of a mathematical problem. The terms represented by $x$ must be agreed upon by
author and reader; the discovery of $x$ must provide the
solution of the inquiry. That is to say—when the reaction
of the specific fictional environment (its workings animated by norms based on the general environment) to
the specifically designated set of desires harbored by
the character shall have been determined, then the work
of literature is artistically complete, for the pattern
will then contain the finished result of the attempted
imposition.

Into the five divisions just demarcated the demands of
the serious reader will regularly fall. On the basis of
them no genuine opposition between the purposes of the
author and those of the reader can be formulated. These
demands do not hamper, check, nor discourage the author
who desires to remain faithful to probability. On the
contrary, they spur him to the height of his intent. They
force upon him the fullest development of his powers of
observation, the most careful discrimination in the choice
and combination of his materials, and the employment of

the fullest resources of the medium. Author and reader are two constantly interacting agents. It was the successful achievements of past authors which taught readers the potentialities of literature. It is the expectations of readers which, in turn, react to constitute demands laid upon present authors. At the base of these demands lie the parallel aims which reader and author, both men with human impulses, entertain against the environment. Here is the inseparable bond between them. In the proportion that his results become important for the author, they cannot fail also to gain significance for the reader.

Now the significance of the work of literature for the author himself has already been noted. The satisfactions it conveys to him are those associated with a satisfactory labor which contains a strong reference to a future whose realization is thoroughly potential and likely.

When the reader experiences a work of probable fiction which complies with his demands, he calls it beautiful. He does so because it depicts an environment considerably like his own in the state in which a man very like himself wishes it to be. It is the judgment of a man upon an environment. Its conclusions and implications are not true to fact; they cannot be applied directly to the general earthly environment as it exists. The work is thus fiction still. But it is a fiction strictly disciplined by the demands of probability. It is not truth; it is verisimilitude. It is not factual truth; it is *poetic* truth[14]—

14 Recognized by Aristotle as constituting the primary function of literature: ''From what we have said it will be seen that the poet's function is to describe, not the thing that has happened, but a kind of thing that might happen, i.e., what is possible as being probable or necessary. The distinction between historian and poet is not in the one writing prose and the other verse . . . . ; it consists really in this, that the one describes the thing that has been, and the other a kind of thing that might be. Hence poetry is something more philosophic and of graver import than history, since its statements are of the nature rather of universals, whereas those of history are singulars. By a universal statement I mean one as to what such or such

"truer than the truth" because purged of abnormal and accidental variations. It is an experimental working out of a problem which exists in the environment, taking the environment itself as the standard.

It thus follows that poetic truth, as attained within a work of literature, is fiction of the kind by which men live. It is a guide for human life. It can be applied by the reader directly to his own life to serve as the aim or goal toward which his efforts shall be directed. It is immediately assimilable to his desires; it promises them future success. For the character in the work is the reader's surrogate, testing out for him the validity of his ambitions. In this way the reader's own future is foreshadowed in the manner which can best profit him. Experience acquired from literature is experience which is retrievable—unlike that of the world which, once definitely entered upon, carries with it a chain of irretrievable consequences. The forecast offered by probability is man's surest, as it is his only, guide for the future. It is by no means perfect; its calculations may be upset by the abnormal and exceptional. But if a man will rely firmly upon its favorable prognosis, he will venture his fortunes to best advantage—and human life is such that every man must gamble in this fashion.

The entire realm of literature or fiction has now been marked out into three distinct divisions. It has been shown that each of the three can satisfy the desires of a distinct type of reader. Fiction which includes the impossible gratifies the reader who wishes to flee the world; that which includes the improbable soothes the reader who wishes to achieve in the world a success incommensurate

---

a kind of man will probably or necessarily say or do—which is the aim of poetry, though it affixes proper names to the characters; by a singular statement, one as to what, say, Alcibiades did or had done to him."—*On the Art of Poetry*, ix (Bywater's translation).

with his circumstances and abilities; while that which is
true to both and so achieves poetic truth animates the
reader who seeks a guide for further aims and achievements within his environment. Works of literature containing each of these three types are, in the degree in
which they satisfy the respective desires of their readers,
beautiful to those readers. As a consequence, the field
of literature contains three distinct types of the beautiful.

A classification by value may now be added to this
classification by kind. For the beautiful in literature is
not an absolute. It is a value existing relative to the
means or materials which have played a part in its creation—to the ability of the author, to the capacity of the
medium, to the purposes of readers, to the human society
in reflects. Consequently, the means exist which may be
utilized for the purpose of declaring one of the three
types of the beautiful superior to the other two.

Now the exact empirical import of such a declaration
must be clearly comprehended. To say that only one of
these three types is capable of producing the highest
expression of the beautiful in literature, does not degrade
the two remaining types. For they justify their existence
in the classification precisely by devoting themselves to
specific and distinctive purposes. Since they may admirably achieve these purposes, their genuine value cannot be
gainsaid. Thus it would be idle and illegitimate to base a
classification by value upon a direct comparison of the
three types. But to compare the types invidiously among
themselves is not the intention of the classification here
to be made. On the contrary, all three must be measured
by a standard erected from the materials which every
work of literature employs—by a standard composed
from the literary means themselves.

*The superiority of fiction disciplined by probability to attain poetic truth is demonstrated by every relevant test which can be applied.*

Suppose, in the first place, that the standard be that of the author himself. It is clearly apparent that the writer of probable fiction must be a man possessed of the most comprehensive experience with the people and things of the world. The extent of the contact he attains with his readers depends directly upon his familiarity with their activities and aims. His ability to observe accurately and discriminatingly the contents of his environment will directly condition his power of reproducing them faithfully within the medium. Moreover, it is demanded of him that he discern clearly the balanced character of the general flow of things, for he must be able to choose data which fairly represent the environment as a whole. And he must be able to discipline his aims by the demands of that environment if he would attain results not disruptive of its bonds. The authors of impossible and improbable fiction are not forced to face the full extent of these exactions.

Secondly, let the standard be that of the medium. Clearly the creation of probable fiction makes obligatory the employment of the utmost resources of language. For the spectacle of human life must be faithfully and minutely depicted. No class of phenomena may be omitted; the favorable and the unfavorable must alike receive representation. The scene to be reproduced is of this world— not of a world ideally adapted to human desires. Consequently, results of significance to this world will be attained only if there is a searching inquiry among its objects and a lifelike reflection of them in language. Impossible and improbable fiction spring directly from the fact that the medium has not fully nor accurately reflected reality, and has thus not been utilized to its fullest capacity.

Thirdly, the standard may be that of the character and abilities of the reader. The reader of probable fiction has not been defeated nor discouraged by life; he needs no soporific or drug. He is the possessor of a satisfactory labor, but his capacities are ever broader than his possessions. The need for oblivion or for narcotic stimulation can be satisfied by simple fare directed to meet a one-voiced demand. The need for further experiences and new aims in life can be satisfied only by a product which can endure the rigorous requirements of many and varied demands. The fact that the serious reader finds in literature the gratification he seeks reflects as much honor on literature as on the attainments and ambitions of the reader. It proves that literature is worthy the serious efforts of men and has a place of value in human life. If there were only impossible and improbable fictions, literature could indeed be a refuge for the defeated and an anodyne for the discouraged. But it could never enter directly the every-day affairs of serious men.

Thus there is, finally, the standard of human life itself —the highest standard possible. *It is through probable fiction that literature gains direct contact with the actualities of life. Poetic truth is the passage by which the department of literature forms a direct junction with the main stream of human knowledge. Consequently, it is its attainment of poetic truth that justifies the existence of literature as a department of human knowledge.* To forecast the future through earnest consideration of the probabilities and potentialities inherent in the present is the power which makes of the author a veritable prophet and seer. And it is this power which gives to literature the proud place it has regularly occupied in the affairs of men. The magnitude of the importance of literature for human life has been proclaimed innumerable times by idealists and empiricists alike:

Thus the history of a nation's poetry is the essence of its history, political, economic, scientific, religious. With all these the complete historian of a national poetry will be familiar; the national physiognomy, in its finest traits and through its successive stages of growth, will be dear to him: he will discern the grand spiritual tendency of each period, what was the highest aim and enthusiasm of mankind in each, and how one epoch naturally evolved itself from the other. He has to record the highest aim of a nation, in its successive directions and developments; for by this the poetry of the nation modulates itself; this *is* the poetry of the nation.—Carlyle.[15]

Literature is a part and a tremendously important part of the environment of the mind. Its influence, though incalculable, is not in the slightest danger of being exaggerated. Its influence is immense. It is daily increasing. It is rapidly becoming the "effective voice of the social government." Just in proportion to its effectiveness as art, it takes possession of the emotions and thus controls the dynamic part of the mind.—Stuart P. Sherman.[16]

In poetry, as a criticism of life under the conditions fixed for such a criticism by the laws of poetic truth and poetic beauty, the spirit of our race will find, we have said, as time goes on and as other helps fail, its consolation and stay. But the consolation and stay will be of power in proportion to the power of the criticism of life.—Matthew Arnold.

The saying of Matthew Arnold that poetry is a criticism of life sounds harsh to the ears of some persons of strong esthetic bent; it seems to give poetry a moral and instrumental function. But while poetry is not a criticism of life in intent, it is in effect,

---

15 *Heroes and Hero Worship.* Quoted by Cowl, *Theory of Poetry in England.*

16 "Unprintable," *Atlantic Monthly,* July, 1923. Quoted by Mr. Van Meter Ames, *Aesthetics of the Novel* (1928), p. 176.

and so is all art. For art fixes those standards of enjoyment and appreciation with which other things are compared; it selects the objects of future desires; it stimulates effort. This is true of the objects in which a particular person finds his immediate or esthetic values; and it is true of collective man. The level and style of the arts of literature, poetry, ceremony, amusement, and recreation which obtain in a community, furnishing the staple objects of enjoyment in that community, do more than all else to determine the current direction of ideas and endeavors in the community. They supply the meanings in terms of which life is judged, esteemed, and criticized. For an outside spectator, they supply material for a critical evaluation of the life led by that community.—John Dewey.[17]

The conclusion is thus clearly designated and (on the basis of the empirical evidence) indisputable: *The most beautiful works of literature are those which, by obeying the full demands of probability, attain through poetic truth an extensive application to the lives of readers— providing them thereby aims which give purpose and direction to their activities.*

One general objection will be made to this conclusion —and indeed to the entire discussion. It will be said that there has been an artificial simplification of one term. In reality there are "readers," not "a reader." And readers are men of widely varied experiences, activities, capabilities, and ambitions. It may be granted (the objector will assert) that serious readers in search of poetic truth constitute a distinct class of their own. But within such a large group the greatest diversity must abound. How, then, can any work of literature which deals specifically with the personal affairs of these readers find application to more than a handful of their number? How, consequently, can there be any agreement about the beauty of

---

[17] *Experience and Nature*, 204.

works of probable fiction if there exists no foundation for an agreement? To base the highest beauty in literature upon the personal aims of readers can thus differ little from basing it on chaos.

If each reader were a unique monad existing in total isolation, then this objection would be of weight. But the very existence of human society turns upon the wide diffusion of common interests. It has been seen (and need not here be reviewed) that, since author and reader are both men in a society, every work of probable fiction will necessarily contain numerous interests common to both— and these will represent the broad, the important, the significant aspects of their membership in one society. When the work advances to depict smaller groups and more personal interests, then indeed it will have more points of contact with some readers than with others. In connection with these specific interests a considerable diversity will exist. The personal aims of readers do not coincide, since each one of them has certain, even if relatively minute or superficial, individual variations, and a total fund of experiences not precisely identical with that of any other reader. It is thus openly apparent that readers will differ as widely about the beautiful in literature as they do about the beautiful in life. What some of them hold up as aims, others will possess as actualities. What is significant to some will be a matter of indifference or aversion to others. Even in the life of one reader, desires will alter with increasing knowledge, experience, and achievement. These things are universally recognized as the normal manifestations of life in a heterogeneous environment. If literature did not reproduce them it could not be a faithful reflection of life.

It will be observed, however, that the elements on which are based the differences of aims between readers are by no means absolute. They are the superstructure of variation built upon a broad foundation of agreements and common interests. The questions upon which men in a society disagree form only a fraction of those upon which they are united and which they assume without dispute as the foundation for their disagreements. The existence of human society rests on the fact that it is possible to compromise, reconcile, neutralize, or submerge those more radical differences which would be disruptive of its best interests. Furthermore, when literature reflects the surface differences among individuals, it does so in a fashion which supplies yet one more common bond. No matter how narrowly personal are a number of the interests with which it deals, the work of probable fiction subjects all its data to the norms exhibited by the general environment in which all readers live. In the norms thus set forth all readers have an interest.

If society at large labors to reconcile diversity among its members, cannot literature do the same among its readers? Is it not possible in literature to reduce even the limited diversity which exists? Among a number of beautiful works of literature belonging to its highest category, is it not possible to designate a most beautiful from their number? Who shall make such a decision? The task can be accomplished, obviously, only by an "expert" reader—a man who can select among many works which report a society, those which report it most significantly. The necessity for such a step clearly exists; the materials for its construction are at hand. A discussion of it leads one, however, from the field of literature to that of literary criticism.

# Chapter VI

## THE ISSUE IN LITERATURE

The disadvantages under which the empiricist labors within general aesthetics were pointed out when that broad realm was being traversed. The idealist's system is complete therein. The empiricist, however, can do little more than indicate the larger implications of his attitude. His system is built up from particulars; it does not descend from the absolute. At the present stage of the discussion, the empirical attitude toward the beautiful, seen from the point of view of the subdivision of literature, has been outlined in accordance with the specific materials upon which such an attitude must repose. Consequently, it becomes possible at this point to oppose the system of the empiricist to that of the idealist without injustice to either.

The purpose of such a display must be to seize upon the fundamental points of opposition and to comprehend their full significance. If the entire subject has received logical or inclusive division, if it is true that there exist two, and only two, ways of approaching and determining the beautiful—then the opposition should be capable of statement in such fashion that a genuine issue results— an issue being, in the words of the New International Dictionary, "the point at which a matter is ready for, or admits of, decision." Concerning any element of the opposition, therefore, one should be able to declare: *either* this *or* this must be accepted as true, since no third possibility exists.

It is no injustice to the idealist to view his principles solely as they relate to literature. Their implications are the same from whatever aspect or under whatever focus they are viewed. The idealist's aesthetic contains all the fine arts, literature included. To deal idealistically with literature one has, then, merely to substitute "beauty in literature" for "beauty in art." The familiar elements of the system then appear as:

I. The beautiful in literature is represented by an absolute, an eternal and perfect idea.

II. The beautiful work of literature contains within it a spark of the absolute.

III. Beauty in literature is created and recognized by a special faculty, in direct contact with the absolute, existing within the mind of man.

To approach, then, the first of these principles. The idealist declares that the purpose of literature is to express, to represent, to mirror, to body forth, the absolute idea. The empiricist declares the highest purpose of literature to be the expression of the probable, the potential, within the general human environment.

There is an apparent similarity between these views. They agree that literature does not aim to reproduce the actual, literal, historical condition of things. Both assert that it strives to represent an ideal. But this surface agreement merely emphasizes the basic opposition between the two contentions. The two "ideals" are entirely antithetical in character. That of the idealist is perfect, static, eternal, and unchanging. It is obviously opposed in every respect to the character of the earthly surroundings. The demands which it may be supposed to impose cannot be realized on earth. The approach to this ideal leads directly away from the environment to the ivory tower of the absolute. It follows that literature must separate itself from all connection with the world. It must have no care for the "real existence of the object"

(Kant); it must not "ape reality" but "leave reality"
(Schiller); it must not "direct itself to any outward end"
(Schelling)—not serve any "end lying outside itself"
(Müller-Freienfels); it must be "of no use" (Schopen-
hauer), and have no connection with the "practical"
(Croce); it must not "serve moral ends and the moral
end of the world generally" (Hegel).[1]

For the empiricist the purpose of literature is likewise the expression of an "ideal." But the empiricist's
ideal is one which has no other-worldly home. On the
contrary, it springs from the closest and truest representation of the earthly environment that the author, and the
subject matter and medium of literature (all of these
being themselves in closest association with the world of
things) can encompass. As a consequence, this ideal is
not perfect, nor static, nor eternal, since none of these
qualities are observable in the environment. On the other
hand, it may be realized by men within the world. Poetic
truth, by reproducing the average or normal workings
of the world and testing specific situations by that standard, constructs a plan by which a man may achieve the
most vivid and pleasurable of human satisfactions—that
of subjecting still more of his surroundings to his personal wishes. Probable fiction points out the potential
which is ever a step—but only a step—in advance of the
actual. It is true that literature may depart from poetic
truth and still remain literature—literature, moreover,
which possesses genuine beauties because it provides
genuine satisfactions. But in the degree in which it mis-
represents the environment by violating probability or
possibility—in that degree it forfeits its chance to join
the highest rank of the beautiful in literature.

---

[1] These are all excerpts from the quotations on pp. 80–83 *supra*.

The antithesis between empiricist and idealist is here a direct one. And it is evident that the question hinges upon the opposing ideas of leaving reality and of remaining within it. The latter phrase bears its meaning on its face; the former phrase requires explanation. It is thus proper to inquire of the idealist what he means by "leaving reality."

Does the idealist's phrase carry any empirical meaning? Can it, that is, be explained in terms of this world? The question is readily determinable. There are only three means by which literature may transcend the environment. It may do so through its medium, through its creator the author, or through its subject matter.

Obviously, literature cannot throught its medium escape the bonds of practicality. For literature of all possible varieties and purposes must be set forth in language; and language is a medium universally employed by men to disseminate their experiences and to further their interests. Language shares with the tool-using capacity the distinction of being man's most practical weapon in his fight against his surroundings.

Can the author escape the nexus of practical reality? The empiricist views the literary artist as a laborer at a vocation which, to be humanly satisfactory, must provide him present, and promise him future, satisfactions. The present gratifications are those of earning a livelihood and of expressing instinctive impulses. The effort to attain them forces the author to consider the demands of his readers, since readers provide the economic market whose quotations govern the realization of the author's aims.[2]

---

[2] This does not mean that the writers of the greatest pieces of literature necessarily make the most money. It *does* mean that starving authors did not enter literature with the desire of starving.

Now it is possible for an author to write without any
thought of earning a living by so doing. But the amateur
author (as he is called) is no less firmly bound to reality
than is his professional kinsman. In the first place, it is
scarcely ever possible to declare in any specific case that
the desire for money does *not* motivate the author's
efforts, since the question of what constitutes a decent
livelihood varies with individuals. Secondly, in the absence of a need for money, other "worldly" motives for
the production of literature exist in increased force. The
desire of winning a lady's favor may be active; or, the
motive may be that of gaining notoriety—social com-
mendation. Finally, it is an historical fact that amateur
literature has introduced no new elements and has provided no new problems. It has always followed professional models. There is indeed one difference between the
two—a characteristic one. The word "amateur" carries
a derogatory connotation; it implies the crude, the non-
serious, the superficial, the generally inferior. Indeed,
it may be seen that the amateur author occupies the same
position relative to the professional author that the non-
serious or amateur reader has been shown to occupy relative to the serious reader. If he is a true amateur,[3] he
engages in literature in order to restore a balance. He
comes to literature from an unsatisfactory labor (boredom being here included) in the world. His writing is a
pastime, a drug, or a therapeutic agent. It is precisely
such an attitude, on the part of reader or author, which
degrades literature by denying it a serious commission

---

[3] The needy writer who is forced—because he lacks experience or ability,
or because he has not yet gained a following—to supplement his literary
labors with more remunerative efforts in other fields, is not a genuine amateur. For he will renounce his outside labors when (and if) he succeeds in
gaining a livelihood solely by authorship. As Charles Lamb succeeded with
the Elia essays, the bonds of his relatively unsatisfactory labors in the East
India House became increasingly irksome to him.

in aiding the advance of human knowledge. But even here —when writing provides the gratifications which restore the personal balance of the amateur author, it ⌐ᴀₛ fulfilled a function eminently practical.

To conclude—amateur literature cannot on any count be declared a "purer" literature. On the one hand, it is by no means less firmly a part of "reality" than is professional literature. On the other, it is not "purer" through any distinctive characteristic or any superior quality. On the contrary, it has shown itself to be generally sterile, artificial, and inferior precisely because there has been one motive lacking in its production—the necessity of earning a livelihood : the element which supplements the others to make of literature a complete and satisfactory human labor.[4]

Does the nature of its subject matter grant literature the opportunity of transcending the environment in an empirically definable manner? Clearly it cannot do so. Clearly every concept fashioned by man must be verbalized in terms of human experience. Empirical reality furnishes the materials even for the products of the wildest fancies and the most delirious dreams, as also for

---

[4] The few idealists who have cared to touch upon this "material" question of literature and an economic livelihood do not agree among themselves. Coleridge (*Biographia Literaria*, Chap. XI) makes the logical idealistic separation between literature and a practical labor: "Now though talents may exist without genius, yet as genius cannot exist, certainly not manifest itself, without talents, I would advise every scholar, who feels the genial power working within him, so far to make a division between the two, as that he should devote his talents to the acquirement of competence in some known trade or profession, and his genius to objects of his tranquil and unbiassed choice." This is the sort of thing I attack in the text above as conducive of amateurism in its worst sense. Yet George Henry Lewes, a disciple of Hegel, directly contradicts Coleridge's view in his *Principles of Success in Literature* (edited by F. N. Scott from the edition of 1892, Allyn and Bacon, 1917): "To write for a livelihood, even on a complete misapprehension of our powers, is at least a respectable impulse. To play at Literature is altogether inexcusable: the motive is vanity, the object notoriety, the end contempt."

concepts designed to express the purest ideality. No idealist denies this truth; it merely proves to him the impossibility of expressing the spiritual through the material. But if language, the medium of literature, is thus bound to the environment, then fiction, the subject matter of literature expressed through the medium, must be likewise confined. Fiction can free itself solely from certain manifestations existing within the environment. The very fact that it *is* fiction means that it has freed itself from the demands imposed by factual truth. It may go further—it may break with probability and possibility. But it can gain no freedom beyond this. And even the most impossible fiction has merely broken with certain readily observable nexus of the environment—not with the environment itself. Nor can fiction, whatever its variety, shake itself free from utility, from practicality, from significance for human behavior. If it attains poetic truth, it becomes a guide to life; if it violates probability, it is still of genuine use as a soothing syrup. Even if it breaks with possibility, it serves the practical and useful purpose of gratifying readers who wish an escape from the consciousness of failure, a diversion to prevent boredom, or play to recuperate from serious labor.

The conclusion is inescapable. The idealist's contention that literature must avoid the practical, must leave reality, must transcend the environment, is one which can have no empirical meaning whatever. Solely upon the wings of spirit can such things be done. The sense in which these phrases are used by the idealist is a purely metaphysical and magical one. To have determined this fact is to have made a decided step in advance. For the opposition between the idealist and the empiricist on this point can now be stated in the form of an issue. *Either literature is as closely entwined with the environment and all the values within it as is any other labor of men—or it separates itself from the environment in some empirically inexplicable sense, and, by a spiritual ascension in obedience to demands purely spiritual, rises above it to the absolute.*

The second of the idealist's three major principles is that a work of literature is beautiful if it contains beauty within itself—if there is an indwelling spark of absolute beauty. In opposition to this, the empiricist declares that a work of literature attains the highest class of literary beauty when its author has employed the resources of medium and subject matter in such a way as to attain through poetic truth the fullest association with the interests and desires of the reader.

The empiricist stands directly opposed here to the idealist's contention, since it is at total variance with his own basic principles. To bring an absolute down to earth and to incorporate it in an object is to deny the relative. If a work of literature, to be beautiful, must contain the spark of divine beauty, then only two conditions are possible: either the spark is present, in which case the work is supremely and eternally beautiful; or it is absent, in which case the work does not come within the range of aesthetics. There is no basis here for a more beautiful or a less beautiful—no foundation for a judgment that a work of literature, although beautiful in certain respects or according to a certain standard, is not so beautiful as another work superior in these respects or constructed in accordance with another and a superior standard. To declare with certain idealists that works of literature may be more or less beautiful as they more or less clearly express the absolute, is to be guilty of the absurdity of setting up a category of the *relatively* absolute.

Now it has been seen that the idealist considers the work of art (which includes works of literature) to be a conjunction of certain material or earthly elements with the indwelling spirit of beauty. The function of the matter is to be in proper subordination to the spirit, so that in the work itself the properly gifted spectator may see spirit shining through matter.[5]  But what if the spirit of beauty refuses to descend and to incorporate itself? Then the.work is obviously mere matter, a corporal body without a soul. And what is the nature of this material substance? It is a mere lifeless *imitation*—a mere slavish reproduction—of natural objects which themselves are only imperfect, rapidly fading copies of perfect, eternal ideas. "The imitative art," says Plato, "is an inferior who marries an inferior, and has inferior offspring."[6] Such imitation, he declares, is thrice removed from genuine (that is, ideal) reality.

Plato's judgment upon "unideal" works of art—works which, lacking the divine spark, are confined to mere imitation of earthly objects—has been echoed repeatedly and consistently by idealists. Works, writes Schelling, in which the artist wishes to "subordinate himself to actuality" and "to copy existing objects with slavish fidelity" will result in "larvae indeed, but not works of art." If the artist, holds Goethe, "following a blind instinct" strives after "an appearance of naturalness," he will lead his work to the "lowest step" of art.[7]  And Ruskin writes: "Unideal works of art (the studious production of which is termed realism) represent actual existing things, and are good or bad in proportion to the perfection of the representation."

---

[5] This conception was discussed on p. 91 f. *supra.*

[6] *Republic*, Book X (Jowett).

[7] These are excerpts from quotations on p. 88 *supra.*

Since idealists are thus generally agreed, it is proper to inquire whether "imitation" has any empirical meaning in the sense in which they conceive it. For the empiricist's interpretation of the term differs *toto caelo* from theirs. Plato's derogatory estimate is completely rejected by the empirically inclined Aristotle. For the Stagirite, *mimesis*—always used honorifically—represents the very purpose and character of literature.

To say baldly that literature is "imitation" has little or no empirical meaning. The assertion is not a synthetic judgment: it adds no predicate by way of logical definition. All the actions of men are imitations.[8] The man who builds a ship imitates other ships. Obviously, when literature describes a ship it does not imitate a ship by actually building one. One must add, therefore, that literature is imitation *through a medium*. But the medium is employed only *in a certain manner*—i.e., fictionally. And one must not forget that the imitation is effected and controlled *by an agent*. Now all these qualifications are extremely important, real, genuine—and (not least) necessary, if "imitation" is to possess any intelligible meaning in reference to literature. When taken together, they present the standard empirical position: Literature imitates the environment through an agent (the author), in a medium (language), and in a certain manner (by use of fiction). Clearly, the idealist can never accept this position in regard to "imitation." For with these materials the empiricist explains the entire work of literature. If the idealist grants their validity, he must submit to their full and complete employment. In such a case, what will

---

8 The declaration that "all art is expression" occupies the same category. It is to be noted that Croce, after making this assertion, then further assumes "expression" to be a purely spiritual entity: "Expression is free inspiration."

become of his absolute? It will be a thoroughly useless appendage whose presence is inexplicable and whose utility is unaccountable.

What, now, can be said of the idealist's view that "imitation" is the spiritless reproduction of material or earthly externals? One observes simply that the idealist is at his old tricks. He chooses a broad, abstract, and hence empirically negative term. He refuses to define it— to accord it the *differentia* necessary to justify its application to literature. Under cover of the mist thus created, he attempts to smuggle in his well-known dualism. The genuine and significant values of a work of literature he ascribes to spirit; what remains is called mere "matter" —which is all that non-ideal works possess. But he cannot explain or define what this "matter" is; it must be something or other which, by his own definition, cannot be much.

To conclude, consequently, that the idealist's "imitation" is a purely spiritual conception incapable of any intelligible empirical meaning, is to have made an important forward step. For the situation has now been forced to an issue. *Either a beautiful work of literature is the imitation of the environment by an author, in a medium (language), and with a subject matter (fiction)—or it is the combination of an empirically absurd element called "matter" with a purely spiritual element called "the ideal."*

The third of the three principles of the idealist is that beauty in literature is created and recognized by a special faculty in the mind of a man. At this place idealism employs the two terms characteristic of it—those of "genius" and of "inspiration." The genius has a special faculty within him through which he achieves direct contact with absolute beauty. Inspiration is the process by which the spark descends from the absolute into that special faculty.

The question here is obviously this: can "inspiration" bear any intelligible empirical meaning? One discovers that the idealist, obeying his dualism, divides the creative efforts of the author into two separate categories. On the one hand are the powers emanating from the spirit; on the other hand are those acquired through the exercise of talent. It is unnecessary at this point to discuss the question posed by this dualism, since the issue has already been determined. It was observed (in a previous chapter) that idealists have differed among themselves over the matter of the validity of talent as an element in artistic creation. It was seen that the "difficult" idealists, who see the necessity of talent, are unable to support their contention against the "easy" idealists, who trust to spirit solely. They are unable to maintain their position for the reason that, if talent is recognized as a means, its capabilities must be utilized to their full extent. When this is done, the need of an absolute vanishes. Consequently, it was declared, the only consistent position of the idealist on this matter is the following: A beautiful work of literature is created by inspiration, which is occasioned by the passing of a spark from the other-worldly absolute into a special faculty in the mind of the genius, a man who is favored with such a visitation.

To the idealist, then, inspiration is a purely spiritual experience, indescribable in terms of ordinary experience. And such a conception, he adds, fits the facts. He points to numerous accounts of the phenomenon by authors and composers who declare that they have experienced it. The tenor of these accounts is very nearly constant. The artist relates that, having determined to create a poem or a musical composition, he has concentrated all his knowledge and abilities (all his "talents") toward that end. But he labors vainly. The product seems destined to be lifeless, disjointed, void of meaning. The artist, accordingly, becomes dispirited and dejected. Suddenly, like a clap of thunder, the situation is transformed. The entire work comes before the artist in a flash. All he need do is to transcribe it as swiftly as his fingers can fly. Thus emerges the finished work. The artist is weary, but he is filled with great exhilaration—with a joy doubly great because of the depth of his previous despair. He feels that he has had an experience exceeding the quality of earthly experiences. He has been a mere blind instrument, a recording agent, through which the absolute has spoken. The combined efforts (he feels) of his earthly talents resulted only in a lifeless and disheartening disjuncture; the spirit suddenly transformed all, breathing into the dead matter its significance, life, form, and perfection.

It is true that the evidence the idealist cites proceeds almost exclusively from artists who are themselves romantic idealists, who are engaging in the congenial task of contemplating their own genius, and who are giving testimony which, by its very nature, cannot be contradicted nor confirmed. Yet the empiricist has no desire to attempt to impugn the witnesses. By no means does he wish to belittle the processes of artistic creation, the products of its workings, or the quality of the satisfaction it affords to the creator. He *does,* however, utterly oppose the assumption that these processes involve the interposition of an other-worldly force, bringing a unique sort of knowledge from the realm of the absolute. For the empiricist there is no difference in method between literary creation and the creation of any new and valid tool for human knowledge. There is only one way of attaining valid knowledge—namely, by the steps involved in all human judgments. The scientist employs these steps; the author follows them no less surely.

The empiricist may, perhaps, be permitted to illustrate his position on this question by means of an analogy (for the idealist employs metaphorical analogy without hesitation). He wishes to compare the phenomena attending literary creation with those involved in the solution of a jig-saw puzzle. Let it, therefore, be imagined that a certain man has made the solving of jig-saw puzzles the main interest of his life—that he finds therein a satisfactory human labor. Upon an occasion, accordingly, he procures a puzzle consisting of three hundred pieces. These he spreads upon the table in his study. His problem now definitely confronts him. His three hundred pieces are his data. They are to be combined into a whole which has meaning and significance. Yet the data have, at first, no apparent relation to each other; they seem isolated and meaningless. How shall the man proceed with his labors? His experience with such puzzles has shown him that the completed whole will probably represent a rural scene or a landscape. Here is a possible clew. He notes that a number of the pieces are colored green. Perhaps they represent the herbage of the scene. He acts on this assumption by separating them from the others and attempting to piece them together. Despite the utmost concentration, his progress is slow and discouraging. All that keeps him at his task is the fact that minor successes in fitting a few of the data together prove to him that he is on the track leading to the solution. Slowly his labors continue. He makes further tentative suppositions: he supposes the pieces colored blue to be a representation of the sky. Gradually, features of houses, trees, animals begin to take form. And then, at one stroke, the entire plan comes before him. The pieces will unite in a picture of a landscape, containing cows, houses, a milk-maid, and a river. At once the data which are still un-fitted acquire new meaning. They have now a bond of unity. The man is now working toward a discerned con-clusion. He becomes excited; he labors speedily and with confidence. He rapidly completes the puzzle. When the final piece is in place, he experiences renewed satisfaction. He has imposed his will upon disjointed data by uniting them into a unified pattern.

The analogy is humble. But its analogic value be-comes pronounced by very reason of its humbleness. For in such a sphere certain obvious elements are brought out —elements which are in danger of being overlooked or ignored when a splendid labor like that of authorship is being considered.

To approach the creation of literature on the basis of this analogy is to note, in the first place, that an author is a man who has deliberately set about to become what he is. Like other men he has accumulated a large fund of experiences within his environment. In addition, he has learned to express his reactions through the medium of language. He has before him examples of the successful achievements of other authors. All these circumstances constitute materials for his labors. Literature becomes his vocation—the source of his satisfactions as a laborer and a human being. Upon his vocation he molds his entire life. Its aims become his aims. In obedience to them he looks upon life from a certain point of view. He is con-stantly searching for "copy"—for aspects of human ex-perience which may be utilized as materials for a work of literature. It follows that, when the author begins his labors upon an intended work, he does not face a pathless wilderness. His aims, his medium, his materials, all send out threads of direction whose guidance he may follow. What he faces is a problem of his own making. He wishes to impose his desires upon an environment represented within his medium by constructing a pattern which shall respect those desires. His data are drawn from his total fund of experience. As data they are by no means blind and without direction. They are modeled after the real environment. If they would obey the demands of probability, they must as a whole fairly represent that environment. The basis on which they are selected for employment in solving the problem faced on an occasion by the author is the degree in which they seem to concern that problem: in other words, it is the intention of the author *to find data which appear capable of having a unified plan imposed on them.*

The selection and observation of the data constitute the author's first step. His second begins when he attempts to combine them so that they will form a unified pattern. This task offers great difficulties. Numerous smaller *liaisons* between data are easily discoverable. But conflicts between groups are frequent, and much of the material stands obstinately aloof. The author does not utterly despair. He knows the direction in which he would travel, and he encounters an occasional earnest of success. He continues to shape, to fit and refit, to combine his data. Then suddenly the "happy thought" comes to him.[9] The rebellious data show themselves tractable; the

---

[9] The "happy thought" which brings to view the plan which will unite the data, arises most frequently, I believe, from the sudden acquisition of a new datum. Goethe was in much perplexity about the incidents of his *Werther*—in particular, about a logical *dénouement*. Then: "All at once I heard the news of Jerusalem's death, and immediately after the general report, the most accurate and circumstantial description of the occurrence, and at this moment the plan of *Werther* was formed, and the whole shot together from all sides, and became a solid mass, just as water in a vessel,

entire group of smaller combinations is caught up and fused. A plan which unifies the entire work is revealed in the full perfection possible to art. The whole character of the author's labors is altered. The data now have place, meaning, significance, and coherence; they converge toward a discerned pattern. The plan he has discovered takes possession of the author, and he feels himself to be only its passive recording agent.

The satisfaction and joy which the discovery of the finished pattern impart to the author are most intense. The discovery has solved his problem. It has meant successful achievement within the vocation which grants him a livelihood. Furthermore, it affords gratification to his instinctive desires as a man. The pattern exhibits the environment in the state in which his aims wish it to be. The author has arranged it so as to win a victory over it. Such victories, it has been seen, are productive of great exhilaration, since they spell success for man in his continual conflict with his surroundings. It is true that the victory has been achieved merely within a medium. But to the author medium and reality are closely bound together. His result may have direct significance for his future conduct. It is of importance, moreover, for the lives of readers, and, perhaps, for human knowledge generally.

The empiricist has thus no quarrel with artists who relate their experiences during the creation of a work of art. He may suspect them of dramatizing the situation somewhat. He suspects that some of them exaggerate the gloom and despondency, the feeling of frustration, which precedes the finding of the pattern, in order that

---

which stands upon the point of freezing, is converted into hard ice by the most gentle shake"—*Dichtung und Wahrheit* (Oxenford's translation, 1:509).

the excessive elation imparted by its discovery may be more brilliantly displayed and contrasted.[10] That they, however, describe the phenomena essentially as they occur, there can be little doubt.

But the idealistic interpretation of these phenomena is quite another matter. The idealist is intent upon inserting his absolute into the processes of creation at the most favorable point. He chooses the moment at which the full plan first bursts upon the creator. Everything else— the training, the preparation, the openly avowed intentions, the circumstances of the problem, the constant attempts to follow out lines of union—it is to the idealist's advantage to disregard. Accordingly, he either ignores these things altogether, or he asserts that they result only in failure and despair—that they are a foil for the spirit. When he quotes as evidence the creative experiences of, for example, Mozart, he does so in a manner that may cause the unthinking person to be scarcely aware that Mozart's entire life was devoted to music, that he knew how to play the piano, that he had learned the technique of composition, that he was familiar with the works of other composers, that he composed not a few but many works at regular intervals, that he had a distinct style of expression, and so on.

The idealist, then, devotes himself to one stage of the creative experience to the exclusion of all else. He asserts the remarkable and extraordinary nature of this stage. What he means is clear. The sudden advent of the finished plan is a miracle. It must come from beyond the earth—from the absolute. And the absolute (*being* an absolute) must accordingly be credited with the entire

---

[10] It is no crime, certainly, for an expert in fiction to interpret a situation fictionally. And an author *should* feel gratified with his own work, and thus be disposed to give an explanation of it which satisfies most liberally his instinctive personal desires as laborer and man.

production of the work. But further—since the absolute is perfect, its presence guarantees the result, the finished work. The worth of the work of literature may thus be judged by the intensity of the agitation and elation the author experiences when he first conceives it entire.

In direct contradiction of the idealist, the empiricist must point out that the phenomena attending literary composition are *not* remarkable in the sense that they are only seldom experienced. On the contrary, all of them regularly attend the creation of works of literature—and literature has always been a well recognized vocation in societies living above a certain minimum level of existence. But more than this. If there is only one method by which valid human knowledge can be attained; if the methods of the author do not essentially differ from those of the scientist, or, indeed, of the layman—then it follows that phenomena such as attend the creation of a work of literature are present in the formation of all human judgments, and the satisfactions which are experienced are felt in some degree by every man when he has found a workable plan by which to solve the problem which has occasioned his labors. If these gratifications are—as they appear to be—more intense in literature, the reason is that authorship is one of the most satisfactory of human vocations. For its successful product is strikingly *beautiful*.

What *is* remarkable about the processes of literary creation is the successful result as exhibited by the quality of the work of literature itself. But the quality of the product is not guaranteed by the alleged magnitude of the pleasures accorded the author in its creation. The excitement and agitation of the author may be declared by him to be great; his conviction of the high quality of his creative experience may be strong and sincere. Yet the resulting work of literature may be entirely mediocre. The quality of the result depends upon the abilities of the author expressed in terms of a standard other than his own satisfaction with his abilities. In fact, the ratio between the intensity of creative excitement and the worth of its product seems rather to be an inverse one. The author of extensive experience and great abilities is far less easily and completely gratified by his labors than is the untried amateur.[11]

The opposing views of empiricist and idealist within the borders of the fine art, literature, have now been reduced to their basic elements, and they have been exhibited in the form of direct issues. The results of this examination may be here restated:

1. Literature is spiritually and entirely aloof from the ordinary earthly environment; or, it is, in all its elements a product of and a part of the environment, firmly joined with, and of significance to, all human interests.

2. The beautiful work of literature is a combination of a spiritual absolute with an inert, indefinable, and empirically absurd entity called "matter"; or, it is a representation of the environment by an author, through the medium of language, by the subject matter of fiction.

3. The beautiful work of literature is, in its entirety, the product of "inspiration" operating through a "genius"; or, it is created by methods identical with (and accompanied by phenomena similar to) those by which all valid human knowledge is acquired.

Further scrutiny of the three issues here set forth reveals the additional fact that they employ a common

---

11 "Vergil, we are told, wished to burn the Aeneid. The undergraduate, on the other hand, often has a considerable conceit of his genius in writing his daily theme" (Professor Irving Babbitt, "Genius and Taste," *The Nation*, February 7, 1918).

denominator by means of which the irreconcilable differences between empiricist and idealist in literature may be reduced to its lowest possible terms—to a single issue, fundamental and all embracing. The idealist's explanation of literature denies, ignores, asserts to be inoperative or of non-significant validity, the materials or means upon which the empiricist erects his own explanation. It appears undeniable that literature, through author, medium, and subject matter, possesses significant connections with the environment and man's activities therein. The idealist denies these connections by asserting the disinterestedness of literature. It seems obvious that literature reproduces the spectacle of man and environment through the same three agencies. The idealist's conception of "imitation" ignores this. Finally, it would appear certain that the experience and training of the author are of major importance in the production of a work of literature. The principles of the idealist can make no admission of this indubitable fact. The conclusion to be drawn from the situation is apparent. *The idealist's explanation of literature, in the character it assumes and the terms it employs, is entirely other-worldly or spiritual. It is an explanation in terms of pure magic.* "The principle of magic," writes Professor Dewey, "is found whenever it is hoped to get results without intelligent control of means; and also when it is supposed that means can exist and yet remain inert and inoperative."[12]

The empiricist is entirely satisfied with this conclusion. He possesses, it is true, no materials with which to attack the absolute itself. For this transcendent essence

---

[12] *Human Nature and Conduct,* 26 f.   Cf. Edward Young's *Conjectures on Original Composition* (1759): "What we mean by genius is the power of accomplishing great things without the means generally reputed necessary to that end."

has, by definition, secured itself against direct empirical assault, since it recognizes no earthly means and conforms to no earthly laws of evidence or verification. But it is not necessary to oppose the absolute itself. The idealist is defeated as soon as it is established that his transcendent entity can have validity *solely* in its transcendent sphere. And this conclusion has now been reached. It has been demonstrated that, whenever the idealist attempts to touch the realm of literature at any point, the inevitable result is a complete denial of all earthly means—so that pure spirit alone is operative.

What the empiricist must point out, therefore, in all idealistic discussions about literature is that they *are* based on pure magic. He must make it clear that the system *does* renounce all empirical materials. He must not allow the idealist (or his unwary reader) to assume those means—to give credit to them occasionally in order to skirt the morass of absurdity. He must insist that, if the means are to be employed, they must be consistently and thoroughly employed. By adopting these measures, the empiricist will in every case completely discomfit the idealist. For the latter, it has been seen, *must* attempt to return to the earth from his absolute. He *must* attempt to reconcile the dualism he has established. For his explanation is addressed to the experiences of men within the earthly environment, and it pretends to possess validity with respect to human conduct. An absolute which has no concern with the earth or with the affairs of men is an absolute deprived of all reason for existence. When the empiricist, therefore, points out the purely spiritual nature of the idealist's explanation, he has demonstrated that the latter's dualism is still unresolved—is forever unresolvable.

The comparison of the two opposing views of literature has left one important issue untouched. The third article of the idealist's system contains, it has been noted, two distinct elements. A beautiful work of literature is not only created by an author; it is also recognized and judged by a reader. Now the empiricist gives full recognition to the influence of readers upon works of literature. The idealist speaks freely about the creation of literature through the "genius" and "inspiration." Does he, however, provide a place in his system for the possible influence of readers? The discussion of this question brings one directly within the field of literary criticism.

# Chapter VII

# LITERARY CRITICISM

*Literary criticism is the process of viewing works of literature from the point of view of their readers.*

The character and importance of the reader's attitude has already been somewhat fully discussed. Its significance consists in the fact that it forms the third and final step of the literary judgment. The third step of a scientific judgment is the application of the hypothesis created in the second step to the environment itself. The final step of a literary judgment is the application of the pattern created by the work of literature to the spectacle of man within the environment. In both cases the interests of the final step are paramount. Its demands impart to the entire judgment the characteristic qualities it possesses. The scientist, knowing that the crucial test of his entire experiment will be the degree in which the workings of the environment support the hypothesis refitted into its frame, selects his materials and disciplines his methods to the end that this supreme test may be successfully met. Since the application of the author's pattern is made through a reader, it is the demands of the reader to which the author must conform. Accordingly, that pattern is characterized by being shot through with human significance. The test of it is the extent to which its conclusions and implications can be fitted into the experiences and activities of readers. Consequently, the most beautiful works of literature, it has been declared previously, are those which attain through poetic truth the most extensive and intimate application to the lives of readers. For, in the eyes of the individual reader, the test of the beauty of a work is the degree in which, by dealing with materials of high significance for him, it provides for him the aims which give purpose and direction to his collective activities.

Moreover, if the reader succeeds in attaining from the author's work the gratification he desires, he will seek experience of additional works of the same kind. His demands will enable the author to find, in the writing of literature, a satisfactory labor in life. For he will be assured of a livelihood from his efforts. It is the reader, that is, who makes possible the existence of literature as a vocation possessing a definite economic status among the numerous other vocations of men.

It is evident, therefore, that the third step of the literary judgment, as represented by the demands of readers, furnishes the controlling and directing force for the author's labors. It supplies the motives which animate those labors; it imposes the conditions under which they are carried out; it sets their limits and defines their objectives. It guides and disciplines the author's methods of employing his materials. It forces him to utilize his medium and his subject matter to the end that the results attained from the materials may be clearly and fully communicated.

On the other hand, the third step does not oppose, thwart, nor discourage the author's own desire for the expression of his instinctive impulses as modified by his experiences. Instead, it extends, clarifies, and strengthens them—forcing them into their most specific and expressive form. For author and reader are basically united; their points of view merge. They are both men with designs on the environment; they share numerous social interests. In addition, there are continual references back and forth between them. If readers make demands which authors must obey, it is, nevertheless, from works of literature produced by authors that these demands arose, since only by these means were revealed the potential gratifications of which literature is capable. And if the reader has power over the author in that he defines the bounds of the author's labors, it is nevertheless true that, within these bounds, the author can attain almost unlimited power over his reader.

Let it be supposed, then, that an author addresses his efforts to the task of meeting the needs and desires of prospective readers in order that he may procure from his work the livelihood which is necessary to make literature a satisfactory field of labor for him. He produces his work. It proves to be desirable to a sufficient number of readers to assure the author a commensurate recompense for his exertions. This pragmatic test proves that a number of individual readers have pronounced the work in some degree beautiful to them. They have passed a favorable personal judgment upon it. They have *criticized* it.

Literary criticism may thus be defined, in a preliminary manner, as the judgment which a reader passes upon a work of literature with respect to its possession of or lack of beauty—a judgment determined by the fact that it has, or has not, provided him in some degree the gratifications he seeks.[1]

But it is at once apparent that such a definition is too abstract to be of definite service. There is not one reader, but innumerable readers. There is not one type of reader,

---

[1] It is evident that the judgment passed by the individual reader will, in the majority of cases, be a favorable one. If the work does not afford him the satisfactions he seeks, he will usually cast it aside largely unread; and he will avoid future contact with works of its class.

but three distinct types, in response to whose demands have arisen three separate categories of fiction—the probable, the improbable, and the impossible. If, therefore, the definition of literary criticism just presented is to have determinable meaning, the nature of the demands of each of these three classes of readers will have to be reviewed. For, if a work of literature is beautiful in the degree in which it meets the demands of a reader, the question immediately arises: the demands of what type of reader?

Readers who seek experience of works of literature which violate possibility are readers desirous of solace for defeat or of play after serious exertion. Their basic demand upon the author is that his work separate them as completely as possible from the normal workings and involvements of the environment. They wish to attempt to restore a personal balance which an unsatisfactory labor (or a too constant absorption in a satisfactory labor) has upset. The works which they read become beautiful to them in the degree in which this demand is met. Under these circumstances it follows that the individual reader is himself the supreme and only judge of the extent to which the work of impossible fiction accomplishes the thoroughly personal function which he demands of it. There is no other standard of judgment involved. The relative success of the work according to this sole standard must obviously be determined by each reader for himself, since no other man possesses precisely his experiences or is aware of his specific reactions to them.

Readers of works of literature which violate probability desire to learn that their present vocations are to a marked degree satisfactory—either by reason of genuine, though not apparent, importance to society, or by reason of the brilliant successes which are possible within them by a regular and easy transition of events. In order to place himself in a position to fulfill such demands, the author, although remaining within the wide confines of the mathematically possible, must break with the norms manifested over an extended period of time by the workings of the general environment. And the measure of the author's success is the extent to which his work serves the therapeutic function of restoring to the reader a personal satisfaction in his present labors and their potentialities. The work is beautiful to the reader as it demonstrates to him that his activities are humanly satisfactory because, in addition to procuring him a livelihood, they allow him the expression of his instinctive desire for present victories over the environment and hold out promising guaranties for the future.

Now the fact that such a work must remain within the bounds of possibility constitutes an additional standard by which it may be judged. It does not renounce the environment; it follows it at a distance. Its materials constitute an imitation—even though distorted—of the basic realities of the human surroundings. Here, then, is an impersonal standard for the criticizing of improbable fiction: a demand that it obey the standards of possibility manifested by the environment.

This criterion is indeed impersonal; but it is entirely too vague and general to be of active service as a canon of literary criticism. For the range of possibility is vast; consequently, its principles make no specific demands. The general concatenations of progression, change, cause and effect, are well recognized by all men who are conducting their lives at a level above that of survival. To demand obedience to them from the work of literature is, in effect, to demand very little. So then—if such an impersonal criterion lacks critical utility, one is thrown back upon the standard erected by the personal desires of each individual reader of the type. He, and he alone, knows the extent of the gratifications the work affords him; he alone is capable of pronouncing the extent of its beauty. Thus, in the case of improbable fiction, one is forced to a conclusion essentially the same as that arrived at in the case of impossible fiction: the standard of judgment is essentially that applied by the individual reader on the basis of personal needs known best to himself.

Works of literature which attempt, by obeying the demands of probability, to attain poetic truth are sought out by readers whose purposes place them, it has been seen, in an entirely different category from those constituted by the two other types. The serious reader does not require the alteration or rupture of the basic manifestations of the environment. He wishes, instead, to procure from literature genuine guidance for the activities of his life. Such gratification will ensue only if literature enters as fully into the involvements of human life amid its surroundings, and reports them as faithfully, as the nature of fiction, its subject matter, will allow. The author who wishes to write a work of literature acceptable to the serious reader is called upon to comply with the specific and difficult demands which the reader's purposes constrain him to make. These requirements (as formulated in a preceding chapter)[2] are the following:

1. The author must present his materials in the form of a representation of a contest between man and his surroundings.

2. The work must gain as many specific points of contact as possible with the reader's experiences and activities.

---

[2] See *supra*, pp. 146–152.

3. The environment presented within the medium must be a reasonably full and complete representation of an earthly environment.

4. The environment depicted must, as a whole, constitute a fair and proportionate representation of the various and conflicting currents within the real environment.

5. The materials employed must be, in their entirety, combined within a pattern (so constructed as to utilize the ability of the medium to express action) which can bring those materials to a state in which they have been subjected to the impress of human desires.

Let it be imagined that the author has been at pains to meet the demands of the serious reader and that he has succeeded in doing so. The reader, consequently, judges the work to be to a considerable degree beautiful. By pronouncing such a criticism the reader has declared the existence of the following situation: Here is a work of literature which presents, from a point of view of maximum significance to me, the spectacle of a man, actuated by motives very similar to my own, imposing desires arising from experiences resembling mine, upon an environment with which I am familiar. As a result of his activities, he succeeds in arranging this environment so that it shows itself amenable to the specific aims he harbors against it. Now I, too, should like to accomplish in the world the results achieved by this character. And I can put myself in his place, if I so desire, and act as he has done in the hope of receiving on my own account the gratifications he is shown to have received. If I do so, however, I shall be obliged to make certain significant changes in my present course of action—my rationale of conduct. My present activities are, judged by comparative and human standards, satisfactory to me; but I

realize that they bear further potentialities which promise even more satisfactions. I am willing, therefore, to
make changes in my conduct if I can find assurance that
they will lead me in the direction of such further gratifications. If I adopt the character's tactics as a guide
for my future life, I must thus be sure that their augury
is bright. I know that a man can never be certain of
future results within a chaotic environment subject to
accidents and exceptional circumstances. But if he can
establish the thorough probability of certain results, he
has secured the safest reliance and the most complete
control of the future possible for men. Consequently, I
seek assurance that this work of literature has given a
fair representation of the dominating elements of the
situation depicted.

The personal judgment of the serious reader is thus
determined by the degree in which the work obeys the
norms of probability as he sees them. All his specific
requirements are directed toward this end. All his gratifications proceed from this source. To what degree, then,
can he be considered an adequate judge of whether
genuine poetic truth has been attained? Obviously, his
opinion will be of most value on those aspects of the work
which concern his narrower and more personal interests
—his vocation, his immediate geographical locality, the
objects and interests over which he possesses a fairly
extensive personal control. With the details of such
topics he has a specialist's familiarity. Here any breach
of probability, arising through omission or commission,
can scarcely remain undetected by his eye.

But every work of probable fiction must deal with
interests far broader in scope than those which come
under the immediate observation and control of the
average reader. It may indeed concentrate upon the

character's specific and immediate surroundings. But it always purports to show the active operation within these surroundings of all the representative forces of the general environment. It cannot avoid judgments upon the major social interests of men, for these are essential elements of any environment. Naturally, then, these interests may be either probably or improbably dealt with.

The average individual reader makes little pretense of being an authorized judge of interests which affect his life but which lie largely outside his control. His activities are restricted to the comparatively narrow interests involving his vocation and the phenomena of his immediate surroundings. He recognizes clearly that these larger interests are of direct importance as the background and the foundation of his personal affairs. But of necessity he permits or delegates other men to determine and to interpret them for him. The character of his education has been determined by others. The social customs of his groups result from growth or tradition, and they are essentially beyond his control. The laws of these groups have been determined upon and codified by others; even their interpretation and application is the business of other men.

At every moment of his life, therefore, every man recognizes the authority of other men to speak for the groups of which he is a member. He accepts their decisions. Upon his willingness to accept depends the entire structure of organized society. That the codes formulated by these men are perfect, the average man does not at all believe. He knows, however, that men who devote all their activities to the interests of a large group have better knowledge than he has concerning the methods by which the affairs of that group may be conducted most profitably for its members. Moreover, he has a practical test of the results of their efforts. They have been relatively successful if they impart to the group a marked degree of stability, and give to its laws a strong promise of uniformity and constancy of operation. Under such circumstances a man has a firm and determinable base on which to build the more restricted and narrow superstructure of his individual activities.

Toward the work of literature the average serious reader occupies a position exactly analogous to that of the average man towards the general environment. The reader desires guidance for his specific aims and individual behavior. They, he knows, must be founded on prescriptions which he has received from others, and which concern interests outside his knowledge and control. Now the reader *is* an adequate judge of the fidelity with which the specific and personal actions of the character within the work are depicted by the author. He alone knows the full extent of their contact with and application to his own personal affairs. But he knows also that these actions are founded on a definite attitude taken by the author toward larger social interests. The latter may not be directly depicted within the work; but they are always involved, since they are the background and the larger motivating forces of the character's aims and acts. The reader is admittedly unable to declare whether these larger interests are full, faithfully, and proportionately reflected by the author. Yet he earnestly wishes this information. If he is to rely upon the work as a guide for his future conduct, he must know whether the entire environment, general and specific, social and individual, is represented in accord with probability.

There thus exists a clear necessity for an expert or "professional" reader. The qualities and training he must possess are also clearly indicated. He must, in the first place, own a broad experience with the various groups of which his society is composed—as well as (for proper perspective) a knowledge of societies of other countries. He must have studied the physical environment of these groups, their social degrees, their occupations and recreations, their habits and characteristic reactions. In the second place, he must be familiar with literature in all its aspects. As an expert reader he will have knowledge of works of literature past and present. He will thoroughly comprehend the nature and potentialities of the literary medium and subject matter. He will be acquainted with technical details involving the character and identity of all subdivisions erected within the field. He will have read what other expert readers have written about works of literature.

*The reader who possesses these difficult qualifications—this knowledge both broad and deep of life, and of literature as well—is called a literary critic.*[3]

The task to which the critic's energies must be devoted is likewise clearly indicated by the necessities of the situation. His critical function involves the application to the spectacle of mankind in contact with the collective interests of the environment, of the results achieved by the specific illustration of that contact presented by the actions of the character within the author's work of literature. His purpose, in short, is to determine the *genuine* third step of the literary judgment. The scientist's third step is the application of his hypothesis to the frame of the environment itself; the purpose is to discover the degree in which the environment supports that hypothesis.

---

[3] "If literature is a criticism of life, criticism . . . . determines the relation of the two, and thus needs as close touch with life as with arts and letters."—W. C. Brownell.

The third step in literature is the application by the critic of the pattern created by the author to the situation of *man* within the environment; its purpose is to determine the extent to which the pattern is supported by the broadest aspects of that relation.

The critic thus constructs the *genuine* third step of literature. It has been seen that the individual reader constructs a third step of his own. But the difference between the applications of the literary pattern made respectively by critic and individual reader now stands clearly revealed. The latter applies that pattern to his own life. It becomes beautiful to him in the degree in which it gratifies his personal desires. He is himself the best judge of the success of the work in this respect. And his judgment constitutes a criticism of the work—an individual criticism whose standards are as various as are the personal needs of individual readers. Such personal judgments are by no means unimportant nor invalid. Upon them depends the existence of the author's vocation. And *within its limits* the validity of such a judgment cannot be questioned.

Over impossible fiction, it has been seen, the authority of personal judgments is supreme. A work which makes no pretense of following the environment can be judged by no standard other than the personal solace it affords each reader. In improbable fiction the authority of personal judgment has been seen to be dominant, although not omnipotent. For fiction of this type may be judged impersonally by the standard it professes to follow—that of possibility. But the vagueness and elasticity of this standard gives the controlling influence to personal reactions within the limits demarcated by the intentions of the work.

The work of literature which attempts to attain poetic truth makes pretensions of a nature far different from those of other types. Its beautiful is to be potential as well. It sets forth the what should be in such terms as to meet the demands of the what may be. In this field the range of individual judgment is highly restricted. It has validity only so far as the narrow and personal interests of the reader extend. And the reader recognizes the inadequacy of his own judgment. He welcomes the aid that the critic can here afford him. For the reader's purposes are serious; he wishes a guide for his actions. It makes a difference to him—a great and significant difference— whether the work is or is not obedient to probability throughout. It is thus the critic's important function to remedy, by his own judgments, the confessed inadequacy of the individual reader's opinions. It is the critic who dominates the field of probable fiction. But the two standards of judgment do not clash. The reader imperatively requires the critic; the critic's express function is to extend and follow out the principles upon which the reader's judgment is based by applying them to the larger social interests which every work of probable fiction inevitably involves.

If the reader requires the services of the critic, literature itself requires them no less imperatively. For it is the critic alone who constructs the third step which joins literature to human knowledge. It is the critic alone who can assess the importance of the results achieved within the field, and who can set forth in significant form the additions which are thereby made to the fund of general human knowledge. If literature bears directly upon human advancement, then and then only is its practice worthy the efforts of serious and intelligent men. Then and then only does it constitute an integral part of, and add a genuine contribution to, the history and progress of human effort.

The character of the critic's labors is determined by, and must conform to, the double command which his function enjoins upon him. The individual reader's judgment owes its inadequacy precisely to the fact that its standards are too narrowly personal. If the critic would remedy that inadequacy, it follows that his own labors must be conducted in as impartial and impersonal manner as possible. If they are not so carried on, then the resulting judgment of the critic will merely be that of another individual reader, and it will hold little more general validity than such a judgment carries. Likewise, if it is true that results are attainable within the field of literature which are applicable to general human knowledge, then those results must be directly assessed and applied. There can be no occasion for the interposition of the critic's own aims and possible prejudices. Accordingly, the two commands thus laid upon the critic converge into one imperative prescription: *The labors attending the carrying out of the function of literary criticism must be performed with scientific impersonality and impartiality. The critic of literature must use the methods of the scientist.*

If the critic is to be a scientist, it is necessary, in the first place, that he have at his disposal well defined and adequate materials with which to work. It is essential, secondly, that he possess experimental control of these materials—the power to utilize them by constructing out of them the three steps which compose the method of every scientific judgment.

The critic's materials are supplied to him by the fact that he is primarily a reader. He demands from a work of literature, therefore, the same definite qualities that the individual serious reader does. But he creates a different criterion for those demands. The fact that he is a critic means that he has had special training in two fields. He possesses a thorough familiarity with what concerns the medium, the subject matter, the technique, the practice past and present, of literature. He has discerned, furthermore, the characteristic and normal manifestations of the group interests within his society. It is by a standard composed of these two matters taken in conjunction that the critic judges a work of literature.

The method of the critic is determined by the fact that he and the author are joint agents in constructing a complete literary judgment. The author composes the first two of the three steps necessary for this result. The first step, it has been seen, consists in the author's selection of data from the environment and his careful observation of them. The second results from his arrangement of these phenomena into the unified pattern which constitutes the work of literature. The critic's function is to compose the third and final step—the application of the results designated or implied by the work to the entire situation of man within the general environment.

The third step is the crucial test of the pattern or hypothesis. Its demands have a backward reference to the steps preceding it. It sets the problems of the author; it disciplines his labors. The fact that his pattern must fit into the complete frame of man within the environment forces him to choose data faithfully representative of the entire environment; it forces him to combine them in accordance with the norms of probability manifested by the general environment. *The activities of the critic are thus directed to the task of determining, on the basis of the materials at his disposal, whether the author's pattern can be successfully applied to the final end or aim which has controlled its construction.* If it can be so applied, then the author's steps are valid and his work has reached the goal it set for itself. If it will not fit, then the first two steps are erroneous at some point or points. In such cases, it is clearly part of the critic's duty to follow the backward reference of the third step in order to ascertain the source of the error.

Let it be supposed, then, that the critic is faced by a work of literature of the present day. His first task is evidently to gain knowledge of the work as reader. Being a reader, he feels so close a connection between actual personal experience and human experience represented within the medium of language that he can to a degree substitute the one for the other. He must, therefore, adopt toward the work an attitude which makes such a substitution possible. He must willingly allow the author his choice of data, the initial conditions he represents, and the limits he imposes both for the action and for the medium itself. And the critic must thereupon follow the materials thus limited and represented to the conclusion of the work. All this is to say that he must *read* the work.

One of the limitations the author has imposed upon himself is of importance as concerning a general subject about which the critic possesses special knowledge. The author's work is not merely a work of literature. It can be further classified as a novel, a drama, or a poem. These three main subdivisions within the realm of literature owe their existence to the fact that they differ markedly as to the specific conditions under which they employ the medium of language.

The novel (prose narrative being now generally known by this term) requires the fullest and most complete expression of which the medium is capable. The novelist must create an entire environment by labors entirely within its bounds; everything that he represents must be fashioned from the unadorned and unsupplemented medium of language. No external aid is granted him. But when he accepts the necessity of the situation, he gains an artist's power over this entire reproduced world. He is not restricted nor governed by materials extraneous to his medium. He can exhibit *quicquid agunt homines* with free and life-like fidelity.

The dramatist enlists the aid of the spoken voice, of the visible presence of his characters, of stage scenery which (at the present time) depicts with great fidelity to the eyes of the spectator the milieu of the work. What the dramatist gains with this aid is obvious: he joins the medium to the actual visible representation of things. In this way he brings his artistic medium closer to actual life by removing its inability (previously noted) to present objects directly to the eye of the spectator in the manner of other fine arts, like painting—while at the same time, he preserves the ability of language to portray action in time. Nevertheless, in securing this advantage, the dramatist imposes certain definite restrictions upon the scope of his labors. He subjects himself to the character and nature of the materials he employs as supplementary to his proper medium. The restrictions herein involved affect the time, the place, the action depicted within his work. Because of the stage properties, the places of the action must be gathered and concentrated; because of the necessarily restricted length of his work, the time of his action must be condensed; because of the stage itself, the actions of the characters must be confined in extent or represented in indirect fashion. Moreover, the "reader" has become an "audience"—a group of people subject to certain group reactions.

Now all these circumstances are genuine elements of the situation. They form the initial self-imposed limitations of the dramatic author. They must be recognized and granted by every reader or listener (including the critic). The judgment passed by any reader upon a drama must, that is, operate only within the limits of the bounds which have been demarcated. No reader demands from the present day dramatist the free range of time, place, and action, nor the representation through language of the physical aspects of the milieu—which the same reader requires of the novelist.[4] On the other hand, the reader *does* expect the best possible disposal of the additional means the dramatist has summoned to his aid. There must exist the firmest collaboration between the supplementary materials and the original medium of language. The former must not distort or destroy the effect produced on him by the latter. The whole must remain a work of literature granting the satisfactions which works of literature are able to dispense. This demand forces the dramatist to possess, in addition to his command of the medium of language, a thorough knowledge of the conditions and necessities of an acted play.

The poet seeks to make language a medium more directly representative of reality by removing its inability to reproduce sound, accent, pitch, and rhythm after the manner of music. In making this attempt the poet takes advantage of an instinctive trait of mankind. To determine a regularity in the manifestations of a tumultuous and cacophonous environment is to impose upon it an auditory pattern of significance to man. By means of such a pattern the surroundings acquire a "tone"—a

---

[4] In Shakespeare's day, stage scenery being almost non-existent, the deficiency had to be supplied by language, the principal medium of the situation.

reference to human actions and designs, which arouses a certain unified disposition to action or behavior. A pattern of this kind is applicable to general human experience in the form of the separate fine art, music. It is applicable also to great numbers of the labors and interests, individual or social, of mankind, and it gives to them an added human significance. It can even be applied to unsatisfactory or mechanical labors to alleviate somewhat the appearance of formlessness and purposelessness which they present to the laborer.[5]

The medium of language is likewise responsive to auditory patterns. Words have stressed and unstressed syllables. They are capable of rhyme and alliteration; they may be made, through onomatopoeia, not only to describe but actually to reproduce sounds. Phrasal inflection directly involves pitch or tonal variation. All these circumstances furnish the means employed by the poet to establish, to accentuate, and to maintain the rhythmic sound pattern he wishes to impose. By means of the pattern he gains for his product the added significance which the steady beat adds to all human activities. He likewise enables his medium to overcome some of its inability of directly reproducing sounds—and this, too, without robbing it of its characteristic ability of portraying action.

But the imposition of the pattern necessitates additional knowledge on the part of the author. In addition to a familiarity with his proper medium of language, the poet must possess an acute sense of rhythm and an adequate comprehension of the various metrical forms, of devices for securing variety within them, of ways for

---

[5] I refer here, of course, to sailors' chanties, Negro melodies, and so on. M. Charles Lalo has given attention to this subject, in his *L'art et la vie sociale*, in connection with what he calls the *anaesthetic* conditions of art (i.e., the social conditions necessary for the existence of art but not explanatory of the work of art itself).

creating what is usually called "tone color," and so forth. Moreover, the existence of the pattern sets certain limits to the work produced, or promotes certain tendencies within it. The finished piece must, for example, be delivered orally if the qualities of the pattern are to be conspicuously displayed. This circumstance, together with the possibility of monotony, tends to reduce the length of the work. The fact that the pattern usually creates a "tone"—which can be created rapidly and cannot long be maintained—exerts a similar tendency. It is also the case that the exigencies of the rhythm necessitate a selection and arrangement of words, and thus a cutting down of the free range of the medium as an implement of expression. And along with the heightened (because rhythmic) significance of the elements of the pattern seems to go a concentrating or compacting of the action—a narrowing, consequently, of the typical ability of the medium. To such conditions the reader of a poem must give an initial acceptance; and his judgment of the work must be applied within the self-imposed limits thus established.

Accordingly, when the critic is faced by a work of literature, he accepts the limits imposed by the requirements of the subclass to which the work belongs. He accepts them as he accepts the author's materials and his formulation of the problem which the completed work is to have solved. In his rôle of reader, the critic then gains experience of the work. As a reader he will receive a distinctly personal gratification from the work—the amount of which will increase with the extent to which the situation of the character in the work finds specific and intimate points of contact with the critic's own experiences and aims in life. Since an extremely broad and varied experience is one of his major qualifications as a critic, the range of these personal gratifications will be wider than that of the average reader. He will be able to comprehend the personal gratifications of readers even when he does not share them—even when the aims of the character portrayed do not closely parallel, nor establish intimate points of contact with, his own. For a wide experience with many varieties of life within his society will extend the critic's comprehension of the aims of readers, just as it increases the ability of the author himself to enter the restricted field of the reader's individual interests and therein to establish, through his work of literature, the fullest contact with those interests.

The personal gratifications received by the critic from the work are by no means unimportant. It is because of them that he finds a satisfactory vocation in reading and judging works of literature. As a reader, moreover, he can procure from literature suggestions pertinent to the conduct of his personal affairs. These gratifications are important, furthermore, because their latitude and degree furnish a criterion by means of which an essential qualification of the critic may be estimated. If he receives but few of them, or if they are markedly restricted to a narrow field, it is thus signified that his familiarity with the manifold interests of the society in which he lives is of a strictly limited variety. In such a case, he is disqualified as a critic, since his judgments will necessarily possess little more validity than those of the average individual reader.

It is one thing for the critic to receive, as a reader, personal satisfactions from the work of literature. It is decidedly another thing for him to allow them a voice when he composes, as a critic, his judgment upon the work. A critic differs from an individual reader precisely through the fact that his judgments are based on grounds broader and more stable than those of personal gratification. Moreover, it has been seen that personal reactions are essentially beyond the scope of criticism; each reader is himself the best judge of their full extent. The critic can justify his existence only through his possession of special knowledge and training which the ordinary reader does not own. It is from the materials supplied by these sources that his judgments must be composed. How, then, shall he bring them into a position of accord with his purposes?

The answer is clearly furnished by an essential prescription of his method. A scientific method must be an open one. Results must be attained by the use of plainly defined materials; and the degree of validity ascribed to those results must be capable of test. Any succeeding investigator must be able to measure the accuracy of the judgment through retracing the steps by which it was formed. Consequently, if literary criticism is to be conducted by the principles of all scientific method, it must deliberately and rigorously exclude the interference of influences arising from the purely personal gratifications received by the critic from the circumstance that he is also a reader. For these private satisfactions are bound up with the critic's personal life; their exact nature as well as their extent and intensity can be known only to him. Here he and the individual reader meet on common ground and judge with equal authority. It is only when the critic turns to the materials which his special knowledge—his familiarity with the general and specific manifestations of an entire society, and with all that concerns literature itself—affords him, that he secures data for a scientific or impersonal judgment. If he would use these data legitimately, he must thus employ all the efforts within his power to avoid the deviation, the distortion, the error, which inevitably accompany the intrusion of elements strictly personal into the steps of scientific judgments.

That it is difficult for the critic to separate his personal satisfactions from the materials with which he is to compose his judgments as well as from his actual method of procedure, is a fact admitting of no possible doubt. That the separation can be accomplished, however, with a marked degree of success is proved by the progress and high attainment of workable human knowledge in those fields in which experimental methods have been set up. Every scientific worker must make the same effort of separation; the validity of his results is directly conditioned upon his success. A chemist receives personal gratification from conducting his labors in his field. He chose chemistry as his vocation for the very reason that these reactions were of unusual range and intensity. He is also animated by the human desire to arrive through his labors at results which will increase his future well-being and elevate his rank in his group. But the chemist, notwithstanding, refuses to allow his materials and his experimental methods to be obtruded upon in any way by influences arising from such personal opinions. It is true that the nature of the chemist's materials makes this exclusion a relatively simple affair; nevertheless, it is one which he must, can, and does make.

The historian faces the same situation, although in his case its elements are far more complicated. He receives from his researches the personal gratifications which a satisfactory human labor provides. He is actuated as a man, moreover, by numbers of individual and group desires which urge him so to shape his professional activities that their results may procure for him an enhanced position within his group. The voice of these personal and group aspirations is strong. To separate them from all connection with his professional labors as historian is a task of great difficulty—especially when the labors deal with situations which involve considerable numbers of these aspirations. Yet the first and by a great deal the most important mandate laid upon the historian is that of effecting the sharpest cleavage between the two points of view that lies within his powers. The existence of history as a reputable department of knowledge hangs upon the historian's ability in this respect. And to point out that personal motives *have* influenced his professional judgments is to destroy the validity of the results of his labors.

The situation of the literary critic is identical with that of the historian. His personal prejudices and ambitions urge him toward judgments expressive of them. Yet the materials and methods with which he is professionally engaged demand the fullest possible suppression of interference from such a source. His achievement as a critic is directly measured thereby. If he gains a high degree of relative success in obeying this command, his judgments will gain direct application to the spectacle of man within the environment. If he fails, his judgments, suffering the distortion and the limitations of personal interests, will lose connection with their proper goal. The problem is one, in short, to whose solution the critic's training and experience continually address themselves. If he would become or remain a reputable critic his effort must never slacken in this respect. For it is a distinctive quality of scientific method that its openly displayed processes render possible the detection of such errors, limitations, and distortions.

One comes thus to the details of critical method. The circumstances upon which that method is founded may at this point endure a brief recapitulation.

It is the function of the critic to effect a complete literary judgment. Every such judgment must be constructed according to the three steps by which all workable judgments are composed. The first two of these are the work of the author. He has been confronted by a problem involving the relations of man and the environment. In order to set about solving it, he has, as a first step, selected, on the basis of his experience with the environment, a number of data which concern the problem. These he has taken apart and carefully observed. He has composed the second step of the literary judgment when he has combined the data into a pattern which solves the problem occasioning the investigation. The standard which has governed both these steps has been one formed from the norms of probability manifested by the environment generally. The author's pattern, expressed within the medium in a manner consonant with the character of the medium, is the work of literature itself. With this product the author has completed his proper task. But the literary judgment has not thereby been completed; the all important final step yet remains. The patterned or hypothesized data must be refitted into the frame from which they were extracted. To this important task the critic of literature must address himself. As a reader he gains experience of the steps constructed by the author. On the basis of his special training he sets about effecting the purpose for which he exists.

The third step of the literary judgment will be found to involve three main questions:

    I. What are the interests into whose frame the literary pattern should fit?

    II. To what degree and in what manner does it represent those interests?

III. What are the consequences of the application of the pattern to the frame composed by these interests?

It is for the solution of these problems that the critic must employ to its fullest extent the knowledge which his special training has provided.

I. In the work of literature the author portrays a specific character in conflict with a particular environment. The completed work exhibits this environment subjected to the desires of this character; he has emerged successfully[6] from a struggle with certain definite manifestations within it. It is rarely difficult to determine the identity of these elements or interests. The author has attempted to create a complete environment, it is true. But, in order to attain in his finished work the state of completeness and finality demanded by art, he has been forced to concentrate upon the character's reactions to certain human interests only. It is these few which constitute the problem posed by the work; it is the satisfactory solution of their demands which, it is understood, brings the work to a state of artistic wholeness. The finished work thus makes the following asseveration: A man constituted like the character portrayed, living within an environment similar to the one presented, will be able to impose his aims upon the particular interests which he has been forced to encounter if he governs his conduct by the methods or tactics here set down.

---

6 It seems more convenient at this point to envisage the struggle as terminating successfully. But the general view here enunciated does by no means exclude tragedy. That subdivision of drama presents no new problems. The conclusion of a tragedy finds the character's surroundings in the state in which, relative to this character, they *should* be. But that state is fatal to the character. Because of some defect in his nature or his strategy, the environment has failed to support the pattern which the tragic hero has attempted to impose. This situation makes no difference in the critical application of the result, as outlined in the text above.

To determine as clearly and definitely as possible what these interests are which have motivated the conflict is the first business of the critic. He will discover that, within his particular surroundings, the character has been engaged in a struggle specifically with the elements of the physical environment, or with circumstances attending the interests of sex, of business or vocation, of education, of family relations, of religion, of advancement of social status, or other definite individual or social manifestations. When the critic has ascertained the interest (or interests) which has set the terms of the conflict, he has procured the materials with which he will be further employed.

II. The interests thus identified and disengaged have a validity or applicability extending beyond the boundaries of the work in which they appear. Their content is not constituted from mere accidental or chance happenings. On the contrary, they are interests which, since they obey the norms of probability, have been made to assume the attitude displayed by the entire environment toward all men irrespective of time and place. They belong, consequently, to the frame of that general spectacle. This is to say that a work of literature submits a particular character within a specific environment to the standard set by the manifestations of the entire human environment toward man collectively—for the laws of probability which govern the selection and combination of the data are founded on these manifestations. Thus the work is an experimental testing out of particulars by the standard of the general. If these universal manifestations have been fairly and adequately represented, then the results of the work will have significance for the large frame which contains these norms. For those results will be the reflection within narrow limits of the attitude of the entire environment in relation to men—the particular arranged in obedience to the demands of the general.

The critic has thus specifically to determine whether the work of literature has, within its limits, given through passage, without hindrance or distortion, to the normal manifestations of the general environment. The materials to be employed in this decision are supplied by the critic's extensive knowledge both of works of literature and of the phenomena of human experience. For the question obviously involves both. If the norms of general probability are to be exhibited at work within a specific environment, then that environment must be reproduced as fully and accurately as the nature of language and fiction will allow. The critic's familiarity with literature informs him of the potentialities of the medium and the subject matter in this respect. And, since the adequacy and fairness of the reproduction of the general interests are in question, the critic must have observed and studied the major manifestations of the human environment. Under this second heading the demands upon the work will be numerous. The work may extend over very narrow limits. It may be a concentrated study of only one or two of the interests of mankind. Yet within these limits the scale of the general must be proportionately maintained. The one or two elements of the conflict of man and environment upon which the attention of the work is concentrated must not be overemphasized nor developed in oblivion of, nor at the expense of, other interests. The influence and validity of other normal human problems must be recognized and provided for, even though they are not minutely developed. And within the field of concentration itself, it is the norms of the probability of the entire environment which must govern the situations that progressively arise during the formation of the pattern.

III. Let it be supposed that the work of literature under examination has complied with all these requirements. What, under these circumstances, is the significance of the result—of the pattern it has composed for its data? The work has been a study under specific conditions of a man's reactions to certain manifestations of his surroundings. But the specific conditions are not disruptive of the point of view of man's eternal fight against his collective surroundings. The man specifically depicted is subject to all the normal manifestations of the general environment toward all men; the elements of those manifestations are arranged to exhibit the character they normally possess. Now the pattern of the work is a demonstration of the tactics employed by the character in imposing his desires upon the interests which compose the problem—so that the completed pattern has brought these elements into the state in which, relative to those desires, they should be. Consequently, the circumstances involved by the pattern are directly applicable to the general situation of man within the environment. And they can be set directly within that frame, since its proportions have been carefully maintained. To make this application—the express duty of the critic—is to determine the contribution of literature, tested by the strictest standards it can impose, to the legitimate plans and aims of human life on earth. It is to point out to men the most reliable guide for the future.

The results attained by a work of literature may be measured not only by their direct applicability to life. For they fall naturally into the same category with those achieved by previous works which have concentrated upon the same human interests. By the results of these previous works the applicability or "workability" of the conclusions of the new work may be further tested. The new pattern will surely be a safer guide for life in one respect than are the older. It will state the problem involved by the interests it concentrates on in terms more recent than those of former works. The data it employs will create a specific environment more nearly representing the conditions of the present day. But if it is to constitute a distinctly superior literary judgment, it should possess an additional advantage as well. It should verbalize the interests it treats more extensively and more accurately than previous works have done. Its pattern may be composed of more carefully observed data, or it may include larger numbers of them. In this way ever better literary judgments are possible (even if not steadily forthcoming), and literature, like science, is able to respond to the progress of general human knowledge and to the constant changes attendant thereon.

It has been seen that the results attained by an historical monograph making an intensive examination within greatly restricted limits are applicable to the larger historical frame. When the *liaisons* are made which unite those results to that frame, it may be found that, although minute in themselves, the results have caused adjustments and changes to be made, not only in those parts to which they are immediately joined, but throughout a large portion, perhaps, of the entire structure—just as the agitation caused by a single stone may be transmitted to an entire pond.

There is a direct analogy here with the results attained by a new literary judgment. If it is more recent or more observant and inclusive in respect to its data, its application to the frame of man and environment may "make a difference" not only in the interests to which it has devoted itself and in those by the side of which it is ranged, but, it may be, in the entire framework. The interests of men are integrally bound together. A changed view toward one interest will almost inevitably involve many more. Thus the literary critic cannot rest content with establishing the immediate *liaisons* of the work. He must follow its conclusions into the broadest social questions known to man, if the conclusions of the work involve alterations therein.

The critic's labors have thus far been described under the assumption that he has, on the basis of his extensive knowledge both of life and of literature, adjudged the pattern or hypothesis which the author's work contains to be directly and genuinely applicable to human life within the earthly environment. In such a case the critic's task is a single one. He has only to make the third step of the literary judgment—to apply the pattern to human life by setting it into the general frame, noting the *liaisons* by which it becomes attached thereto, and tracing the alterations it may make necessary therein. The critic need not minutely consider nor retrace the first two steps of the judgment—the steps which led to the formation of the pattern. For that pattern has proved its soundness by the fact that it was found applicable to human life. The author, that is, submitted his labors to the discipline imposed by the demands of the final step; consequently, his hypothesis is not an erroneous one.

Under such circumstances the labors of the author and of the critic ably supplement each other. The author composes the hypothesis; the critic completes the literary judgment by applying its results to the goal at which it aims, showing their validity with reference to that goal. If the author, then, has (like the scientist) obeyed the demands of the final step during his labors, he has relieved the critic of a portion of his function and duty. *In this sense,* it may be said that the author is his own best critic.

There is a final question which may be asked of the critic after he has completed his task of applying a valid hypothesis. The beauty of a work of literature consists, in the critic's eye, in its ready and valid applicability to the frame of human life. Now it was noted that the author sets the limits of his problem when he enters upon his labors. Those limits may be narrow; there may be an intense concentration upon only one or two of the large number of general human interests. On the other hand, the author may set for himself the task of attempting to reproduce, under specific circumstances, almost the whole of the spectacle of man within the environment in order to show the reactions of his character to the collective elements of his surroundings. Works of literature thus tend to range themselves around two poles. Is the critic, then, to be called upon to decide the general question of whether works of narrower or those of broader scope and limits are entitled to the award of the highest beauty literature is capable of imparting to its products?

The literary critic is unwilling to make an invidious comparison between works of these two types. The beauty of a work of literature must be judged within the limits its author voluntarily sets for it. Its results can be measured directly and legitimately only with those attained by other works which have set the same limits— which concentrate upon the same human interests. Thus there can be no genuine comparison between the two types. They do not oppose each other. Each has its distinctive values and merits; each is subject to distinctive disabilities.

The work of literature which, while allowing for all the ordinary influences of the environment on man, devotes its special attention to a problem directly involving only one or two of those interests, has one obvious advantage in its favor. Its singleness of purpose enables it to develop with great fulness and accuracy the problem it has set. It can display the minutest elements and most intricate manifestations of the phenomena included in that problem. It becomes a special study with limits of self-imposed narrowness—a monograph of literature. As a consequence, a work of this type provides for the reader whose desires it meets the most specific and valuable guidance for his plans of encountering successfully in life the human interest to which the work devotes itself. It anticipates almost every element that the total situation can present. Moreover, the data the work employs are to a considerable degree homologous; the field being small, these data can be almost exhaustively surveyed; and the resulting pattern will consequently provide the most searching and valid judgment, within the limits imposed, that literature is capable of supplying.

But the very character of the type necessarily implies certain limitations and disabilities. There is a concentration upon only one or two interests, and the circumstances attending these are set forth in great detail. Accordingly, it will nearly always be the case that the work will be beautiful to a restricted group of readers only. For the interests developed are not equally significant to all readers, and the explicit circumstances depicted can have extensive points of contact with only a limited number of them. The work thus tends to become one of aesthetic importance only to "specialists" among readers. Again, the fact that the interest concentrated upon is extensively developed means that its manifestations are set forth in a minute reproduction of the circumstances under which they occur in the author's own day. The work is thus a full and faithful reflection of the minutiae of the environment of its day. Now it is precisely such minutiae which are the most fleeting and ephemeral elements of any active society; therefore a work which sets them forth will pass "out of date" with relative rapidity. In a comparatively short time it will no longer be, in its entirety, an adequate guide for its reader. It may remain significant for historical reasons, but it no longer serves with complete adequacy the purpose for which it was intended.

The work of literature which attempts to portray a man acted upon by a conjunction of all (or nearly all) the influences of the general environment, has some obvious limitations. Its author, being unable to represent each of these human interests in detail, is forced to choose out of a great number of manifestations those that will be truly representative of each. His lack of experience with some of them may thus lead him to select data which do not fairly represent their normal workings. In such a case his complete picture will be erroneous; the conjunction of interests depicted will be distorted, overbalanced, or inharmonious. Again, it will follow, from the fact that each interest is necessarily given less detailed development, that the work will not establish extensive, deep, and intimate points of contact with the more personal activities of readers. It will not provide them with the specific materials which would guide their plans within any one interest.

The strength and merit of a work which attempts a comprehensive study of the whole situation of man and environment are, on the other hand, genuine and striking. If such a work sets up fewer points of contact with individual readers and is thus of less significance as a guide for their narrowly personal affairs, it nevertheless enters the circumference of the interests of the broadest group of serious readers. It deals with a composite situation which every reader must face in life. It comes to grips directly with what has previously been declared to be the basic and universal aspiration of man—to secure as much satisfaction for his collective instinctive desires as the environment can be impelled to grant. For it demonstrates how far the united instincts of mankind can be harmoniously associated and gratified within the environment. It deals with man and environment as a whole. It devotes itself, not to the tactics of individual interests, but to the grand strategy of life. It attempts to "grasp this sorry scheme of things entire." It sees life whole— for to see life whole is to view the collective manifestations of the environment in their normal and regular workings, so that one may lay plans for a life which shall touch the centers or norms of as many of these interests as can be enveloped. To formulate such plans is the supreme aim of literature. There can be no greater.

Moreover, a work which views life whole can be little affected by the withering hand of time. It is not based upon the fleeting minutiae of an age. Its core is, on the contrary, the basic and major instincts, impulses, and desires of mankind. These are subject to little change throughout the centuries. The works which deal with them cannot lose significance for men. They are passed on as valued heritages from generation to generation. They are reinterpreted in the light of the special circumstances of each age; they admit of reinterpretation since they stand apart from such special circumstances. Thus they are at home in human society as long as it shall endure.

The critic will acknowledge, then, that the supreme aim of literature, responsive to the universal desire of man, proclaims the superiority of the type of literature which views man and environment as a whole. Yet there can be no direct opposition between the two types. Both are valuable and necessary to the best interests of literature: the one proves itself a fitting supplement to the other. The supreme purpose of historical study must be the reconstruction of the major events and circumstances of the past. Yet the historian who attempts to reconstruct important and extensive historical situations does not flout the efforts of the writers of historical monographs. On the contrary, their works form his principal reliance. In like manner, the author of a work of literature which makes an intensive study of one interest does undoubtedly aid the author of a work of the broader type. His study reveals the normal character, the essential identity, of the single interest. To the other author, who must select as data only the central manifestations of such an interest, the results of the intensive study are of the utmost value.

Let it now be imagined that the literary critic has read a work of literature, has identified the interests which its pattern involves, has applied them to the frame of the environment, and has pronounced, on the basis of his knowledge of life and of literature, that they do *not* fit into that frame. His decision declares that the results implied by the literary pattern cannot endure the test of the third step of the literary judgment. Consequently, one or both of the first two steps must be erroneous. The author has failed to discipline his labors in them by the demands of the third step. Under such circumstances it is the critic's duty to retrace the author's labors in order to discover the source of the error.

It will be found that the errors of the author, like those of the scientist, can be traced to two general causes. The author is either unable or unwilling to remain obedient to the norms of probability manifested by the general environment. He has composed an erroneous pattern either because he *could not* or because he *would not* compose a valid one. These two sources of error involve both the author's experience with life and his ability to handle artistically his medium and subject matter. They may be present, moreover, in his first step of observation and selection of data, or in his second step of organization of the data into a completed literary pattern.

The author cannot compose a valid literary hypothesis if he lacks sufficient experience as a man with the interests which that pattern involves. His limited experience may have enabled him to see only the accidental, not the normal, workings of the environment through these interests. Again, if his experience cannot supply him with the data he requires for his pattern, he will be forced to compose them, wholly or in part, on the basis of the character he thinks they *should* possess. Data thus composed are almost inevitably spurious. The author will manufacture them out of materials belonging to interests with which he *is* familiar—in which case they will be an artificial reflection of those other interests. Or, he will attempt to procure his data directly from some other work of literature—in which case they will be limited and vitiated by the fact that they have been removed from the context or pattern for which they were specially selected and made to serve in another and perhaps very different one. In either of these cases, the result will be a distortion. Data so manufactured will not be a fair or an adequate representation of reality. The data which compose a literary pattern must be observed directly and intently, and they must be verbalized with fidelity. If this has not been done, they will not form genuine, integral, and independent elements within the pattern.

An invalid literary hypothesis will result, also, from an author's lack of ability and training in connection with his medium and its subject matter and technique. In the first place, the selection of data for a literary pattern requires more than an extensive experience with life. The prospective author must view his collective experience from the point of view of his vocation. He must be able to recognize the problems and situations of life which have literary or fictional significance. Without this ability he cannot be an author; without similar ability in his vocation, no man can be a successful worker. In the second place, the author must have the ability to verbalize the data which his experience supplies him. This task, which calls also for the power of accurate observation, is one of no little difficulty and importance. Considerable training is necessary if one is to see the data clearly, and find the *mots justes* which will report them unequivocally and with unblurred sincerity. Upon accuracy of verbal reproduction depends the reader's ability to associate the medium with life—to substitute it, even, for life. Moreover, a great portion of the value of the work will be contributed by the fact that the author has verbalized a section of the environment, perhaps, in a manner more accurate, extensive, and minute than that of any former author.

Finally, the author must be able to construct a fictional pattern which shall adequately represent his data. Such a pattern must meet the collective demands of the situation; it must do full justice to the clash of interests involved. It must evolve itself from the normal workings of the data in combination, and it must include all of them. The framework of the pattern must be the norms of probability manifested by the general environment. If the author is untrained or unskilled in composing patterns, he will have a tendency to be too conscious of, and too much in haste to arrive at, a goal which will furnish a solution of the problem which motivated his labors. Accordingly, he will be tempted to ignore, manipulate, or coerce certain of his data with the purpose of attaining that goal more directly. Again, his lack of ability may lead him to seek a pattern from another work of literature. He may attempt to force the borrowed pattern upon his data, they being unable naturally to receive it. In either case his completed pattern will be manifestly erroneous.

The second general source of erroneous literary patterns is the author's unwillingness to construct a valid one. His experience has been wide and varied, and his observation is keen and discriminating. But he is possessed by some personal or group interest which colors and biases or prejudices both his selection and observation of data and his grouping of them. Every author is faced at the outset with a problem to solve; but the prejudiced author has already decided, wholly or in part, the character the solution of the problem must present. He is under the sway of certain taboos. He pretends to choose representative data and to construct for them the pattern which their own probable workings clearly indicate. Yet he has (and not unconsciously) weighted the materials of his two steps so that the validity of those taboos will never be questioned nor impugned. And he may wish, for reasons known best to himself, actively to advocate the results reached by such weighted evidence. He may wish, that is, to produce propagandist literature. Obviously, in all such cases the finished pattern will be erroneous for the same reason that renders erroneous any scientific hypothesis: the creator has interposed ulterior motives of his own directly within the workings of his data and the framework of his pattern.

When the literary critic has traced and discovered in a work of literature the source of the error which has occasioned the failure of the third step, he has definitely passed judgment upon the work. He has criticized it adversely. It has pretended to be a valid literary judgment involving interests of serious import for men. The critic, on the basis of definitely cited evidence, points out that it contains errors which remove it from the class of literature which obeys the laws of general probability. Its results cannot be assimilated to the aims and desires of men with prospect of realization. The work is an untrustworthy guide for human conduct. The critic pronounces this judgment on the basis of his extensive knowledge of life and literature—not on the basis of his individual desires. Thus those judgments can be surveyed, retraced, and attacked by any succeeding investigator. They have been formulated in obedience to open and impersonal principles; they are not personal reactions animated by motives known fully only to himself. Finally, it is unquestionable that the critic is in duty bound to pronounce his judgment. The demands of the all important third step of any judgment contain the clearest and most imperative backward references to the first two steps.

It is fitting, perhaps, at this point to take a general view of the purpose and function of the literary critic. He has been shown to be the interpreter between literature and life, acting in behalf of serious readers. As such, his influence both upon literature and upon life is important.

The critic makes the work of literature more beautiful for the reader than it would otherwise be. The reader tends to interpret beauty in literature from the point of view of his own narrowly personal needs. The critic recognizes and allows for such interpretations. But he employs his special knowledge and training for the purpose of fitting the results of any work of probable fiction into the great frame of man and environment. By pointing out the connections of those results with the general interests of men, the critic makes the work more significant for readers whose interests are given attention. But he also thereby makes the work of significance to readers with other interests, for he demonstrates that these other interests may be genuinely, if indirectly, involved. In short, he increases the depth and the scope of the beautiful in literature—the quality of the gratification it affords and the quantity of those who share it.

The literary critic interprets life in the interests of literature's concern with life. Science attempts to view the environment strictly apart from human desires upon it. Literature regards the entire situation of man within the environment. It does not avoid the human; it *is* the science of the personal equation. Thus the literary critic determines, interprets, and pronounces the degree of validity of the individual and group aims of men. He determines the what *should be,* which always conforms more nearly to instinctive human desires than the what *is.* He subjects the aims he deals with to the strictest standard that the situation affords—the demands of probability. These aims are thus tested aims; they are the what should be expressed in terms of the what normally will be. As such they are of eminent value for men; they become motives for conduct. It is the critic, therefore, who gives specific formulation to the proud duties of literature: to point out the goals to which human effort may legitimately aspire; to provide the human motives which shall actuate the tool-forming labors of scientists, and thus to humanize knowledge; to guide and direct, in short, the course of human civilization.

It is fitting also, at this point, to sum up in article form the reasons which impart to the labors of the literary critic a thoroughly scientific character:

1. He possesses data — works of literature — upon which to expend his efforts.

2. His special training in life and literature has provided him with the ability to comprehend and to work with his data.

3. His judgments are composed in accordance with the three steps by which all scientific knowledge is attained—even though his special concern is with the third of these steps.

4. He is able to proceed impersonally—to separate his personal preferences and dislikes from his method and his professional activities.

5. He has experimental control of his materials—for he may reconstruct and thus test the first two (the author's) steps of the judgment.

6. His method is strictly empirical and inductive. His results are based solely upon materials empirically supplied.

7. He arrives at results which do not deny, ignore, or clash with the continuous flux and change of the earthly environment.  Those results do not pretend to stand apart from subsequent alterations, in literature and in life, of this universal sort.

8. His method is an open one; consequently, his errors may be detected and attacked by any succeeding critic.

An inquiry must now be made for the purpose of discovering what provision there is, in the system of the idealist, for the reader and the critic (the expert reader) of literature. It is clear that they must be provided for by the terms of that article of the system which reads: the beautiful work of literature is created *and recognized* by a special spiritual faculty of the mind. But this article of faith makes no distinction between author or creator, on the one hand, and reader and critic on the other. Both are classed together in the same category. And there can be little doubt which is the more important of the two. It has been seen that the main force and emphasis of idealism rests upon the conception of the genius and his creative inspiration. It is impossible for this genius to have a rival of any degree of importance.

The idealist, it can be seen, provides no distinct point of view for reader or critic. For the empiricist the reader plays an integral and important part in determining the character of any work of literature; the creator is obliged to consider his aims, needs, and desires. But it is impossible for the idealist's creator to have any concern about readers. He follows solely the dictates of the absolute as he receives them during his inspired moments. To consider the earthly, material, practical desires of readers would be to make spiritual inspiration impossible. It would mean a concern with the useful and practical—realms from which beauty in literature is sharply and completely divorced.

*The result is, then, that, for the idealist, creator and reader (and critic) are one, and the creator is that one.*

If the author will not make advances toward the reader, naturally the reader and the critic are obliged to go to the author. If the latter has no concern with anything exterior to the special and inviolate realm of literature, then reader and critic must enter that realm if they would establish any contact with the author and his work.

But it is important to realize what such an action involves. To go to the author, the reader and critic must leave the world of ordinary reality to enter an ivory tower wherein the absolute and its high priest, the author, are supreme. They must leave the realm of earthly experiences and human values expressed in their terms. To gain admission to the spiritual realm they must shake off all traces of their own desires on earth—all references to the world of the practical and useful—all hope of gaining experiences which can be absorbed into their fund of normal experience—all expectation that literature will be of significance for their future conduct. They cast off, in other words, every one of those values which, for the empiricist, determine the character, the significance, and the beauty of a work of literature. And a further distinction is thereby abolished. The critic differs from the ordinary reader precisely for the reason that he has a superior acquaintance with the "earthly" references of literature. If these references are strictly interdicted, there is then little or no explicable difference between the ordinary reader and the literary critic. The latter cannot, on the basis of special qualifications, lay claim to a right to speak with superior authority about a work of literature.[7]

After the critic is within the sanctum of the temple, what function can he perform in connection with the mysteries therein enacted? Can he judge the author and the work of literature which he encounters there? Obviously he can do so only in a very special sense. For he has

---

[7] I shall, consequently, employ only the term "critic" throughout my discussion of idealistic criticism. It should be remembered, however, that this critic has no means of distinguishing himself from any other reader, and that he has no authority beyond that of any other reader.

no standard of his own by which to measure the work; he has abandoned all such criteria upon entering the author's domain. Nor can he proclaim the *relative* merits of any literary product; to do so would involve references to values outside the realm of pure beauty. Thus he cannot judge the technique of the work with reference to literary technique in general, the validity of its contents relative to the materials employed, the human applicability of its results. The critic's only standard, consequently, is that of the author. The latter follows the gleam of the absolute. The critic must do so, too. This is to say that the critic must seek spiritual experience of the kind the author undergoes in creating his product. He must so dispose himself that the absolute will strike *his* special faculty with a spark of the inspiration which has animated the genius of the author. On the basis of such an experience the critic becomes qualified to determine whether the work of literature he has under consideration does or does not contain the spark of absolute beauty which spiritualizes it and guarantees the aesthetic purity of the result.

Thus the critic is faced with only one decision: Does the work contain the spirit of the absolute, or does it not? If he decides that the work *does* contain such a guaranty, then his task is supremely simple. In such a case the work is eternally and perfectly beautiful. It will exhibit that beauty, unmarred by change of time or circumstance (since it stands totally aloof from such practical, earthly influences), to all ages and ranks of men. If they fail to perceive its beauty, the fault is entirely theirs. By this failure they have pronounced themselves lacking in the spiritual capacity or attunement which would have given them a proper appreciative experience of the work. Had they possessed such a capacity, the spark inhabiting the work would have struck out an affinitive spark within their own special faculties. Spirit would have leaped to spirit; the vibrative resonances of the absolute imbedded in the work would have elicited sympathetic vibrations within their own souls.

It is the spiritual and inexplicable experience of this sort in the presence of the work, which determines the critic's own decision. If his response is positive, he declares the work one of perfect beauty. His task is in this case one of affirmation and assent; it can scarcely, under any interpretation of the word, be called a judgment. Moreover, the critic's decision is not at all necessary. The work is perfect because the absolute has consented to dwell in it. The proclamation of assent in its perfection made by the critic has no influence of any sort upon its beauty. The critic merely places a thoroughly unnecessary endorsement upon an already certified check.

The critic may, on the other hand, fail to receive in the presence of the work the stimulus which he takes to be the reaction of the spirit upon his special faculty— his soul, his emotions, his feelings, his imagination. He declares, consequently, that the spirit of beauty does *not* dwell in the work. This, assuredly, is a judgment upon the work. Its absolute nature must be noted. The critic's decision does not assert that the work is not beautiful merely to him or to readers like him; nor does it mean that the work is of little value or beauty relative to the interests it treats, the form it assumes, or the technique it employs. The critic's judgment means precisely that the spirit of beauty does not at all reside within the work—that no reader nor critic, consequently, can ever discover it there. As a result, the work is nothing. It cannot be considered as of any import whatever to art or to literature. It does not belong in the ivory tower, for the spirit does not own it; it must be cast into the outer darkness as an empty, purely material shell.

What validity or finality is to be attached to the idealistic critic's condemnation of a work of literature? It has been based entirely upon a personal experience indescribable in ordinary language; it can support itself by no evidence external to that experience. Yet the judgment declares unreservedly that there is no beauty in the work: that the author, in creating it, was not acting under inspiration from the absolute.

Is the critic here an adequate judge of the genius of the author? On the face of the question he seems not to be. The author asserts that he created his work under inspiration. Since this is a spiritual, unique, individual experience, he knows far better than the critic can whether he has genuinely received it. As evidence of it, moreover, he displays its product, the work of literature, in which he declares the spirit to be imbedded. Now the critic approaches this situation from the outside. *He* has not produced a creative effort. His only qualification for judging it is his ability, when in the presence of the work, to receive from it a reflection of the spark whose full force the inspired author alone has felt and placed there. Now if the critic does not experience this spiritual reaction, it may indeed be the case that there is no spark in the work. But it seems far more likely that the fault lies with the critic himself. The offended author will naturally declare that the critic has received no stimulus because he does not possess sufficiently refined or adequately attuned spiritual organization. Or, perhaps, the critic did not approach this one work *in the proper spirit*. Consequently, there was a short circuit because of the non-conducting nature of the critic's attitude. Upon the basis of the situation—the critic being forced to adopt (idealistically speaking) the author's point of view by entering the realm wherein the latter is supreme—it seems impossible to deny that, whenever any disagreement arises, the author is right and the critic is wrong. The final retort of the author can always be that *he* has produced the work of literature. Could the critic have done as much?

If the literary critic's pronouncement of the perfection of any work is useless and unnecessary; if his condemnation of the work can always be legitimately called in question and disproved by the author—then it may well be asked: why should there be a critic at all? *The answer unmistakably returned by the system of the idealist is that there is no need for the existence of critics, since there is no function for them to perform which can have the slightest influence on the situation.*

But if the critic humbly pleads with the idealist for a chance to live, he may then, perhaps, be granted his plea provided that he is made distinctly to recognize his status. He must come empty-handed into the creator's ivory tower. His criticism will thus become creator's criticism. Within the tower he must know his place. He can have no part in the mysteries performed by the hierophant, the creator. As critic, he cannot call down lightning from Olympus. But there may be conceded to him the humble office of wand-bearer to the priest.[8] In this capacity he can be admitted to the inner ceremonies. Perchance, when the fire of the absolute descends and hovers over the presiding genius, an errant flash of it may glance into the special faculty of the critic. Thus, through a spark of the inspiration whose full force entered the creator, he becomes able to speak with appre-

---

[8] *Phaedo:* "There are, say those who preside at the mysteries, many wand-bearers, but few inspired."

ciative comprehension of the resultant work of literature. His accents of admiration, hushed and full of awe, are what constitute literary criticism.

The danger in the situation is that the wand-bearer, familiar after a time with his humble duties, may allow himself to speak profanely of the miracles and contemptuously of their product. He may even venture to frame rules of his own for the ceremonies and thus attempt to measure himself with the creator—whereas it is obvious that there can be no comparison whatever between the theories of a disobedient attendant and the official ministrations of the presiding priest.

But perhaps the wand-bearer is only a critic in disguise. Perhaps he is a potential creator, a potential high priest. In such a case his status is indeed altered. For then the spark from the absolute (which is a *creative* force) will strike a special faculty fully attuned to creation. The result will be that the humble wand-bearer will become an author—a being infinitely higher than a critic. He will himself become, in turn, the hierophant presiding at his own mysteries. He will himself produce original works of literature. To alter the metaphor—the function of an experience with a work of literature is, for the potential creator, to inaugurate a creative energy which shall itself produce new and independent works. But such a product—even if it deals with the work which called it forth—can scarcely be called a criticism; for it is essentially, and it may be entirely, a new creation. It may indeed, since it was brought into being by experience with another work, be called "impressionistic criticism." But this is criticism indistinguishable from independent creation. The new work exists completely in its own right, and not as the reflection of another work. Its creator is an author, not a critic.

One asserted function of idealistic criticism thus stands revealed. Since it is a creator's criticism, it is of great importance to creators themselves—creators only passingly disguised as critics. But it is well to note that the "criticism" produced in this way is of no importance *as criticism*. One has yet to discover a function for pure criticism—a *raison d'être* for the entire critic who is unable or unwilling to become an independent creator.

Further consideration must thus be given to the activities of the pure critic or non-creator. His task has been stated, figuratively, to be that of receiving within his special faculty a spark of the creative inspiration which enabled the author to produce a work of literature in which the spirit thus received is embodied. The critic, that is, must gain experience of the spirit of the work through his emotions, his unconscious, his intuition, his soul—or whatever other name be given to the special faculty, conceived as an independent metaphysical entity, which he is supposed to possess. By means of such a faculty, unconnected and entirely opposed to the lower or "material" faculties (such as the understanding, the reason, intelligence, the conscious processes), the critic gains an "insight"—an ability to penetrate the outer material wrappings to come to the animating spirit beneath.

Now the situation which the idealistic critic faces presents two objects which may be spiritually penetrated. The author must have possessed the spirit within himself in order to produce the beautiful work of literature. And the beautiful work itself contains a spirit which has subdued and unified its material elements. If the critic would exercise his insight, he must, accordingly, bring his special faculty into contact either with the author or with the work.

All idealistic criticism must take, therefore, one of the two forms here indicated. It attempts to experience spiritually either the author or the work. The critic, that is, substitutes himself for, or *becomes,* the author or the work itself. Illustrative examples of this universal and necessary idealistic situation are readily afforded by the precepts of two modern systems of idealistic criticism: that of *Einfühlung* or empathy, in which the critic penetrates or becomes the work; and that promulgated by Benedetto Croce, in which the critic penetrates or becomes the author. It is instructive to examine more closely each of these idealistic systems.

The theory of Einfühlung (empathy), first definitely brought forward by Theodor Lipps, may be conveniently viewed through the intermediacy of Professor Langfeld, one of its present day adherents. Professor Langfeld thus describes its fundamental conceptions:

There are two main forms of motor attitude that may be assumed in regard to an object, one of which particularly concerns aesthetics, the other not. The one is an adjustment toward, the other an adjustment in the object. When one sees a tree swaying in the sunshine, one can either have the motor impulse to put out one's hand to stop the motion, which is in a sense a defensory attitude, or one may have the impulse to sway with the moving tree and thus to realize the true nature of its motion. It is this latter form of adjustment that has been described by Lotze, and it will probably be recognized from what has gone before that it is such a reaction that is found in aesthetic enjoyment. It will be recalled that two attitudes may be assumed toward the outstretched hand of a statue: either one of grasping the hand or of feeling the "outstretching" of the hand. It is through this latter attitude, which gives us the feeling of the tension and the weight of the arm, the angle at which it is raised, and the bend at the elbow and wrist, that we can get the true aesthetic effect. We can feel these qualities of form and motion only by carrying out the movements or experiencing somewhere in the organism a tendency to such muscular adjustments and movements. It is only by such a movement within ourselves that we can have the experience of aesthetic pleasantness or unpleasantness of things.[9]

There is little doubt that Professor Langfeld has described what empathy *wishes* to be. Doubtless it desires, as do many other idealistic systems, to base itself upon spirit and yet to make free use of empirical terms and data. Unfortunately, the empiricist must accuse Professor Langfeld of employing means to confuse the situation and to misrepresent the obvious character of *Einfühlung*. He has, in the first place, called empathy a "motor attitude," and has said that it predisposes to, or causes, muscular adjustments within the subject or observer. Now the former is precisely what it *cannot* be, and the latter is precisely what it *cannot* do. In the second place, he has so represented matters that there seem to be only two possibilities—an aesthetic reaction to an object in the manner of empathy, or a complete indifference or hostility to the object. He thus identifies empathy as *the* aesthetic reaction. This representation does not fairly portray the situation.

The empiricist must point out that Professor Langfeld's distinction between the two attitudes of "adjustment toward" and "adjustment in" an object is merely the familiar, arbitrary, idealistic dualism of the useful or practical versus the purely beautiful. An object is useful when it contains any reference to a value external to the object—to another object, or *to the behavior or conduct of the spectator*. An object is beautiful, on the contrary, when it exists solely for its own (i.e., the absolute's) sake.

---

9 *The Aesthetic Attitude*, 112 f.

With this familiar idealistic contention in mind, let Professor Langfeld's illustration of empathy be viewed again. If a man sees a tree swaying, he may indeed raise his hand to ward off possible injurious contact with it. Everyone will agree that his defensive attitude is not aesthetic. But this scarcely meets the issue. Let it be supposed that, under no apprehension of danger, he sees the swaying tree and admires it. It represents to him what a tree should be. Consequently, he associates his experience of it with the fund of experiences he possesses. It sets up a disposition to action, a motor attitude, which may influence his future activities. This, it has been seen, is the empiricist's attitude. Since it relates the beautiful directly to the "practical," it is totally opposed to the idealist's view. Here, then, is the crucial question with which the adherent of empathy must be confronted. This spectator receives from his experience with the tree an "adjustment toward" (and not "in") the object. This is an aesthetic attitude. *Is it empathy?* It cannot be. Professor Langfeld has ruled it out as non-aesthetic. He has thus denied the entire empirical position. What he has left is "adjustment in" the object. It must be inquired whether this expression is capable of bearing any empirical meaning.

When one gains "adjustment in" the object, writes Mr. Langfeld, one gains "feeling in the object." "One's own personality is merged and fused in that of some external thing."[10] Accordingly, empathy can contain no reference to a subject or spectator, because, after he has undergone this miraculous transition, he no longer exists. He has become the object. Subject and object have been made identical. One sees again why, in this system,

---

[10] P. 137.

"adjustment toward" an object cannot be an aesthetic attitude. But further: What is the meaning of the declaration that one becomes "merged and fused" with the object? There are two possibilities here, and two only. "One's own personality" is either one's *real* ("material," "earthly") or one's *spiritual* ego. To imagine that one's material ego becomes the object—as Lot's wife became a pillar of salt—is a manifest absurdity. The alternative which remains, sets the clear stamp of pure idealism upon the system. *Einfühlung* is the process by which a special faculty of the mind—one's entire spiritual ego—leaves its material shell and pierces to the spark of absolute beauty inherent in a beautiful object. If the object is not already beautiful, the process cannot occur, since spirit does not then call to spirit. This situation being clearly established, it can matter little what name is given to the special faculty (one's personality, ego, soul, unconscious, and so on), or what poetic metaphor (to become the object, to merge or fuse with it, to feel within it, to obtain adjustment within it, and so on) is used to describe in earthly language an inexplicable spiritual experience.[11]

Indeed, *Einfühlung* is as old as the naïve anthropomorphism or animism of the savage. It is a pleasing mythology. It is the pathetic fallacy. It is romantic "sympathy"—traceable in a direct line at least as far

---

[11] Lipps and Volkelt have expressly denied that *Einfühlung* is "association." Vernon Lee, in *Beauty and Ugliness* (1912), objecting to the "metaphysical mythology" of Lipps, has conceived the following alteration of the system: ". . . . it seemed to me that what I afterwards learned to think of under that convenient and misleading name of *Einfühlung* was not a purely mental process, and that at the base of aesthetic preference there lay not mere ideas of a motor kind, but actual muscular sensations and even objective bodily movements." There is general agreement that Lee's alteration would thoroughly destroy the entire groundwork of empathy. In his *Les Sentiments Esthétiques* (1910), Charles Lalo, in a thorough and masterly analysis, exposes the purely metaphysical and sentimental nature of *Einfühlung*.

back as Novalis. It is Shelley becoming the west wind; it is Geoffroy Saint-Hilaire reclining on the banks of the Nile in order to become a crocodile. The idea of empathy is present in the writings of numerous idealists who had never heard its name—as, for example, in the following passage from Guyau (who supposes himself to be a scientific sociologist):

In order to understand a sun's ray, one must vibrate with it; one must also, with a ray of the moon, quiver in the evening shadows; one must twinkle with the blue or the golden stars. To comprehend the night, we must feel the quivering of dark spaces, of vague and unknown immensities, passing through us. To perceive the springtime, one must have in one's heart a little of the lightness of the wings of butterflies—the fine powder of which we breathe in appreciable quantity in the spring air.[12]

The other—and more usual—method adopted by idealistic criticism is that of forcing the critic to become the author. This method is well illustrated by the aesthetic opinions of Benedetto Croce. The basic principles of Croce's system have already been identified as those in general use among "easy" idealists. Moreover, the system as a whole has been well advertised by his English and American disciples, E. F. Carritt and J. E. Spingarn; and it has been much discussed by other writers on aesthetics. A brief résumé will thus be sufficient here.

For Croce all art is expression; all expression results from intuition; and all intuition is spiritual. The work of literature is thus necessarily perfect, since it is guaranteed by the absolute itself.[13] If it were not perfect, expression could not have taken place: the work would not

---

[12] *L'art au point de vue sociologique* (ed. 2; Paris 1889), pp. 14 f. My translation.

[13] *Aesthetic*, 119: "Expressive activity, just because it is activity, is not caprice, but spiritual necessity; it cannot solve a definite aesthetic problem save in one way, which is the right way."

be in existence. It follows, likewise, that the work of literature is purely spiritual in character. It can have no conceivable connection with, nor dependence on, anything outside its own unique, individual essence. It contains no reference to physical reality,[14] to conceptual (i.e., "earthly") knowledge,[15] to utility, to morality. It does not even call up questions concerning its medium (since, when not clothed in language, it does not exist at all),[16] its technique (which would involve "conceptualistic" references), or its literary kind (since it is a unique individual without a species). Thus it remains pure spirit thoroughly sufficient in and for itself. The agent of its creation is an author who, as high priest, has brooded over the mysteries until the spiritual fervor seized him:

The individual A is seeking the expression of an impression which he feels or anticipates, but has not yet expressed. See him trying various words and phrases which may give the sought-for expression, that expression which must exist, but which he does not possess. He tries the combination $m$, but rejects it as unsuitable, inexpressive, incomplete, ugly: he tries the combination $n$, with a like result. He does not see at all, or does not see clearly.

---

[14] *The Essence of Aesthetic,* trans. Douglas Ainslie (London, 1921), p. 9: "And if it be asked why art cannot be a physical fact, we must reply, in the first place, that physical facts *do not possess reality,* and that art, to which so many devote their whole lives and which fills all with a divine joy, is *supremely real;* thus it cannot be a physical fact, which is something unreal." The italics are in the translation.

[15] *Ibid.,* 18 f. Conceptual knowledge involves consideration of the reality or unreality of an object. "But intuition means, precisely, indistinction of reality with unreality, the image with its value as mere image, the pure ideality of the image; and opposing the intuitive or sensible knowledge to the conceptual or intelligible, the aesthetic to the noetic, it aims at claiming the autonomy of this more simple and elementary form of knowledge, which has been compared to the dream (the dream and not the sleep) of the theoretic life, in respect to which philosophy would be the waking."

[16] *Ibid.,* 42–44: "In reality, we know nothing but expressed intuitions: a thought is not a thought for us, unless it be possible to formulate it in words; a musical image exists for us, only when it becomes concrete in sounds; a pictorial image, only when it is coloured." Again: "Poetry is born as those words, that rhythm, and that metre."

The expression still eludes him. After other vain attempts, during which he sometimes approaches, sometimes retreats from the mark at which he aims, all of a sudden (almost as though formed spontaneously of itself) he forms the sought-for expression, and *lux facta est.* He enjoys for an instant aesthetic pleasure or the pleasure of the beautiful. The ugly, with its correlative displeasure, was the aesthetic activity which had not succeeded in conquering the obstacle; the beautiful is the expressive activity which now displays itself triumphant.[17]

Surely there is nothing at all new nor unexpected in the system thus briefly outlined—except, indeed (a fact which moves the empiricist's admiration), the candor with which the full implications of "easy" idealism are accepted. The only matter of importance here, consequently, is the following: What is the function of the critic with reference to a piece of literature thus produced and thus characterized?

The answer is that the critic must become the author in the same sense in which the critic capable of *Einfühlung* must become the object. "The artist," writes Croce, "produces an image or a phantasm; and he who enjoys art turns his gaze upon the point which the artist has indicated, looks through the chink which he has opened, and reproduces that image in himself."[18] Or, this process may be viewed more intently. It will be remembered that the "individual A" is the author who has successfully achieved intuitive expression.

Now if another individual, whom we shall call B, is to judge that expression and decide whether it be beautiful or ugly, he *must of necessity place himself at A's point of view,* and go through the whole process again, with the help of the physical sign supplied to him by A. If A has seen clearly, then B (who has placed himself at A's point of view) will also see clearly and

---

[17] *Aesthetic,* 118.   [18] *Essence of Aesthetic,* 8.

will see this expression as beautiful. If A has not seen clearly, then B also will not see clearly, and will find the expression more or less ugly, *just as A did.*[19]

Certainly, in the latter part of this passage, the empiricist must defend Croce against himself. He will not allow him to deny his own words or to rupture the basic texture of his system by asserting at this advanced stage that the critic is to discover whether the work of literature is beautiful *or ugly*. Surely no work of literature can be ugly. Croce's whole case rests upon the spiritual necessity of successful expression—and all expression that exists *is* successful. A work of literature thus guaranteed by the absolute must be absolutely beautiful. Ugliness is merely non-existence.

One notes that the critic (B) must take A's "point of view"—that he must "look through the chink" A has opened. It is necessary to point out once more that these metaphors are capable of two diametrically opposed interpretations. There may be, to employ again Professor Langfeld's convenient terms, "adjustment *toward*" or "adjustment *in*" the author. The former would mean that the critic associates himself, on the basis of his own experience with life and literature, with the author's product. It is obvious that this is the genuine empirical attitude, but it is equally obvious that it is not an attitude which Croce's critic can be allowed to assume. For references to life and literature are wholly "conceptualistic"; they violate the spiritual integrity of art. They constitute a break with the author's point of view. Accordingly, only one possible interpretation remains. The critic must, through his special faculty, magically and spiritually merge and fuse himself with the spiritual personality—

---

[19] *Aesthetic*, 119. The italics are in the translation.

the essence of genius and inspiration—possessed by the author. But when this metaphysical transmutation has taken place, there certainly exists no longer an "individual B." He has no function to perform as an individual. He can make no references to anything on the basis of his individuality. He is entirely walled up within the limits of the personality of the author. When he looks through the chink A has opened, he does so as A, not as himself.

The conclusions which follow here are unmistakable, and Croce bravely accepts them. There is no reason whatever for the existence of a critic: "since it is clear that, since no critic can make an artist of one who is not an artist, so no critic can ever undo, overthrow, or even slightly injure an artist who is really an artist, owing to the metaphysical impossibility of such an act."[20] On the other hand, there are many reasons why critics should not exist. Sometimes they set themselves up as magistrates and pretend to pronounce concerning the beauty or ugliness of a work. Thus they make themselves ridiculous by pretending to decide something which has already been irrevocably decided. For: "The production itself of art is never anything but this distinguishing, because the artist arrives at purity of expression precisely by eliminating the ugly which threatens to invade it." Thus: "Criticism, conceived as a magistrate, kills the dead or blows air upon the face of the living, who is quite alive, in the belief that its breath is that of the God who brings life; that is, it performs a useless task, because this has previously been performed."[21]

---

20 *The Essence of Aesthetic,* 83.

21 *Ibid.,* 86 f. Here, in Croce's own words, is the disproof of his assertion, quoted previously, that the critic can ever encounter ugliness in a work of literature.

But the "critic" may become more obnoxious still. He may set himself up as an oracle and presume to give out rules and commands to govern the creation of literature. Such people are wild beasts and should be slaughtered ruthlessly. The motive of their activities is jealousy; for they are

. . . . artists who have failed and who aspire to a certain form of art, which they are unable to attain, either because their aspiration was contradictory, or because their power was not sufficient and failed them; and thus, preserving in their soul the bitterness of the unrealized ideal, they can speak of nothing else, lamenting everywhere its absence, and everywhere invoking its presence.

In short, there is only one kind of work in connection with literature which has some faint reason for existence:

. . . . the criticism of interpretation or comment, which makes itself small before works of art and limits itself to the duty of dusting, placing in a good light, furnishing information as to the period at which a picture was painted and what it represents, explaining linguistic forms, historical allusions, the presumptions of fact and idea in a poem; and in both cases, its duty performed, permits the art to act spontaneously within the soul of the onlooker and of the reader, who will then judge it as his intimate taste tells him to judge.

But such work, having no connection whatever with the spirit of art, can scarcely be termed criticism—particularly when "that sort of work already possesses its own name of interpretation, comment, or exegesis."[22]

One arrives thus at the conclusion that there is no such thing as literary criticism and no place for what is called a critic. It is true that experience with a work of literature may cause the properly endowed experiencer

---

[22] *The Essence of Aesthetic,* 88 f.

to become himself an independent author. But such a result, by its very terms, has no connection with "criticism." Accordingly, by command of the idealist, one must view criticism as mere Platonic non-being which can gain reality only when it thoroughly renounces itself —only when the critic, by a spiritual metamorphosis, becomes *the* author, or when he becomes an author on his own account.

The empiricist's admiration for Croce is sincere. For Croce has candidly accepted, with scarcely any false pretensions or evasions, the full implications of the idealist's system. He has not attempted to hide behind the empiricist. He has declared: "Art is spirit; that is all one knows or needs to know." But the thoroughgoing nature of his idealism has not only occasioned the animosity of "difficult" idealists; it has also vaguely alarmed those who proclaim themselves his disciples but who yet have the uneasy feeling that certain things—for example, their master's wholesale slaughter of critics—constitute a *reductio ad absurdum*. Mr. E. F. Carritt feels that the critic has received hard measure. But his attempts at stopping somewhat short of full length succeed only in subverting essential and fundamental elements of the system.[23] A. E. Powell (Mrs. E. R. Dodds) likewise suffers misgivings about the "communication theory."[24] Mr. Spingarn asserts that Croce's system is well illustrated by the following formulae enunciated by Carlyle after Goethe: "what the poet's aim really and truly was, how the task he had to do stood before his eye, and how far, with such materials as were afforded him, he has fulfilled it." This is an ancient ruse, but it will not succeed at this late stage.

---

[23] *The Theory of Beauty* (ed. 2; 1923), particularly pp. 195–200.

[24] *The Romantic Theory of Poetry. An Examination in the Light of Croce's Aesthetic* (London, 1926).

The idealist will not be permitted to hide behind a formula which *appears* to possess empirical respectability. In what capacity, it must be demanded immediately, does the critic ask these questions—as critic, or as the *Doppelgänger* of the author? The answer one confidently expects (and which exposes the absurdity of Mr. Spingarn's pretensions that a Crocean can give to such formulae the validity they seem to bear) is provided almost immediately thereafter by Mr. Spingarn:

> When Criticism first propounded as its real concern the oft-repeated question: "What has the poet tried to express and how has he expressed it?" Criticism prescribed for itself the only possible method. How can the critic answer this question without becoming (if only for a moment of supreme power) at one with the creator?[25]

The critic, after having become the author, asks himself *as author* what the author has tried to express!

---

[25] "The New Criticism," in *Creative Criticism* (1917).

# CHAPTER VIII

# THE ISSUE IN LITERARY CRITICISM

The present discussion has at length reached the stage at which the historic questions, asked and debated whenever the status and character of literary criticism have been under consideration, are capable of intelligible treatment. It has previously been declared that any attempt to confine a discussion of judgments in literature strictly within the limits of literary criticism proper must result in futility and superficiality—in arguments at cross-purposes, in an utter inability to determine issues decisive of the matters under debate.

It has now been demonstrated that a judgment in literature is inevitably an aesthetic judgment, and that it is, equally inevitably, a philosophic judgment. It has been shown that the field of philosophy has always been pervaded by the irreconcilable opposition between the idealist, who places his values within a region standing totally apart from the world as it presents itself to men, and the empiricist, whose values all grow from and partake of the manifestations of the earthly environment. From these two collective views, it was pointed out, arise the historic attitudes toward beauty, toward beauty in art, toward beauty in literature, and toward judgments concerning beauty in literature. It was proved, moreover, that these two views are, irrespective of the subject under discussion, totally at odds with each other—that the presence of the one involves the utter absence of the other; and that, consequently, any project of reconciling them is certain to result in failure.

All these matters are strictly relevant at the present juncture. They are the necessary preliminaries of any rational consideration of judgment in literature. By connecting idealistic and empirical judgments in literature with the fundamental principles of all idealism and all empiricism, they have set the terms by which the main problems in criticism may be intelligibly determined and described. By their complete and logical division of the question, they have supplied the issues into which those problems may be resolved. By demonstrating the irreconcilable opposition of the two systems, they have furnished the motives to necessitate a decision on the basis of the issues.

More particularly, the previous discussion has supplied two specific conclusions which are of primary importance for any treatment of literary values:

1. It has shown that the idealist's explanation of the character of literature is couched in terms of pure spirit; and that, accordingly, it denies, ignores, or declares of non-significant validity, all those empirical materials upon which the entire explanation of the empiricist is based.

2. It has demonstrated that the idealist, in declaring that creation and criticism (genius and taste) are one and that that one is creation, denies, in effect and intent, that there is such a thing as literary criticism—an occupation with a subject matter, a point of view, a validity, and an identity, of its own.

The significance of these two demonstrated conclusions is obvious. If any subject is to serve as a legitimate topic for debate, it must provide for the opposing contestants a certain number of basic points of agreement. The opponents must unite in accepting certain things as evidence; they must concur about the amount of evidence which shall be necessary to constitute proof of the matter at issue. There can be, that is, no disagreement within any department of knowledge without a previous agreement; on any other terms no decision within the limits of that department is possible. This being the case, the situation brought about by the opposing attitudes toward literary judgments becomes clear and apparent. *There exists no basis whatever for an argumentative contest between the idealist and the empiricist within the bounds of literature and literary criticism.* There is not one element of agreement therein. The methods of the one system entirely deny the processes of the other.

One is dealing here, then, not with a difference of degree, but with a complete difference of kind. The clashes of empiricist and idealist in literary criticism are the clashes of two systems, not merely of two divergent views of judgment in literature. It is one *Weltanschauung* opposed to the other. It is the struggle in a narrow field of opponents whose main armies have been contending all over the broad regions of human knowledge. The terms under which the contest is waged in literature and literary criticism are the following:

1. Is literature a spiritual or an ''earthly'' phenomenon?

2. Is there such a thing as literary criticism, or is there not?

These are the terms which clarify all the issues which arise. From these two questions those issues have sprung; to them they may all be reduced. The character of this general situation, a matter of paramount importance, must never be lost sight of in the ensuing discussion.

The attention may now be directed to the first of the major objections of the idealist to the empiricist's explanation of the character and function of literature and literary judgment. The empiricist pronounces the hegemony of works of literature which strive to attain poetic truth and to become of the greatest and most direct significance to human behavior by achieving the fullest and broadest association with the environment wherein that behavior is operative. In doing this, it will be contended, the empiricist effectively proclaims the inferiority of those types of literature which have set other aims for themselves. He proclaims, in effect, that all romance is an inferior form of literature. But more—his very definition of literature practically ignores an extremely important type of literary expression—namely, lyric poetry. On its own terms, the idealist will say, the empiricist's definitions and judgments of value are manifestly inadequate.

Here, then, is an issue, a definite and complete opposition. It will be the empiricist's duty to lay bare its elements and display the motives and necessities which animate the clash. Since it concerns the question of the character of literature, he will show that it can be reduced to the fundamental terms of the opposition in this department. Those, it has been declared, are the following: Is literature a spiritual or an earthly phenomenon?

The idealist considers the supreme purpose of literature to be that of furnishing an adequate vehicle for expression of the absolute. His entire attitude toward literature is determined, it has been seen, by this belief. The first necessity of the situation, accordingly, is a description of the character of literature which will declare its intimate association with the absolute. Such descriptions have frequently been made by idealists:

For all good poetry is the spontaneous overflow [spirit] of powerful feelings [special faculty].—Wordsworth.

The poet, described in ideal perfection, brings the whole soul [special faculty] of man into activity, with the subordination of its faculties to each other, according to their relative worth and dignity. He diffuses a tone and spirit of unity [spirit], that blends and (as it were) *fuses* each into each, by that synthetic and magical power to which we have exclusively appropriated the name of imagination [special faculty].—Coleridge.[1]

Poetry, in a general sense, may be defined to be the expression of the imagination [special faculty].—Shelley.[2]

All, that is literature, seeks to communicate power [spirit]; all, that is not literature, to communicate knowledge. Now, if it be asked what is meant by communicating power, I in my turn would ask by what name a man would designate the case in which I should be made to feel vividly, and with a vital consciousness [special faculty], emotions which ordinary life rarely or never supplies occasions for exciting, and which had previously lain unawakened, and hardly within the dawn of consciousness—as myriads of modes of feeling are at this moment in every human mind for want of a poet to organize them?—I say, when these inert and sleeping forms *are* organized—when these possibilities are actualized,—is this conscious and living possession of mine, *power*, or what is it?—De Quincey.[3]

Poetry, strictly and artistically so called . . . . is the utterance of a passion for truth, beauty, and power [ideal forms], embodying and illustrating its conceptions by imagination [special faculty] and fancy, and modulating its language on the principle of variety in uniformity.—Leigh Hunt.[4]

It [literature] places before the reader symbols which represent the absent facts, or the relations of these to other facts, and

---

[1] *Biographia Literaria,* Chap. XIV.

[2] *A Defense of Poetry.*

[3] *Letters to a Young Man,* III.

[4] "An Answer to the Question, What is Poetry," in *Imagination and Fancy.*

by the vivid presentation of the symbols of emotion [spirit] kindles the emotive sympathy [special faculty] of readers.— G. H. Lewes.[5]

The simplicity of these "definitions" is indeed admirable. But it is obvious that it is gained only by the fact that they see in literature no more than the idealist wishes to see there. They all declare that literature is spirit calling to spirit. And this, for the idealist, is a sufficient definition. For him literature cannot be characterized further. He cannot grant the validity of any "earthly" complications. He cannot recognize literary types; he cannot distinguish between poetry and prose literature. He cannot, in brief, include in his "definition" of literature a single one of those characteristics which, for the empiricist, are constituent parts of its nature. Thus, in the empiricist's view, he is not faced by the necessity of *defining* literature at all. His "definition" is the proclamation—sometimes open, sometimes concealed—of a mystery. Naturally, it is not to the idealist's advantage to dwell upon the pure other-worldliness of his description. It is better to allow the unwary reader to imagine that empirical constituents *are* accorded validity. In this way the inevitable dualism is less open to the vulgar gaze. And it will be only rarely that an inquisitive reader asks embarrassing questions—as does Ruskin, for example, in the following passage:

Here is a word [poetry] we have been using all our lives, and, I suppose, with a very distinct idea attached to it; and when I am now called upon to give a definition of this idea, I find myself at a pause. What is more singular, I do not at present recollect hearing the question often asked, though surely it is a very natural one; and I never recollect hearing it

---

5 *Principles of Success in Literature*, 37.

answered. In general, people shelter themselves under metaphors, and while we hear poetry described as an utterance of the soul, an effusion of Divinity, or voice of nature, or in other terms equally elevated and obscure, we never attain anything like a definite explanation of the character which actually distinguishes it from prose.[6]

After the idealist has described the character of literature in the only terms possible for him to employ, his next step lies clearly before him. In order to find the works which must embody the highest literary beauty, he has only to discover what type of literature (although he cannot officially recognize "types") provides the most fitting abode for the spirit.

In this search the idealist must obviously discard or pass by the great bulk of literary expression. The longer works are all greatly encumbered by "material" trammels. Their material husks (i.e., structural forms) give them too much of an earthly character. They have too much regard for the "practical." They establish far too many communications with human behavior; they repose too strongly upon the earthly environment and thus seem to grant its reality and validity. Of course, in these instances, the idealist may affirm with Croce that *even though* such works of literature concern the practical, the useful, the ethical, yet they concern them merely as appearance and not as reality.[7] Nevertheless, this is a

---

[6] *Modern Painters*, vol. 3, Chap. I. The best definition Ruskin can compose, however, is the following: "I come, after some embarrassment, to the conclusion that poetry is the suggestion, by the imagination, of noble grounds for the noble emotions." Now not only is this definition couched in the same terms as those metaphysical explanations he condemns, but it also fails to differentiate poetry from prose—the very consideration for which he attacks those others.

[7] *Essence of Aesthetic*, 14 and 16 f.: "An artistic image portrays an act morally praiseworthy or blameworthy; but this image, as image, is neither morally praiseworthy nor blameworthy." "But intuition means, precisely, indistinction of reality and unreality, the image with its value as mere

desperate measure, to be lightly entered into only by an *enfant terrible* of idealism.

However, such a measure of desperation is not necessary, since there exists a type of literature which meets the greater portion of the idealist's demands. This type is that of lyric poetry. A lyric is regularly brief; thus it cannot collect many "material" impediments. It can utter a "single pure tone"; consequently, it is, according to Plato, "not relatively but absolutely beautiful."[8] All it need do (and herein lies its supreme idealistic merit) is to supply the poetic symbols which may serve as the channel through which the other-worldly absolute may attain direct contact with the special faculty of man.

The conclusion is clear and unavoidable. It may be viewed to best advantage, perhaps, in the words of a contemporary idealist. "The sole purpose of poetry," writes Mr. John Drinkwater,[9] "is to produce the virile spiritual activity that we call aesthetic delight." When this activity has been set going, it is found that the earthly product (whose perfection is guaranteed by spiritual necessity) is thus characterized:

We recognize in the finished art, which is the result of these conditions, the best words in the best order—poetry; and to put this essential poetry into different classes is impossible. But since it is most commonly found by itself in the short poems which we

---

image, the pure ideality of the image. . . . . And indeed, whoever, when examining a work of art, should ask whether what the artist has expressed be metaphysically and historically true or false, asks a question that is without meaning and commits an error analogous to his who should bring the airy images of the fancy before the tribunal of morality: without meaning, because the discrimination of true and false always concerns an affirmation of reality, or a judgment, but it cannot fall under the head of an image or of a pure subject, which is not the subject of a judgment, since it is without qualification or predicate."

8 I refer here to a passage in the *Philebus* which I have quoted on p. 59, *supra*.

9 *The Lyric* (London, Martin Secker).

call lyric, we may say that the characteristic of the lyric is that it is the product of the pure poetic energy unassociated with other energies, and that lyric and poetry are synonymous terms.[10]

But more must necessarily follow. Poetry cannot be idealistically distinguished from prose literature except by the fact that the latter, according to the foregoing terms, is no fit habitation for spirit. Consequently, the lyric is synonymous with poetry, which is synonymous with literature. When the idealist turns his attention to literature, he seeks works which can contain the absolute. These works he will not classify by type, for he recognizes no types. Accordingly, what is empirically designated as lyric poetry is not a type to be judged by its own standards. On the contrary, it is supreme over the whole field of literature. And since it alone embodies the absolute, every other class is non-ideal—that is, of no value whatever. Lyric poetry, then, *is* literature. *When the idealist speaks of or describes literature, he is talking solely about what the empiricist calls lyric poetry.*

The intimate and necessary connection between idealism in literature (i.e., romanticism) and lyric poetry has often been remarked. Professor Gustave Lanson has written:

What is romanticism? To this difficult question one may reply, after observing the trait which is apparent in, and common to, romantic works: romanticism is a literature dominated by lyricism.

And further:

Romanticism (and this is its glory) is shot through with metaphysical elements. From this springs the character of its

---

[10] Coleridge, in enumerating the reasons for the greatness of Shakespeare's plays, mentions his ''interfusion of the lyrical—that which in its very essence is poetic.''

lyricism—in which, amid sentimental expansion and picturesque scenes, we are presented with meditations, or symbols of the universal or the unknown.[11]

For the idealist, the lyric is practically synonymous with the very essence—the single spiritual propulsion— of inspiration. From this point of view, indeed, *every* visitation of the absolute on earth strikes a lyric note. Thus F. Baldensperger writes:

> One may say without paradox that every genesis has to be *lyrical*—which is to say that at the moment in which the germ capable of development establishes itself in the mind, it takes on, before all else, the characteristics which are regularly attributed to the subjective inspiration in poetic creation.[12]

And since it is almost pure spirit, the lyric poem contains very little "matter." This very circumstance is its glory. This is what makes it beautiful in its own right and completely self-sufficient. What, indeed, except the dead dross of matter can be added to its spirit?[13] Consequently, what marks the inferiority of all other types of literature is precisely such material additions. For they

---

[11] Both excerpts (my translation) are from his *Histoire de la littérature française* (Paris, 1909), 930 f. Cf. Belis's words in the Introduction of his *La critique française à la fin de XIXe siècle:* "La sensibilité et l'imagination romantiques se sont donné libre carrière—il est à peine nécessaire de la rappeler—dans la poèsie lyrique. Il était naturel qu'une époque d'individualisme exprimât l'essence de ses inquiétudes et de ses rêves dans les poèmes où l'âme de l'auteur, se débarrassant de toute contrainte, nous fît voir à nu le prestige de ses enchantements, et le charme de ses mélancolies, et aussi, hélas, la profonde plaie secrète, source commune des uns comme des autres."

[12] *La littérature* (Paris, 1913), p. 21. My translation.

[13] Mr. Drinkwater asserts that, in addition to the pure "poetic energy," there are other energies, such as those of morality, and of "profound intellectual control of material." When a poet, he declares, possesses these other energies in addition to the poetic energy, "his work very rightly is allowed an added greatness." In view of the familiar necessities of the idealistic attitude, there is something delightfully and refreshingly naïve about Mr. Drinkwater's idea. One is irresistibly impelled toward parody: A and B are both genuine poets, but B's poetry has an "added greatness"—for he, being a dentist, has the added energy of the ability to extract teeth!

cause a clouding, a curtaining of the pure spirit. The disparity between the senseless hulk of matter and the intensity of the spiritual form becomes too apparent. The absence of this unequal association is the supreme greatness of the lyric. For, writes Walter Pater:

The ideal types of beauty are those in which this distinction is reduced to its minimum; so that lyrical poetry, precisely because in it we are least able to detach the matter from the form, without a deduction of something from that matter itself, is, at least artistically, the highest and most complete form of poetry. And the very perfection of such poetry often seems to depend in part, on a certain suppression or vagueness of mere subject so that the meaning reaches us through ways not distinctly traceable by the understanding.[14]

The empiricist may remark at this point that, from the idealist's point of view, it is no doubt an excellent thing to have dismissed from the literary pale all works except lyric poems of a hundred lines or less.[15] This, the empiricist will continue, is a good start. But the process should be carried to an even greater measure of perfection. After all, even in a short poem, numerous "material" elements, like meter and a certain measure of structural form, still persist. Surely, these things should be eliminated out of respect for the absolute. Literature should be further reduced to a few poetic symbols which will catch the overtones of the absolute. But further— even words have unfortunate basic "material" involvements. They are inevitably "imitations" of the environment; they have "conceptual" meanings. Assuredly, all literature should therefore either be abandoned in favor of some less basically "material" art; or it should consist of meaningless syllables—for these will not cause the

---

[14] "The School of Giorgione," in *The Renaissance.*
[15] I choose this number in deference to Poe's *Philosophy of Composition.*

listener to be distracted by practical associations, whereas the "suppression or vagueness of mere subject" is admirably achieved.[16]

It is clear that a number of romanticists have felt this further impulsion. Moreover, a few of them have followed it to a logical conclusion. The road thereto is plainly marked out. The clue is supplied, for example, by Wordsworth, who, in an enumeration of poetic kinds, writes: "3rdly, The Lyrical,—containing the Hymn, the Ode, the Elegy, the Song, and the Ballad; in all which, *for the production of their full effect, an accompaniment of music is indispensable.*"[17] The lyric must regularly, then, be set to music. And is it not possible to declare that *music* is an art which contains all spirit or form, accompanied by no "matter"? Walter Pater emphatically so pronounces. The logical deduction from this becomes apparent: "Music, then, and not poetry, as is so often supposed, is the true type or measure of perfected art." Consequently (he declares in italics): "*All art constantly aspires towards the condition of music.*" And thus literature (i.e., lyric poetry) attains final perfection when it renounces itself and becomes pure music—which is a separate fine art! The empiricist would inquire whether this conclusion,[18] thoroughly logical in view of the premises, does or does not constitute a pure *reductio ad absurdum.*[19]

---

[16] One hears of sculptors who place the works they possess in the inverted position in order that they may contemplate pure line alone, without being annoyed by the resemblance of the works to the human figure.

[17] Preface to the Poems of 1815. My italics, except for the word "full."

[18] Pater was by no means the first thus to conclude. Novalis, Tieck, and, in particular, Wackenroder, had held the same opinion. See the chapter "Wackenroder: Romanticism and Music" in Brandes' *Romantic School in Germany.*

[19] It seems safe to make the sweeping assertion that those idealists (Schelling, Schopenhauer, Pater, etc.) who have proclaimed the aesthetic supremacy of music over the other fine arts on the ground that it is unen-

It remains now to examine this entire subject from the point of view of empiricism.

A lyric poem, empirically considered, is a non-narrative[20] piece of literature which, by the employment of metaphors, symbols, "tone color," and metrical pattern, arouses in the man who recites it or hears it certain vague dispositions to conduct. By means of vagueness, mystery, and rhythm, it furnishes an outlet for the romanticist's *Hang zum unbegrenzten.* Now what is the nature of such a desire? It is one felt at times by everybody. It is the wish to give ultimate and supreme expression to instinctive human desires. The lyric wishes to utter a literary (that is, fictional) judgment which shall respect the utmost assertion of such desires: the gaining of a state in which all things become benevolently disposed toward all the desires of men and are guaranteed to remain eternally in that state.

Judged by the standards of human experience such a state is *impossible* of attainment. The work which pronounces or envisages its existence must necessarily be composed of impossible fiction. The lyric openly manifests this character. It removes itself as far as it can from contact with the actualities of human experience and

cumbered by "material" impediments, knew very little about music. What led them to such a proclamation was, undoubtedly, the fact that music aroused in them certain vague excitations. This is exactly the reaction of the musically ignorant. An intelligent comprehension of a piece of music involves a knowledge of its structure and of musical technique generally. Every piece of music has a "material" pattern. The most modern compositions have them no less than do the works of the old masters. But there are many who declare that the inferiority of modern "tone poems," etc., consists precisely in the fact that, instead of a pattern evolved from the basic nature of the musical medium, these pieces have forced upon them patterns from other arts: they are made to tell a story, to depict a scene, to imitate an object (e.g., a locomotive).

20 If ballads, which are essentially narrative, are declared to be lyrical, it is the idealist's and not the empiricist's cause which is thereby embarrassed. I am trying to adopt a view of the word which shall meet the idealist squarely on his own ground.

with the conditions under which literature can legitimately report and direct that experience. It seeks vagueness of subject matter in order to conceal its break with the basic texture of the environment. It employs language, but it ignores the characteristic ability of that medium, the portrayal of action. It makes a fictional pronouncement, yet it refuses to apply the standards by which fiction judges its own pronouncements. As a result, the lyric is fiction which is completely walled up within its own borders. For the only outlet of fiction upon workable human knowledge is poetic truth—and the fiction contained within the lyric is at the furthest possible remove from this.

The lyric poem, consequently, arouses in its reader a disposition toward conduct, an impetus to inaugurate action, for it suggests or holds before him a supreme and beautiful goal toward which all men would strive if they were able to gain a sufficient familiarity with its status in reference to them. But that impulse must remain frustrate. Every avenue leading toward the classification, the comprehension, the development of it has been deliberately cut off. The abscission is essential, for any further effort of the reader to associate the goal more definitely with his own fund of experience would immediately disclose the impossible fiction which has artistically created it. Thus the goal causes a vague excitation of the reader's fund of experience. But there can be no absorption into or association with this fund. The reaction must indefinitely maintain its original status of vague and frustrate excitation.

From this status flow the merits of lyric poetry. They are those associated with all impossible fiction. Lyric poetry grants in an admirable manner and with remarkable fulness the gratifications which that type of fiction is capable of imparting. To a far greater extent than can a novel or a drama belonging to the same fictional category, it can divorce itself from association with action or experience. As a result, it provides greater gratification for the reader who wishes, by reason of defeat or temporary weariness to flee from action and experience. It is much shorter than the novel or drama; accordingly, it can impart its narcotic stimulus in unified and concentrated form. Moreover, the lyric takes from poetry the additional significance which pitch, rhythm, metrical pattern, and oral delivery, afford. Furthermore, it unites itself easily with music in the form of song. Thus delivered and experienced, it gains the social significance which the steady beat adds to human activities: it adds meaning to a mechanical labor; it provides the bond of union which makes a temporary human group of the chorus which chants it. Again, the quality and manner of its appeal make it eminent in its class. It produces its greatest effect upon readers who possess experiences and reactions which society designates as "refined." For, unlike novels and dramas of this class, it does not gain the *incredulus odi* of intelligent readers for the reason that it rigorously avoids fictional form and references to daily experience. Finally, an enjoyment of it may even be a good augury for the future earnest conduct and vigorous action of the enjoyer. The refreshment it affords the possessor of a satisfactory labor makes him able to return to his vocation with renewed energy. The fact that an adolescent youth enjoys it may be a very bright forecast for that youth's future life. No doubt it is an excellent thing for an inexperienced young man to have "high (i.e., impossible or other-worldly) ideals." He will be obliged soon enough to temper these ideals to accord with his own and the world's potentialities. But the unbounded strength of their original impetus shows the force with which the youth responds to the challenge of life; and it is this force which, although duly tempered to actualities, will keep him continually dissatisfied with what he possesses—continually in search of the beautiful.[21]

In view of the many undeniable advantages lyric poetry owns, the empiricist concludes that it represents the highest achievement within impossible fiction. It is supreme in its own field. The type to which it belongs affords satisfactions at intervals to all human beings. It refreshes after toil, and it consoles for defeat. It is thus of considerable practical significance to human life. By their very nature such satisfactions must be intensely and narrowly personal. Accordingly, lyric poetry stands almost wholly outside the range of impersonal critical judgments. Its achievement can be measured only by its success in imparting narcotic or recreational solace. And it is the receiver alone who can know the full extent of the gratifications it affords. Moreover, since it is impossible fiction, lyric poetry makes its own laws, which are not those of the environment. And it should be judged within the limits it deliberately lays down for itself. A lyric poem should be directly compared only with others of its kind. It must not be held to standards to which it makes no pretence of conforming. That he pronounces its type to be not the highest class of fiction—not the kind which is of direct significance to human knowledge and serious activity—does not, to the empiricist, mean the degradation of the type. It should be judged, to repeat, by its

---

21 It is perhaps unnecessary to say that the words above do not mean that there is an absolute concealed within this youthful impetus, nor, certainly, that human society is or should be constructed to accord with the impetuosity and inexperience of youth. That these two last-named qualities do unfortunately exist together is well attested by the proverb: *Si jeunesse savait, si vieillesse pouvait.*

own limits. Within them it is genuine literature. The empiricist, unlike the idealist, is not obliged to say that a work or type is *either* perfect *or* of no literary or aesthetic import whatever. He deals with classification, with comparative and relative judgments.

To call lyric poetry supreme in its own department of impossible fiction is thus, for the empiricist, to accord it a genuine function and to give full recognition to the markedly superior quality of its potential achievement in the service of that function. *Such a pronouncement, however, can, under no conditions, prove acceptable to the idealist.* And the circumstance which compels his rejection of it pierces immediately to the heart of the irreconcilable opposition between the two views of literature. The idealist cannot grant the existence or validity of species, categories, or kinds in literature. What is empirically designated as lyric poetry constitutes for him the only adequate expression which *literature* can accord to the absolute. Consequently, works of this class constitute the supreme and perfect—which mean for him the only—representatives of the fine art, literature. And the absolute is, for him, by no means an impossible fiction. His philosophic and aesthetic system is based on the declaration that the absolute harbors the realities, the significant values, of human life. It follows that the quality of works of literature which express the absolute are guaranteed by the absolute. Thus the idealist is forced to proclaim not only that lyric poetry is the sum total of literature. He is further obliged to insist that it expresses, not fiction, but *the* truth. It is, in short, philosophy. As such, it is the bulwark of human values and the only guide for human behavior.

The empiricist would insist, consequently, that the point directly at issue in this controversy be correctly apprehended. He himself judges lyric poetry as a type of literature (i.e., fiction); the idealist pronounces it to be a direct revelation of spiritual (i.e., perfect, eternal) truth. The issue, then, is not the question of whether lyric poetry is superior or inferior *literary expression*. It is precisely the familiar and inevitable one of whether literature is spiritual or "earthly"—or, more explicitly, that of whether or not the absolute exists.

The desperate and implacable nature of this conflict thus immediately emerges. The idealist's entire faith is at stake. To doubt the divinity of lyric poetry is to blaspheme the absolute. The lyric provides the idealist with the intense and narrowly personal gratifications to which the circumstances of his life incline him to cling with the ardor of the devotee. Through them he feels that he is of the spiritually elect—that he alone can interpret the lyric mysteries. The poem itself becomes for him a litany—melodious, rhythmic, sonorous, hypnotic—to be chanted with fervent zeal as a proclamation of faith. Tell him, under these circumstances, that a lyric poem is fiction and not the highest rank thereof, and that, by failing to recognize this, he is hugging a delusion which will result disastrously for him—and he will turn on you with a zealot's rage. You are a heretic. Every man's hand should be against you, and the fires of the *auto da fé* should be kindled for you.

The empiricist is pained but not dismayed by this attitude. He is pained because he comprehends the idealist's need. The man who shows a need for retreat from the affairs of life must be allowed that retreat. He must be allowed, also, the full personal gratifications which his renunciation of those affairs affords him. While he is enjoying them his cry of *procul, O procul este, profani* should be respected. But the case is entirely altered when

the inhabitant of the retreat promulgates laws for the
world based on the conditions within his cave. Since the
actualities of the world cannot support these promulga-
tions, the result is the familiar and disastrous dualism.
Such a situation the empiricist must necessarily denounce.
To give credence to the idealist's dualism is to assert that
the best life is one conducted at a contemplative level. It
is to say that the only important values of the world are
attained by making plans in gratification of instinctive
human desires, and by carefully abstaining from putting
any of the plans to the only test known to man—that of
"workability" within the human environment. It is to
set up dispositions to action, but to frustrate them
through a refusal to dispel their vagueness by defining
them in terms of human experience. Consequently, such
a dualism strips human activity and conduct of all real
values. If genuine values are to be gained by contemplation alone, then the practical, week-day affairs of the
individual are necessarily to be carried on without ethical
reference.

Accordingly, the empiricist—to conclude this entire
question—sees no reason to alter his declaration that the
best type of literature is that which attains the firmest
connection with, and makes the fullest use of, the empirical materials to which it has access. In obedience to this
necessity, it must employ its subject matter, fiction, to
attain poetic truth, the sole type of fiction which endures
direct translation into human experience. Such literature, moreover, is perhaps most strikingly characterized
by the principal ability of its medium. *It has fictional
structure or fictional form.* It conducts the elements of
the environment depicted through action in time, in order
that it may demonstrate the advance within that fictional

environment of plans constructed by the aims of men on the basis of their experiences.

A second major objection which must of necessity be urged by the idealist against the empiricist's account of the character of literature is that it does not in any case explain *all* of a work of literature. He will magnanimously grant that it explains certain material manifestations of the work. But in every beautiful work, he will add, something—call it what you will—eludes empirical description. And it is precisely this elusive something which spells the difference between mere formal correctness and genuine beauty, between the skeleton and the living body, between talented ability and genius. Its revolt from analysis, its refusal to abide by rules, means that it must be experienced and cannot be described. To fail to grasp this situation when examining a beautiful work is to miss its essential significance and thus to disqualify oneself as a judge. It is to make impossible, too, a full estimate of the individual differences of merit among authors. For empirical standards, by their impersonality, cannot plumb the depths of individual achievement.

It must be evident that these contentions are forced upon the idealist by the necessities of his dualism. He forcibly and arbitrarily strips a work of literature of the significant values it possesses in its own right. These he ascribes to spirit. He calls what he asserts to remain after this abstraction the mere "material" qualities of the work. He contends, quite correctly, that these are incapable of explaining the work. *Then he declares that they compose the data on which the empiricist's account of literature is based.*

The empiricist must therefore retort immediately that what the idealist calls the "matter" or "material form" of a work of literature is an artificial and non-empirical conception. A work owns all its elements and its significant human values; deprive it of them and one has a residue which cannot be described in empirical terms. The interest thus shifts to another question. If the empiricist refuses to recognize these "idealistically material" elements, and if the idealist brings them in only to reject them—then what function do they perform? Obviously, they serve as pawns for the familiar strategy of idealism. They are the smoke screen which is to conceal the inevitable dilemma. They lead the unwary to believe that idealism can give full weight to empirical data and can include them harmoniously in its formulae. The further direct implication is that the idealist resorts to his absolute only when all the empirical elements have, in any particular case, had their opportunity to explain a work and have been found manifestly unequal to the task. It is apparent that the idealist can well afford his magnanimous gesture of including "material" elements in his account of the character of literature.

Once more, therefore, it must be pointed out that if empirical elements are to be utilized in explaining a work of literature, they must be genuinely empirical and they must be fully operative. The idealist can by no means accept them under such terms and his mutilation of them renders them thoroughly invalid. Thus his conception of literature is entirely spiritual and non-empirical. Accordingly, the empiricist declares that another question has been reduced to the fundamental terms of the general opposition: Is literature spiritual or "earthly"?

One frequently reads assertions that the work of some author does not attain the first rank of greatness because it lacks a *nescio quid,* a *je ne sais quoi.* In the empiricist's view such a proclamation constitutes a refusal to construct an adequate judgment on the basis of a sufficient analysis. The appeal is made, instead, to a mystery. Behind every drawn curtain of this kind lurks the probability that a human error has been operative. There is a suspicion that the creator of it is either unable or unwilling to construct an adequate evaluation. He is unable if he lacks training; he is unwilling if he is under the sway of some personal prejudice—the fact, perhaps, that he did not receive from the work he is considering the personal gratification which his temperament or his circumstances cause him to seek.

To explain a work of literature empirically is by no means to fail to do justice to the author's individuality and the full extent of his achievement. It *is* to assert that these qualities become evident only through the manner in which he handles the materials he has employed and conducts himself within the limits he has set for his labors. To say that a man's accomplishment in any vocation is to be judged by the manner in which he utilizes and controls the materials necessarily involved in that vocation, seems to the empiricist to be the utterance of the merest commonplace. This is the basis of all earthly judgments of individual merit. Moreover, the many materials of the vocation of authorship afford scope for the widest variation in achievement. The immense difference between a work produced by an inexperienced and inexpert writer and one created by an excellently trained and broadly experienced author who employs the same sort of data and sets for himself the same limits—is so startling as to appear well-nigh inexplicable. And the difference itself expresses precisely the difference in the individuality and personal achievement of the two men. For, writes the late W. C. Brownell: "In a work of art, it has been observed, personality is not what you put in but what you can't keep out.''[22]

A third objection by the idealist to the empirical conception of literature is that it leads one outside the work of literature itself to other and artistically extraneous interests. Instead of devoting his attention to a description of the individual poem or drama before him, the empiricist, it will be said, immediately begins to travel away from the work—to describe it in terms of other works, to consider the elements which it owns in common with them, to associate it with the desires of men, with morality, with human society generally.

The empiricist is not at a loss to comprehend the motives and necessities which animate such a contention. Suppose that one attempts to describe a work of literature solely in terms of the qualities possessed by *that* work. By this act one has ruled out at one stroke any consideration of medium or of technique, of aim in reference to human activity or of effect in reference to the reader's experience as a man. In short, one banishes all empirical data (for the ''material'' elements in the work are non-empirical). There remain only a *something* in the work and a state of excitation in the ''mind'' of the reader. Under these circumstances, one type of description alone is possible: the work is spirit calling to spirit. The entire question is thus urged by the first of the idealist's three principles—that literature is ''disinterested,'' complete in and for itself, and totally aloof from practical or earthly references. It is the old matter of the beautiful *versus* the useful.

Accordingly, the empiricist sees that acceptance of the idealist's contention means the acceptance of his system

---

[22] *Standards* (1917), p. 68.

*in toto.* It is to say that a beautiful work of literature has an other-worldly reality, and that the search for it is the only function of critical effort. When the idealist asks what a work of literature *is*, he is inquiring its status in reference to a transcendent reality. His question, asked in the same terms of any object, involves of necessity the same answer. What *is* a pencil, if one is not, in reply, to be allowed references to the facts that it is a utensil for writing, that it is composed of wood (from trees), of graphite (a chemical composition), and so on? Obviously, the empiricist will not play this absorbing but onesided game. His analysis of the idealist's motives in proposing it has revealed that it is simply a variation upon the inevitable issue. It is the idealist's objection to all the earthly references of a work of literature.

If spirit is not the sole constituent of art, then a work must be defined by its genus and differentiae. Its relation to the materials it employs must be clearly ascertained. This is the precise purpose of a scientific classification. The individual is defined on the basis of its groups. Only in this way can one separate the characteristics it possesses in common with its successively more specific and smaller groups from those which it owns more particularly as an individual work. As a result, its individuality and originality are fully assessed; the new is formulated and estimated on the basis of the old.

There arises in this connection the endlessly debated question of the relation of literature to morality. To the empiricist, morality is anything which has to do with the aims of human beings within the environment (chiefly, of course, with reference to other human beings), and with the actions instigated by those aims.[23] The term is thus as

23 Cf. Buermeyer, *The Aesthetic Experience*, 131: "More positively, we may say that morality consists in realizing the maximum of good for the

broad and inclusive as human activity itself. The judgment uttered by every work of literature is inevitably a moral judgment—an indirect one, it is true, in the cases of impossible and improbable fiction.

Now the purpose of poetic truth is to formulate the aims of men. Consequently, such fiction is a test of morality by the standard of probability. If the author can demonstrate, in strict obedience to the demands of probability, that the collective interests of mankind are best served in his day by acts which his society holds to be immoral—then those acts *ought not* be considered immoral any longer. The ethical principles of the group should be altered so far as they concern these acts. Accordingly, the express purpose of a work of probable fiction is to question existing ethical formulae. One may go farther. If the author regards certain ethical precepts as not subject to question, and thus refuses to subject them to his tests, he is introducing into his work a familiar type of human error. His result is propaganda literature, which cannot be harmoniously related to the frame of man and environment. On the other hand, it is evident that, after the author has depicted the successful termination of acts considered immoral, it may be discovered that he has arrived at such a conclusion only by suppressing certain of the normal accompaniments of the situation or by refusing to follow out the normal consequences which are observed to flow from such acts. In these cases he has been guilty of a breach of probability. He has thereby disqualified himself with respect to his serious fictional intentions.

---

individual and for society through the adequate expression of human powers. These powers are, originally, natural impulses. Impulses, however, conflict, and none of them knows until taught by experience and example, the form of expression which will most satisfy it.''

The empiricist believes that he adopts an attitude which satisfactorily relates literature and morality. The idealist cannot, of course, accept it. To have literature inevitably concerned with morality would mean to admit that its face is turned toward earthly and not toward spiritual purposes. It would make literature practical and useful.

But this is by no means all that is involved in the question. Why is the idealist—the romanticist, the *l'art pour l'art* adherent, the disciple of Croce—so savagely contemptuous of any relation between literature and morality? Apparently he feels that there is an absolute antithesis between the two. Certainly he cannot conjure up such desperate opposition from the empiricist's attitude. If he were opposing only general empirical concepts, there would be no special reason to single out the term *morality*. For in this general opposition the relation of literature and morality forms only a part of the more fundamental spiritual-practical issue. One concludes that when the idealist speaks of morality, he does not mean what the empiricist understands by that term. Instead, he means *idealistic* morality. Between literature idealistically envisaged and idealistic morality—between the ideally beautiful and the ideally good—the conflict is indeed savage and irreconcilable. But the empiricist would observe that the peculiar intensity of the struggle results from the fact that it is a civil strife among idealists.

The idealist interested in morality is a man who has empirically observed and reacted to some set of activities (chiefly those associated with relations between the sexes) in his environment. These observations then serve as a springboard to the absolute; on the basis of them he constructs an ideal morality. And this absolute, the Good, now has eternal and unalterable characteristics and demands. Certain earthly acts represent it; these are forever good and moral. Other earthly acts deny it; these remain eternally immoral. At one stroke all progressive, relative morality has been swept away. For the temporary, historical expression of it within one social group has been eternalized in spite of the fact that the social conditions and clashes of human interests which evolved it have inevitably gone on changing and developing thereafter.

When, under these circumstances, a work of literature attempts to swim with the current by examining and reinterpreting the ethical principles of a society—for this is what literature *does,* whether the fact is granted or denied by idealists—it faces the insuperable barrier of moral commands involving (it may be) an outgrown historical situation. Such commands, being formulated by an absolute, cannot be altered or called in question by men. The result, naturally, is a contest between absolutes. On the one side is the beautiful which commands literature to go boldly afield in sole search of expression of the beautiful. On the other side is morality, which lays claim to eternal possession of a large area of territory, and which warns off all trespassers who have not entered through the prescribed gateway.

Now the struggle of one perfect absolute to overthrow another perfect absolute must surely be a strange and Gargantuan affair.[24] But whenever the issue has been joined, the Beautiful has regularly proved to be the

---

[24] Perhaps one should rather envisage it as the struggle between the Beautiful and the Good for the possession of the True. It has been shown that the idealist considers literature (i.e., lyric poetry) to be a direct expression of eternal truth.

weaker sister—and naturally so, since art must necessarily be less fundamental and essential to human society than is the ethical compact. Thus the Beautiful (art, literature) has frequently been routed, subjugated, or decimated by the Good.

For Plato, the poet may indeed be the inspired prophet. Yet when the philosopher has observed that the literature of his day comes into conflict with morality, the poets are unceremoniously and rigorously excluded from the Republic. Another idealist, John Ruskin, writes:

> The great arts—forming thus one perfect scheme of human skill, of which it is not right to call one division more honourable, though it may be more subtle, than another—have had, and can have, but three principal directions of purpose:—first, that of enforcing the religion of men; secondly, that of perfecting their ethical state; thirdly, that of doing them material service.[25]

It is true that Ruskin subsequently declares, in the same essay, that art's "service in the actual uses of daily life" are "its main business of all." But this is a meaningless compliment. By categorically separating his third division from the first two, Ruskin has identified the practical with the non-moral. And if the two conflict within a work of literature, there exists no doubt that the "practical" would immediately be made to feel its humble status.

Tolstoy (to take only one more example) is a third idealist who depicts the inevitable outcome of a contest between the Beautiful and the Good. His tactics are to survey the field of literature from the point of view of the moral or religious absolute:[26]

---

25 *Lectures on Art* (New York, 1880), p. 37.

26 The present work has no intention of entering the field of religion. On the other hand, it must be pointed out that the fact that an idealist gives the name of religion or of God to his moral absolute should not remove his methods and his system from the realm of discussion—even though he may intend that result to follow.

And if a religious perception exists amongst us, then our art should be appraised on the basis of that religious perception; and, as has always and everywhere been the case, art transmitting feelings flowing from the religious perception of our time should be chosen from all the indifferent art, should be acknowledged, highly esteemed and encouraged; while art running counter to that perception should be condemned and despised, and all the remaining indifferent art should neither be distinguished nor encouraged.[27]

Now the results of a search for a sincere art prove that:

. . . . of all those novels, stories, dramas, comedies, pictures, sculptures, symphonies, operas, operettas, ballets, etc., which profess to be works of art—scarcely one in a hundred thousand proceeds from an emotion felt by its author, all the rest being but manufactured counterfeits of art, in which borrowing, imitating, effects, and interestingness replace the contagion of feeling.[28]

But even this wholesale slaughter will not suffice. After having determined the works which have a sincere purpose, one must further inquire which of them have a good moral purpose. The result of this question is a further wholesale elimination. In fact, in literature, very few works remain after these reductions. The survivors are such as the following:

. . . . "The Robbers," by Schiller; Victor Hugo's "Les Pauvre Gens" and "Les Misérables"; the novels and stories of Dickens,—"The Tale of Two Cities," "The Christmas Carol," "The Chimes," and others; "Uncle Tom's Cabin"; Dostoievsky's works—especially his "Memoirs from the House of Death"; and "Adam Bede," by George Eliot.[29]

The idealist in aesthetics will naturally reject and contemn this great slaughter of art in the name of

---

[27] *What is Art?*  Trans. Aylmer Maude (New York, 1899), p. 138.
[28] *Ibid.*, 124.
[29] P. 145.

morality.[30]   The character of the surviving literary remnant will, quite probably, also incite his rage.  But to what standard can he have recourse?  On what grounds will he base his refutation?  Tolstoy has preëmpted his only possible means.  He has already appealed to an absolute in another world and a "contagion of feeling" in author and reader.

The opposition up to this point has concerned the matter of the character of literature itself.  The attention may now be directed toward questions involving judgment in literature, or literary criticism.  Naturally, these two major issues are closely bound together.  The idealist's spiritual explanation of literature carries with it the further necessity of proclaiming the supremacy of the type wherein the spirit is supposed to reside in its greatest purity.  The empiricist's description of literature involves a classification of its materials—which is necessarily a judgment upon them.

It has been declared that the issue between empiricist and idealist over the question of judgment in literature is the following: Is there a form of human knowledge such as literary criticism or is there not?  This is to assert that the idealist's attitude banishes all possibility of independent and reputable judgments in literature.  The only possible literary criticism is, consequently, an empirical criticism.

It was demonstrated, furthermore, that the character of the issue results inevitably from the general principles of empiricism and idealism.  If literary criticism is to

---

30 He will call it "comstockery."  Cf. the words of Anthony Comstock: "Art is not above morals.  Morals stand first.  Law ranks next as the defender of public morals.  Art only comes in conflict with law when its tendency is obscene, lewd or indecent. . . . .  The closer art keeps to pure morality the higher is its grade."—Quoted in *Anthony Comstock*, by Heywood Broun and Margaret Leech (A. & C. Boni, 1927).

exist along with other kinds of trustworthy human knowledge, it must have a function to perform, a subject matter to deal with, a method to pursue. It must be capable of attaining tested and valid results. For all these basic necessities there is ample and careful provision within the empirical attitude. The idealist, on the contrary, cannot make such provision. By contending for the spiritual constituency of literature, he rules out all empirical considerations with regard to it. What the empiricist calls literary criticism thus becomes to the idealist merely the useful or practical associations of literature—and these, not being integrally related to the essence of literature, are entirely incapable of serving to define it or to become data for judgments within the field. But the idealist's own system cannot, it has been shown, provide a place, a point of view, ior a literary critic. Within it, an intending judge of literature must lose his identity as a person by merging spiritually with the author or the work; in this fusion he loses all references to himself as a person or the representative of a method. He can retain his individuality only by using the work he has experienced for the purpose of exercising his own creative abilities. In either of these cases, the existence of criticism is impossible.

The necessities of the idealist's position must never be lost sight of when judgments in literature are being discussed. They are the motives which give voice to the objections which he has always urged against the materials upon which criticism must be founded. There can be, he asserts, no valid empirical knowledge of a work of literature. In pursuance of this contention, he finds his arguments readily supplied to him. For the idealist in philosophy holds that *no* empirical knowledge can be knowledge of genuine (spiritual) reality. The measures he adopts to attempt to discredit the empiricist's data are now familiar. He assumes, on the basis of his own system, that human knowledge is either perfect or non-existent. Accordingly, when he surveys empirical knowledge, he points out that it is strictly relative and non-permanent. Men experience the greatest difficulty in determining it and concurring about it. Necessarily, it is based on the general flux of the environment. It is subject to all the varieties of human error. To the idealist the indicating of these admitted characteristics constitutes a sufficient repudiation of all empirical findings. Over the "ruins" of the system thus supposedly overthrown, he leads in his absolute, whose qualities are directly antithetical in nature. *It can be seen that the idealist in literature will adopt the same tactics toward empirical knowledge of literature (i.e., literary criticism) that the idealistic philosopher employs against empirical knowledge in general.*

As a consequence of this situation, one of the first contentions of the idealist against literary criticism[31] will be that it is manifestly impossible for the reason that no two people can ever concur in their judgments about a work. Anatole France gives voice to this objection:

Objective criticism does not exist any more than objective art, and all those who are pleased to think they put something else than themselves into their work are dupes of the most fallacious philosophy. The truth is we can never come out of ourselves. It is one of our greatest misfortunes. What would we not give to see, for one minute, the skies and earth with the facet-eye of a fly, or to understand nature with the rude and simple brain of an orang-outang? But this is quite forbidden us. We

---

31 Since empirical criticism has been shown to be the only form of literary judgment which can receive the name of *criticism*, the adjective "empirical" will no longer be prefixed.

are shut in our personality as in a perpetual prison. The best thing we can do, it seems to me, is to recognize this sorry condition with a good grace and to admit that we speak of ourselves every time we have not the strength to hold our tongue.[32]

The familiar situation here involved needs no long restatement. The idealist admits only two degrees of comparison. For him a man's judgments can be either thoroughly identical with those of another man, or they must be totally dissimilar. He can acknowledge no other degrees of similarity or difference, for these are necessarily based on empirical distinctions.

Undoubtedly every man possesses a total fund of experiences not precisely identical with those of any other man. For that fund includes numbers of narrow interests and reactions to specific environmental circumstances which give rise to certain socially narrow or personal aims. The fact that literature, which deals with all human experience, is able to gratify personal aims and desires is a fact of great importance for its status. For the number of its readers is thereby made unlimited; it becomes a satisfactory labor for an author and a vocation of concern to human life. Naturally, any method of judging works of literature must take this situation into account. The empiricist's attitude expressly does so. Impossible and improbable fiction, which direct themselves almost exclusively to the gratification of personal needs, have been declared to lie almost entirely outside the range of criticism—except, indeed, as that is involved in their classification. The justification of these types is the degree of success with which they accomplish their mission—and only the individual himself can fully pro-

---

[32] From his essay on Jules Lemaitre, quoted in D. Nichol Smith's translation of Brunetière's "Impressionist Criticism," in his *Brunetière's Essays in French Literature* (1898).

nounce concerning this matter. Moreover, even within the realm of probable fiction, individual judgment has a genuine, if restricted, range and validity.

But the greatly preponderating portion of any individual fund of experience is composed of elements which the man shares with his larger or smaller groups. It is these elements which are the basis of society—just as it is the function of society, through its customs and laws, to determine, extend, and standardize them. A work of literature which would represent human life with the greatest fidelity and most significant effect of which its subject matter is capable, must obey the demands of the group elements of that life. If it would represent social interests truly, it must submit itself to the highest standard it possesses—that of probability. A literary judgment upon such a work will properly be concerned with the purposes the work has erected—the degree of success it has attained in reflecting the total interests of life, and the disposal it has made of its materials to effect this end.

It is over probable fiction, judged by the aims it has set for itself, that literary criticism has authority. The critic who assesses the results of these aims does not rely on the personal gratifications which he receives from the work as a reader. His duty is to exclude them from his labors as completely as he possibly can; he succeeds or fails as a critic in so far as he does or does not make this exclusion. He must judge, on the authority of the special knowledge he possesses, solely those materials with which the aims of the work he is examining concern themselves.

That the judgments of contemporary critics upon a work of literature will often differ is undoubtedly true. The empiricist should be allowed to minimize this truth no more than the idealist should be allowed to exaggerate it. In such cases, the important matter is not that differences *do* occur. What is of importance is their nature and extent, and the background of agreement against which they are displayed. A difference whose specific nature is once comprehended is in a fair way of being solved. For the opposing critics have both arrived at conclusions by employing clearly defined materials within an open method. Their labors can be surveyed; the errors can be traced—whether they result from the interposition of personal prejudices or from the lack of sufficient training and experience. Moreover, such differences must, by their nature, be capable of a reasonable composition. For they are not based on personal gratifications—reactions which are not arguable.

A second general contention of the idealist, closely allied with the one just examined, will point out the temporary nature of any critical agreement. Let it be granted, it will be said, that critics of one age are in essential agreement about the merits of a work of literature. Nevertheless, the passing of a few decades, a few significant changes in social conditions, will to a great extent invalidate the judgment agreed on. Accordingly, the labors of criticism will have to be performed over again, and all the difficulties of coming to a new agreement will be again faced.

To the idealist, whose principles oblige him to maintain the unalterable perfection of any beautiful work to all readers and all ages, such a situation does indeed seem fatal. To the empiricist the fatality would rather be the fact that the work of literature did *not* become to a great extent out of date. If the function of the highest class of literature is to express the legitimate and potential aims of society, and if the progress of a society depends upon its successful endeavors to achieve its aims (its ideas of the beautiful)—then the great merit of a work of literature must be the circumstance that the aims it depicts have been largely achieved and replaced by others: that it has stood directly in the path of the progress which soon encompassed and absorbed it. Obviously there is involved here the entire question of the attitude of literary criticism toward works of the past—the question of historical criticism, scholarship, or research.

The literary critic who is faced with a work of the past must endeavor to reinterpret it in terms of the present. It is only within the present that the past (and the future) can exist, for it is only in the present that it can attain translation into human activity. This circumstance governs the critic in two respects. In the first place, it means that, no matter how intense his interest in a certain period of the past may be, it is this past *as seen in the light of the present,* which is what his researches will necessarily determine. Consequently, he must possess and retain those qualities which make him a critic in his own day—his broad knowledge of contemporary life and his familiarity with literature written up to and within his own times. To translate his labors with the past into results of significance to the present is the final end of his labors. In the second place, it will cause him to select, as the subject of his critical efforts, works of the past which will endure transference into the life of the present because they are still of significance to the present. It was previously noted[33] that a certain class of works of probable fiction can well endure such a translation. Works of this class deal with the broad and practically unvarying interests of men in such a way that their patterns are not pronouncedly stamped with the special circumstances of the time. These are the works

---

[33] See *supra,* p. 219.

which are capable of "remaining alive" indefinitely;
their beauty, once established, gives promise of enduring
with no serious modification.  Other works, however, tend
in varying degrees to restrict themselves to one or two
specific interests, which are, in their nature or their
manifestation, closely connected with the special circumstances of their day, and which are developed by their
authors with a fulness which involves the complete par-
ticipation of such historical conditions.  Naturally, these
works most resist reinterpretation.  Their significance
largely confines itself to the circumstances they record.
If they are examined by the critic, it will be for reasons
entirely or mainly historical.  Their only connection with
the present, that is, may be the fact that they played an
integral part in the historical sequence of works of literature, or that they exerted a marked influence upon an age
which still retains certain significant connections with the
present one.

In face of this situation, the critic enters upon his
labors.  *He must attempt to perform for the work in
reference to its own past age the same service that he
accomplishes for a work of the present.*  He must ascertain its historical significance—its relation to the life and
literature of its own day.  There devolves upon him, consequently, the necessity of possessing the broadest familiarity with the life and literature of the period in which
the work appeared.  On the basis of this knowledge, he
will attempt to fix the status of the work with reference
to the desires of its readers—to find out whether it
belonged to the impossible, the improbable, or the probable fiction of its day.  Such a question naturally involves
the training of the author, the materials which he has
employed, his avowed purposes with regard to them, his
relation to the interests he depicts, the influence of other

authors and of other times upon him. If his work was intended as probable fiction, it must be ascertained whether, on the basis of the materials and technique available to him in his day, he has properly represented the interests of his time. The significance, both to the life and the literature of his time, of the judgments expressed or implied in his work, must also be computed. In these questions will be involved considerations respecting the author's ability to control his medium, and the possible personal or class prejudices which have influenced his pattern. Moreover, in serving as the present day interpreter between the work and the interests of its time, the critic will make use of the historically audible reactions to the work by readers and critics of that time.

When the critic has thus set the work in its proper historical perspective, he may assess its importance to the literature and life of the present day. Its relation with the present may be—to repeat—direct or mainly historical. If, after the special circumstances which accompanied its production and determined its character have been subtracted, the work still treats significantly interests of importance to life today, then the work is as directly relatable to the present as is any work produced in the present. The reader of today should be able to attain from it a number of the gratifications he seeks; the work should, consequently, be "revived." On the other hand, the work may belong so completely to its time that there is little or no residue after the special circumstances have been extracted. In such a case, it may attain importance by being fitted into its proper historical frame—for it may have influenced more extensive phenomena, whether of literature or of life, which themselves show a clear relation with the interests of the present.

Now it is clear that the idealist can give no genuine recognition to the methods just outlined. His beautiful work of literature, being spiritual, stands totally aloof from all circumstances of time, place, and public favor. Moreover, since it *is* spirit, it is perfect and unalterable. It disregards all attempts at historical alignment. If its perfection happened not to have been conceded at various periods, this was merely the result of the deficient spiritual insight of the readers (or critics) of those periods. Such readers, consequently, deserve only ridicule, no matter what may have been the time, circumstances, and specific grounds or intent of their adverse or qualified judgments upon it. It is true, indeed, that certain idealists may, in the way usual with them, magnanimously concede that a work of the past has certain attachments to the nebulous *Zeitgeist* they ascribe to its period—that certain of its "material" qualities belong to time and place. They may thus appear to grant some approval to historical criticism. But when the usual questions are asked concerning the extent of such criticism and its validity in explanation of the work, it is immediately discovered that this apparent concession is—as it must be— entirely meaningless. Such an idealist, when questioned, may, like Croce, seek refuge in metaphor to declare that this criticism has the "duty of dusting, placing in a good light"[34] the works of the past. But further inquiry discloses only his refusal to assign to such phrases any non-spiritual meaning whatever.

It should therefore be noted that *the empirical attitude alone grants validity, purpose, and justification to methods of historical research in literature. Scholarly research is the methodizing of the empirical attitude in*

---

[34] See *supra*, p. 244.

*literary criticism.* A failure to recognize this indubitable and basic fact and a consequent disposition to accord a place to the idealist, can only result in the nullification of literary scholarship. An example of this situation may be offered. At the beginning of his *Problems and Methods of Literary History,* Professor André Morize writes as follows:[35]

Literary history thinks that it can help literary criticism; can clear a path for it; can lighten its task of understanding, judging, and classifying literary works and the great movements of human thought. It offers its services as a devoted auxiliary, modest and self-effacing. It has no imperialistic designs: it covers enough territory already to have no need to encroach on that of a neighbor. It prepares the material for the critic but puts no restrictions on the way he should use it. If he has faith in impressionistic criticism, if he believes that the literary critic should surrender himself to the emotion produced by the book he is studying and then should express this emotion with precision and delicacy, he is free to do so. Literary history asks him only to base his personal reaction on facts that have been historically verified, to define his position clearly, and, when communicating a purely personal reaction to the public, not to believe or to make others believe that he is giving any added information about the work or its writer. "Impressionism," says Lanson, "is the only method that puts us in touch with beauty. Let us, then, use it for this purpose, frankly, but let us limit it to this rigorously. To distinguish *knowing* from *feeling,* what we *may know* from what we *should feel;* to avoid *feeling* when we can *know,* and thinking that we *know* when we *feel:* to this, it seems to me, the scientific method of literary history can be reduced."

One is faced, in this excerpt, by a series of desperate contradictions. If impressionism (idealism) is the only method of ascertaining beauty in literature, then historical research is useless and foolish. To tell the idealist

---

[35] Ginn and Company (1922), p. 1 f.

that his system is sound, but that he will please make it strictly subservient to the empirically determined facts which the system must deny or ignore, is to demand that he surrender his idealism. To declare to him that he must remember that "feeling" (i.e., communing with the absolute) must be clearly recognized as something distinct from and inferior to "knowing" (i.e., gaining empirical knowledge) inasmuch as it is mere personal opinion (and not absolute aesthetic knowledge), is to demolish his entire attitude and to arouse his undying animosity. On the other hand, if literary history is to arrive at valid results, it must obviously have a firm and solid foundation. This it will by no means possess if its findings can be at any time contradicted or disregarded by the supreme authority of spirit. In short, the case cannot possibly rest in this state of chaotic contradiction. Literary history *is* literary criticism. As such, it must undertake the complete control of its field by banishing all opinions whatsoever which are not based on empirical evidence.[36] If it cannot assume full charge of its department of activity, it should confess its inadequacy and abandon its efforts altogether in view of the inevitable unsoundness of whatever results it may attain.

Another major accusation of the idealist against all judgment in literature is that it must necessarily consist of dogmatic and arbitrary rules which are to be indiscriminately applied to all works of literature. He wishes it to appear that criticism is a Procrustean bed which forces all works of literature to measure up to certain

---

[36] This necessity is realized by M. Gustave Rudler, who writes, in the *avant-propos* to his *Les techniques de la critique et de l'histoire littéraire en littérature française moderne* (1923), the following: "L'impressionisme ne s'enseigne pas; il échappe par définition à toute méthode, sinon à toute discipline. Je le laisserai donc en dehors de cette étude sans essayer même de définir sa fonction et de mesurer sa place dans la critique."

violently imposed dimensions applied by rigid measuring-
stick methods.  It is thus concerned, he declares further,
only with the question of whether its rules are obeyed
or violated.  The significant merit, the genuine beauties,
of the work must escape the critic's comprehension.
He restricts himself, accordingly, to a querulous fault-
finding.  The idealist, in illustration of his contention,
will thereupon point out a number of these rules—the
three unities, the Horatian precepts of five acts, of no
more than three speakers, of the avoidance of violent
action on the stage—and will quote a number of remarks
(those of whose absurdity he is most convinced) made
by critics like Rymer, Boileau, or Jeffrey.  He will then
assert that every genuine work of art has ignored or
repudiated these rules, and that such denials constitute
the victory of freedom over dogma.  The impression he
wishes to convey is that he is fighting a noble fight for
the integrity and freedom of literature against the purely
negative, destructive forces of pedantry and bigotry.

To the empiricist, the motive behind these manoeuvres
is openly apparent.  They constitute the idealist's efforts
to carry the war into enemy territory.  They are his
attempts to conceal or justify the fact that he attempts
to slaughter all criticism by contending that criticism is
itself an attempt to slaughter all literature.  The basic
issue is thus the well-known and unvarying one: the idealist's declaration that no criticism is possible.  His griev-
ance here is that criticism has a firmly founded and valid
point of view, and a necessary function.  Moreover, it
goes about fulfilling that function; it *does* judge.  These
are the circumstances that infuriate the idealist and
animate his attack.  As for the particulars of his charge
—they are exceedingly familiar, and they are, by his
system, inevitable.

Naturally, if one must hold that criticism can have no organic status with reference to literature, one must declare that all critical formulae are arbitrarily composed and are universally inapplicable. Naturally, too, if one is an adherent of a system whose values and essences are static and immutable, one can give no recognition to the fact that literature changes and develops along with the society in which it appears, and is observed and judged in conformity with, and in reference to, those changes and development. Again, if one is forced to assert that every new work of literature is unique and that it can belong to no species, then every new work of literature has *no* similarities with any preceding work. Finally, numbers of the unwary may indeed be deceived by a strategy which uproots from their time, their context, their system, their general background, a number of specific empirical observations; which considers them as static and abstract; which declares that they compose the entire empirical attitude; and which demonstrates that they have been violated by works (of whatever period or category) whose beauty is unquestioned.

When the idealist picks out various critical formulae and pronounces their unsoundness with reference to the practices of authors, he has made an appeal to historical criticism—to the history of literary criticism. The empiricist welcomes such an appeal, for his attitude rests upon and conforms to practice, past and present. Recourse to history is recourse to the empirical attitude. Accordingly, in making such appeals, one must accept in full the conditions under which it becomes possible to utilize data empirically acquired. Clearly, the idealist cannot accept these conditions. His general principles forbid all possibility of this. Thus his attempt to discredit the empiricist by appealing to the latter's own

principles becomes thoroughly illegitimate and any discussion of the question he attempts to raise is futile.
There are no bases, no terms, no common agreements, by
which a discussion can be carried on.

Now it is by no means to be declared that those critics
who have endeavored to describe and evaluate literature
empirically have always been sound and accurate in their
labors. A critic is as subject to errors as is an inquirer
within any department of human knowledge. Not the
least of the errors of historical empiricism in all fields
has been the proneness of its practitioners to erect, on
the basis of their findings, a closed system admitting
no progressive changes. But to become an absolutist
(i.e., an idealist) is in any case to depart from empirical
standards. It is to commit error—error which vitiates
the results of empirical investigation, but which does not
refute empirical methods themselves any more than any
scientist's error proves the falsity of scientific method.
When the critic is at fault, the important thing is to determine the nature and extent of his error. This can be
done, but only by the thorough employment of empirical
tests—through a survey of the historical circumstances
and a retracing of the steps of the critic's judgments
in obedience to the collective demands of such an
investigation.

More specifically, it is necessary, before pronouncing
the falsity of a critical formula, to possess information
on the following questions:

1. What is the status of the formula with reference
to the critic's entire attitude? What is the precise scope
and extent of its application? Over what group or sub-
group within literature does it profess to have validity?
The answer to such questions involves a knowledge of
the critic's general principles and a classification of the

formula with respect to them. Its status thus determined, it must be considered, applied, and discussed
*solely within the limits wherein it is supposed to possess
validity.*

2. What, within its limits, is the relation of the
formula to *literature?* Is it the expression of a phenomenon which clearly flows from and is inseparable from
the empirical materials with which literature is concerned? In other words—since language, fiction, the circumstances faced by subclasses like poetry and drama,
all imply or necessitate certain modes of employment or
manner of operation, it must be ascertained whether the
formula under observation, is the expression of one of
such basic principles. If it is, then it may be declared
fundamental, permanent, and necessary, with respect to
the empirical position. It is of interest to note, in these
circumstances, whether the formula has been followed by
previous critics—in practice, if not with conscious and
formulated intent.

On the other hand, the formula may rest almost
entirely on observation of the works of literature of the
critic's own day. In this case there must be an examination of the works the critic had in mind, in order to discover whether the formula accurately reflects the practice
of those works. The validity of formulae thus evolved
obviously rests upon the literary taste, the concerted
agreement, of the authors, readers, and critics of the age
in question.

3. What, within its limits, is the relation of the
formula to *life*—that is, to readers within an environment? Does it embrace demands which are essential to
the basic requirements of readers of the type and intentions specified? Does it concern those fundamental
human desires to whose gratification literature must con-

tinuously direct its activities in order to possess significance for life—in order to possess readers at all? If so, the formula may be pronounced basic, integral, and permanent with respect to the empirical position. The formula may, on the contrary, be (in part or entirely) the codification of demands of readers resulting from special and temporary historical circumstances within their social groups. In this case, it is important to ascertain whether the formula clearly reflects the demands arising from such interests.

In short, there must be the clearest differentiation between the formula's status as integrally expressive of empirical method or as expository of a set of historical circumstances. A formula under the former classification must be generally applicable; under the latter, it must be considered strictly in relation to the historical circumstances attendant upon it. If, in either category, the formula is discovered to be inapplicable, then it is of interest to find the source of the critic's error. It will be found to result from two circumstances: the critic's lack of ability and training, or the fact that he harbors taboos whose validity he will not submit to question. The testing of a critical formula of the past can be seen to require, on the part of the critic of the present day, the fullest and most discriminating employment of the special knowledge which gives him his position as critic.

It is unnecessary, surely, to devote serious attention at this point to the idealist's accusation that literary criticism is only "fault-finding." If a work of literature is a perfect and a spiritual entity, then of course, all comment on it is profane. Everything short of the most enthusiastic approbation must be a carping over minute and irrelevant particulars which have no organic connection with the work since they concern only its "material" phenomena. On the other hand, if one idealistically "becomes" the author or the work, then, indeed, it has been seen, there can be little opportunity for "fault-finding" for the reason that there is no basis for criticism at all. The idealist's accusation, accordingly, means that the critical attitude is not the idealist's attitude. Thus his aversion to "fault-finding" is imbedded in his basic position. The idea of "sympathy" by "feeling in" (*sich einfühlen*) or "seeing in" (insight) an object, and that of *tout comprendre, c'est tout pardonner,* are the commonest manifestations of general romantic idealism.

Another (and, it would appear, the final) contention of a general sort urged by idealists is that literary criticism denies to the author the all important status which is properly his. Literature, it will be said, owes its existence to authors, not to critics. Were it not for the former, the latter could not exist. Between the two there can be no comparison; the author is immeasurably superior. To turn his production over to the mercies of a critic is therefore an unendurable procedure. It is to allow an inferior (almost certainly one who has tried but failed to become an author—for who would remain a critic when he can achieve creative expression?) to judge the work of his superior. The only proper judge of an author's work is a man who has himself produced works of literature.

Once again, the source of this position in the imprescriptible articles of idealism is readily apparent. When the idealist severs literature altogether from life, he has abolished the foundation on which criticism must repose. When he declares that the author is the utterer of divine and perfect knowledge attained through inspiration, he has cut off all possibility of submitting the author's work to the judgment of an earth-dweller. But if these two beliefs are not given blanket approval, then the idealist's entire position on the question under discussion becomes impossible and absurd.

The empiricist agrees that there can be no direct— and, he would add, no invidious—comparison between author and critic. The author is the expert in *fiction*, the what should be. Literature is indeed based on life as firmly as is any other vocation of men. But it is characterized and differentiated by its subject matter—fiction. It is within the bounds of this subject matter that the activities of the author are exerted. Its outlook, attitudes, points of view, become his. He directs his entire life to the discovery and observation of data which will lend themselves to fictional recombination. His products are not truthful but fictitious. The function of the critic, on the contrary, is to evaluate the fictional judgment in terms of the *factual* conditions of life. He does, indeed, receive his materials from fiction. But his methods, aims, and standards are all imposed by the factual demands of the general environment. The importance to life of human interests gives him his authority to judge. His point of view and his training turn him in the direction of factual realities. His product must be, not fiction, but truth—valid knowledge as directly relatable to life and as workable as the conclusions of the economist, the historian, the natural scientist.

The often repeated assertion that the best authors make the best critics, or that no one has authority to be a critic who has not produced a work of literature of a similar kind and of not greatly disparate merit with the work he is criticizing—is thus clearly seen to be false. Author and critic are engaged in labors of a different character; they are oriented within different fields. The author looks upon life as the source of materials for fiction; the critic looks to fiction for materials of direct

and valid significance for life. Both possess a knowledge
of life and of literature, but that knowledge is employed
in pursuance of different aims. It is not, of course, to be
declared that a man who has written fiction can never be
a critic. But it *is* to be said that such a man must make
a clear and sharp distinction between his labors in the
two fields. For this very reason it can scarcely ever happen that a highly talented author can be also a capable
critic, since, if his abilities are completely dedicated to
authorship, he will continually interpret life in the interests of fiction. He will continually see it as the battle of
a man against an environment. He will always be "taking sides"—be indulging his personal desires and reading them into this conflict. Such an absorption in the
personal and the what should be will disqualify him as
a critic. As for the critic, he must submerge his personal
aims and desires. He must interpret the interests of life
impartially and impersonally. His achievement is to be
judged by his training and knowledge as they are exhibited in his judgments. His function of relating literary
patterns to workable knowledge gives him, usually, a
somewhat more pronounced interest in life than in literature. The great critics—such as Faguet, Brunetière,
and Arnold—have been profoundly interested in social
questions.

But if the fundamentally distinct purposes of author
and critic render impossible any direct comparison of
their labors, it is yet by no means to be declared that the
two exist on different planes or in different realms of
existence. On the contrary, both accord recognition to
certain principles or standards, and thus gain definite
bonds of common agreement and association.

The critic, in the first place, is a reader voicing the
demands of readers. It has been seen that author and

reader are interdependent.[37] The critic (the expert reader) is indeed dependent on the author for materials with which to complete the literary judgment. But the author himself is no less dependent upon readers for the existence of literature as a satisfactory vocation. The author's great merit is that of stating the aims of his society on the basis of its character, its circumstances, and its interests. But it is the critic, nevertheless, who points out these circumstances and interests through a searching examination and analysis of the society itself. Criticism determines the dominating motives of society; thus it sets the problems and guides the activities of authors. It is (as third step of a judgment) the background from which literature springs and the goal to which its results must be applied. Matthew Arnold writes: "Criticism first; a time of true creative activity, perhaps,—which, as I have said, must inevitably be preceded amongst us by a time of criticism,—hereafter when criticism has done its work."[38] But, indeed, there can be, in this matter, no clear first and second. The fortunes of both have been intertwined throughout history. Criticism has animated and guided the efforts of creators; but the achievements of creators have set additional canons or standards for criticism.[39]

In the second place, author and critic unite, within the realm of probable fiction, on a common standard. They are joint workers toward one end—the creation of a valid literary judgment. This means that the author, as well as the critic, must discipline his labors by the demands of probability emanating from the third (the critic's) step

---

[27] See *supra*, p. 153.

[38] *The Function of Criticism at the Present Time.*

[39] To ask which comes first, therefore, is as intricate a question as that about the priority of either the hen or the egg.

of the literary judgment—for the third step of every judgment sets the discipline for the entire judgment. The author who is striving to achieve poetic truth must obey the standards which his aims impose upon him. If he does so, then the critic, who adopts these aims as the basis of his judgment upon the work, will be relieved of a considerable portion of his task—for the first two steps of the literary judgment will be sound. In this respect, therefore (but only in this respect), it is true that the author of probable fiction is the best critic of his own work.

There remains to be viewed the idealist's contention that a discussion about a work of literature itself constitutes a new and independent literary creation. A good expression of this idea appears in Oscar Wilde's *The Critic as Artist:*

To the critic the work of art is simply a suggestion for a new work of his own, that need not necessarily bear any obvious resemblance to the thing it criticizes. The one characteristic of a beautiful form is that one can put into it whatever one wishes, and see in it whatever one chooses to see; and the Beauty, that gives to creation its universal and aesthetic element, makes the critic a creator in his turn, and whispers of a thousand different things which were not present in the mind of him who carved the statue or painted the panel or graved the gem.

Is it not possible to declare, from the empirical point of view, that a writer may use, as the data for a work of literature, his experience with another work of literature? Instead of going to some phenomenon in the environment in order to write an essay on the pleasures of taking walks or the beauties of the springtime, he wishes, instead, to tell of his personal reactions to a work of literature he has read. What he produces will be a familiar essay freely indulging his personal idiosyncrasies. One may call it a prose lyric. Are not such essays enjoyable to readers? Do they not constitute genuine literature?

The answer is, of course, that a familiar essay of this type *is* genuine literature and that it *may be* thoroughly enjoyable and desirable. What the empiricist wishes to point out, however, is the position of such essays with respect to literature itself, and the circumstances under which their merits may be legitimately displayed.

The writer of a familiar essay dealing with a specific work of literature is a man possessing experiences within an environment. His reading of the work has struck up a number of associations with his total fund of experiences. These chance contacts and personal reactions he sets down in his essay in any manner it pleases him to arrange them. This situation makes it evident that such essays cannot belong to the highest class of literary expression. They concern the spectacle of a man in reaction with his environment. But they do nothing further with this relation. They do not connect it significantly with human life generally, for such an accomplishment would require the aid of fictional structure and poetic truth. For the same reason, such essays cannot be of practical or positive value to what has been called the serious reader—the reader anxious to construct definite and satisfactory plans of action in life. In short, the familiar essay imparts almost the same variety of recreational or narcotic stimulus as that afforded by lyric poetry. It deals with personal human reactions, but it maintains them in separation from deliberative human activity. Thus these personal associations afford narrowly personal gratifications to individual desires of readers. The reader himself is the best judge of their success in affording him the satisfactions he seeks.

Since a familiar essay about a work of literature is the expression of chance personal contacts, it becomes important to consider the abilities of the one who writes it. For upon him lies the entire burden; the essay is a fragment from his autobiography. Anatole France's well-known words emphasize this fact:

As I understand it, . . . . criticism is, like philosophy and history,[40] a species of romance for the use of intelligent and inquisitive minds; and every romance, properly understood, is an autobiography. The good critic is he who recounts the adventures of his soul among masterpieces.[41]

What, then, is this "soul" which goes adventuring among masterpieces and thus recounts its autobiography? To the empiricist, it is a person—or what is called a personality. And, in the empiricist's eye, the important matter is the quality of this personality. It may be first-rate; it may be second-rate or fourth-rate. But what constitutes the difference between such grades? Precisely this: the first-rate personality is one which has gained the broadest experience with both literature and life. Now it is true that a broad acquaintance of this kind can be exhibited within a familiar essay only to a very limited degree—for literary or fictional structure is absent, and (as later demonstrated) it cannot be valid literary judgment. Accordingly, when assessing the personality of the writer of a familiar essay on a work of literature, the reader must regularly take into account what he knows of the other literary achievements of the writer. Shelley,

---

[40] The inseparability of idealism in literature from general idealism is here recognized. Brunetière, commenting on Anatole France's position, notes (in his "Impressionist Criticism") the same fact: "Impressionist or subjective, when criticism borrows arguments from metaphysics, without even taking the trouble to consider their bearing, it forgets that the value of these arguments is purely metaphysical."

[41] *La vie littéraire*, ser. I, p. iii (my translation).

one knows, is a poet capable of artistic expression and fictional structure. What he has to say about poetry, therefore (in his *Defence of Poetry*), is eminently worth hearing. Anatole France, having proved by his numerous novels the high quality of his literary "soul," may be certain of attracting numerous readers to accompany that soul in its voyages among masterpieces. In brief, the first-rate personality of a familiar essay concerning a work of literature is one which has proved its qualities by demonstrating elsewhere that it is capable of accepting and working with the materials of literature and of obeying its demands with reference to life. Under such circumstances the essay becomes an interesting disclosure of the general *fictional* attitude of this writer—a disclosure which increases the reader's (and the critic's) knowledge of the writer's basic reactions toward his materials in those other works. If the author has not thus certified the quality of his abilities, and if the essay he writes does not disclose an extensive knowledge of literature and of life (and its potentialities in this respect are strictly limited)—then the essay is merely a collection of narrowly personal opinions about literature expressed by an individual reader. It becomes the gossipy assertion of individual literary preferences as determined by personal gratifications. As such, it deserves no higher place than that accorded to small talk and persiflage generally. It *may* amuse an idle hour.

Finally, it is evident that a familiar essay about a work of literature is fiction purely. The desires that the writer of it reads into the work cannot constitute authentic information, critical analysis, of that work. The essay is, admittedly, the record of chance personal reactions. Its value, therefore, is concentrated within those types of fiction over which personal estimates have most authority.

Concerning impossible and improbable fiction, which lie largely outside the range of criticism, the type of essay under discussion may furnish evidence of the large number of private gratifications offered to a first-rate personality. Thus it is an interesting and valuable tribute to the power of literature over readers. But over probable fiction, these essays can obviously possess no critical authority. They do not accept any of the preliminary requirements, the standards, the tests, of criticism. The critic must endeavor to eliminate, not to surrender to, personal preferences of the kind expressed by individual readers.

It might be supposed that the idealist would not feel called upon to oppose the empiricist's estimate of familiar essays about works of literature. For that estimate appears to violate none of the idealist's canons. His system declares that the spiritual spark which the author has placed within a beautiful work of literature generates a sympathetic *creative* spark within the special faculty of the spiritually attuned reader, causing him to write about the work. The resulting essay, although originated by the work of literature, is by no means confined to it nor forced to follow any plan of development. Altogether, it constitutes a new and independent piece of literature. As a result, one has two original literary (i.e., fictional) productions. And it is as a work of literature that the empiricist classifies the essay. He adds that it does not profess to be, and obviously is not, a criticism of the work which generated it. The idealist, one would imagine, cannot object to such a classification.

The idealist, nevertheless, *does* violently object. He is impelled by two circumstances. In the first place, to declare to him that the utterance of chance impressions about a work of literature is not criticism, is to express a meaningless sentiment. For he does not recognize the existence of literary criticism; he declares the impossibility of attaining valid empirical knowledge about literature. Accordingly, the record of fleeting associations aroused by a work is, for him, the *only* information which can be gained about that work. If the term *criticism* is therefore to be employed at all, it can be applied only to essays in which such excursions among masterpieces are set down. In the second place, the idealist's absolute is involved in the situation. The spirit in the work of literature has reacted upon the special faculty of the essay writer and has been reflected into the essay. Consequently, even though the writer of it may seem to be indulging his whims and his fleeting impressions, it is nevertheless true that the hand of spirit guides him. And his product thus has its authenticity guaranteed by the absolute. To say that such an essay *is* literature but *cannot be* criticism, appears, to the idealist, to be the intolerable assertion that the power of the absolute is limited. To admit such limitation is to declare the incompleteness of idealism and to allow the superiority of empirical or critical standards.

Thus it happens that the idealist—even though his system declares that criticism and creation are one (i.e., that criticism *is* creation), and that criticism has no existence as criticism—yet feels obliged to maintain that impressionistic essays about works of literature *do* constitute criticism, and are entitled to be so denominated. Oscar Wilde and Anatole France both call (in the excerpts quoted above) by the name of criticism the voyagings of "souls" among books. Other idealists call such essays creative criticism, impressionistic criticism, or appreciative criticism[42]—always, be it noted, using the word *criticism*.

This crowning pretension on the part of the idealist is one which the empiricist must oppose directly and with all the emphasis at his command. There is no criticism, declares the idealist; there is only individual opinion which sets down any personal associations the work may call up. And yet these personal opinions are, in the sequel, to be given the name of criticism! After contending that experience with a work of literature produces a separate and independent work of literature, he yet declares that this independent work is also a valid judgment of the first work! After pronouncing the impossibility of judgment, he yet *does* judge; for when he declares the critical authority of impressionistic essays, he asserts the necessity of the entire idealistic attitude.

The cause of the idealist's predicament is readily apparent and has already been suggested. He cannot admit that a beautiful work of literature is *fiction*. On the contrary, since it contains the absolute, it must be *truth*. Now he realizes that criticism has always existed; he knows that it consists of judgments which refer the work to some standard. But his own system allows no such references. A perfect absolute cannot be tested by being referred to anything external to itself. Accordingly, he declares the impossibility of criticism. But this

---

[42] The late Professor Lewis E. Gates, in his *Studies and Appreciations* (1900), attempts to distinguish sharply between impressionism and appreciation. He renounces the former and declares himself a disciple of the latter. Now it is certainly true that, so far as the term itself is concerned, there is no reason why "appreciation" should not be (empirical) criticism. To "appreciate" means to place a proper value on. But the term, historically, has been invariably identified with idealism; it has been interpreted to mean the placing of a *spiritual* value on the work by the operation of romantic sympathy. Gates's principles themselves bear out this contention: his appreciative criticism is an idealistic criticism. His distinctions between it and impressionism have no clear basis.

forces him to explain the nature and status of (for example) an essay which discusses a work of literature. He thereupon pronounces it a spiritual reflection of the spark within the original work. *It is the absolute referring back to itself—for spirit can call only to spirit.* Moreover, if the essay would contain a true reflection of the absolute, it must conform to the terms exacted by that power. There must be no effort to interpret personal reactions in the light of collective human experience, for this would appear to judge the absolute by practical and earthly standards. There must be a vague, free, unorganized flow of emanations from the special faculty of the individual: that is, in empirical language, there must be numerous suggestions of associations established between the work and the individual's fund of experiences; yet these associations must remain inchoate, frustrate, cut off from references to empirical materials or to human activity, the standards by which all literature must be judged. Hence the impressionistic essay *must* assume the form it does assume. But further—the reflection of the absolute in such an essay assures the soundness, the *truth,* of the information it contains. It has been produced by the spirit of the original work impinging upon a special faculty and causing (since it is a creative spark) a new creation which it guides and guarantees. As a result, the essay becomes criticism (truth).

Once more, therefore, the situation reverts to the familiar question: Is literature spiritual or earthly? If it is spiritual, then a beautiful work of literature can only be referred to itself in a literary production which allows free and unlimited expression to the intuition, the unconscious (and so on) of the man who has been in contact with it and is recording that contact. If literature is earthly, then it must be judged by earthly (empirical)

standards. Then literature is fiction which can attain
direct and fruitful union with factual realities only
through poetic truth. Then criticism is the interpretation
of literature in the interests of truth. And the standards
of that truth are the factual circumstances of the relation
of man to his collective surroundings.

To the empiricist, criticism consists of attaining workable truths through fiction. What the idealist does is to
refer one fiction (the work of literature) to another fiction (impressionistic criticism). The result, as the empiricist declares it, is forever to wall up literature within
the borders of fiction—forever to deny its influence on
the realities of life. Precisely here is where the empiricist can brook not one iota of compromise. A discussion
of literature which cuts itself off from the factual circumstances of life and yet pretends to go abroad among men
as a valid judgment of literature and life—this is an
intolerable thing. And since the alienation from life is
made imperative by the commands of the absolute, it is
the absolute itself with which the empiricist is at length
brought face to face under circumstances which admit of
no compromise.

For the evidence, so far as literature is concerned, is
now all in. The necessities and ramifications of the entire
idealistic scheme of things in the field of literature and
literary judgment have now been displayed. It has been
shown that this scheme, disguise itself as it may, rests
wholly upon the assertion that there is an absolute, a
spiritual form, a Platonic idea of beauty in literature.
What, then, is this absolute? What is this ideal which is
at the same time real, with a reality which can never be
realized on earth, but which, nevertheless, declares the
unreality of all earthly reality? this actuality which is
never actual? this immanent experience which transcends

experience? this unknown which is yet so surely known
that it alone is knowable? this eternal and all powerful
unity which is never apparent to men except as a duality?
What is this enthroned paradox?

To the empiricist the answer is not hard to find. You
have only to formulate, on the basis of your experience
with the environment, a state of things which you desire
to see realized—a world of the what (for you) should be.
This becomes your ideal. Now you know empirically that
such a state, in order to gain realization, must conform
to the potentialities of yourself in contact with the environment. But you refuse to put your ideal to this necessary test. You declare that the test is needless because
this ideal *is already real.* This assertion being clearly
absurd with regard to the actualities you are forced to
accept in everyday life, you assert further that the reality
of your ideal is its own guaranty—or (what is the same
thing) that its reality is assured by a force which exists
to insure its reality. With reference to your future conduct, your ideal is now an illusion—an untested theory
perhaps fatally divorced from earthly reality. And this
illusion can exist unshattered only by keeping it apart
from all references to collective human experience.
Hence, whatever question (art, morality) is being debated on the basis of that illusion must first be taken
apart from all practical, experiential associations. And
you yourself must bear it company.

But the matter of first importance at this juncture is
the question of what the absolute is when a belief in its
reality is seriously held by an idealist. What is its status
as the source of a system of knowledge—about literature,
for example? Obviously it is the "ghost theory." Obviously, the absolute is the ghost which has occupied all
fields of human knowledge prior to the establishment in

them of valid empirical methods—the ghost which wages a continuous fight against those methods. It is the primeval mumbo jumbo of the savage. Because its power can be exerted only over ghosts, it demands that man and his environment become ghostly. No science—no valid, reputable, cumulative knowledge—has ever been possible in any department until this ghost has been laid and the witch doctors expelled. The natural sciences have long since attained their freedom; history has done so only recently; philosophy, in the opinion of the pragmatist, is affecting its escape even now. Literature, apparently, remains within the toils; the ghost still hovers over it. It will do so as long as any writer can seriously assert that a literary judgment exists on a different plane from any other human judgment.

Naturally, this ghost, which pretends to exist outside experience, cannot be directly assailed by knowledge based on experience. This is a fortunate circumstance. For, concerning the character and habits of ghosts who proclaim (not their fictional but) their factual reality and validity, no intelligent man, it may be said, can have the slightest interest. What *does* concern the intelligent man, however, is the stultifying effect upon the field of literature of a belief in ghosts, and of the consequent determination to lay plans for an attitude toward literature based entirely upon this belief. The many absurd and intolerable results which follow imperatively thereon have been recorded at various times throughout the present discussion. They may now be given a brief and final review.

1. When the idealist, at the command of the ghost, proclaims that literature has no connection with the life and the environment of man, he has declared a manifest absurdity. Its preposterous nature can be concealed only

by an ardent appeal to ignorance. On the side of ignorance the idealist in literature is regularly to be found. He must attempt to attack and discredit all human knowledge. He must seek to create a mystery under whose cover he may slip in his ghost. He finds, accordingly, every phenomenon whose empirical observation and classification offer at least temporary difficulty. He invariably refuses to define his terms; definition would reveal the dualism. He exults in paradoxes.

Needless to say, his appeals to ignorance are excellent *ad captandum* arguments. The mob is on his side. To tell an ignorant man that no one can know anything through worldly means since all such knowledge is vain, is to win his immediate acquiescence, for it is to give him the pleasing information that he and all wise men are at the same mental level. For readers slightly higher in comprehension, the idealist has his paradoxes. If they are used judiciously and frequently, the reader may temporarily lose sight of distinctions between objects and ghosts. Again, a religious appeal is often of effect. The ghost who watches over creation in literature may be called God.[43] For readers capable of more subtle distinctions, the idealist may employ the tactics of, for example, Professor Freud. He may decorate his system with numerous pseudo-scientific adornments. He may declare that it is a strictly scientific (empirical) hypothesis. Readers may thus be led to believe that these adornments have a certain status in the ghostly hierarchy.

---

[43] Carlyle, for example, in his essay ''Characteristics,'' takes his ''unconscious'' through literature and other fields, and then discloses that it is indeed God. Many idealists are not reluctant to have it appear that the empiricist, in denying an earthly system built on an absolute, is denying God. The genuinely sacrilegious element of the matter is the circumstance that these idealists, although believing that the qualities of Deity infinitely transcend the comprehension of man, are yet willing to introduce God at any time to bolster their personal preferences in art or ethics.

When the idealist dedicates literature to a ghost instead of to life, he inflicts lasting injury upon both literature and life. Life, indeed, goes on without literature;
but it is deprived of the aid it might receive from one of
the departments of human knowledge. The aid literature
is capable of rendering to life cannot be overestimated.
The formulation of the practical aims of men in reference to their experiences is a task worthy of the devoted
labors of the most earnest and intelligent men. It is to
point the way along the path of human civilization. But
the separation of literature from life is particularly fatal
to literature. Deprived of direct contact with the grow-
ing, changing affairs of human life, it must sink into the
quiet back-waters of "spirit"—that is, into impossibilities and improbabilities. Here it will furnish recreation
for "tired business men" and consolation to the handi-
capped and defeated. It will furnish museum pieces for
collectors and delicate stimuli for "lovely souls" within
ivory towers. Certain of these functions are, perhaps,
not unimportant. But a dedication of itself to them will
not keep literature alive for serious men among authors
or readers.

2. When the idealist, under ghostly compulsion, pronounces a work of literature to be a spiritual essence
bearing no genuine nor direct reference to men and their
surroundings, he has uttered a pronouncement which is
openly contradicted by the most limited observation.
From this initial absurdity flow many sequent absurdities.

It is an absurdity to declare that a beautiful work of
literature, being spirit, is perfect at all times and to all
readers. This is simply the abandonment of all judgment. And the fate of these "perfect" works has been
well set down by Professor Babbitt:

What we see in America to-day, for instance, is an endless procession of bad or mediocre books, each one saluted on its way to oblivion by epithets that would be deserved only by a masterpiece. We have, in fact, been having so many masterpieces of late that we have almost ceased to have any literature.[44]

It is an absurdity to proclaim by simple fiat that a work of literature is devoid of spirit, and that it is, consequently, not only not beautiful, but also of no literary significance of any sort—that it is to be totally dismissed from consideration.

It is an absurdity to contend that a work of literature is either perfectly beautiful or practically non-existent. This is to think in terms of melodrama. In the world one is never called upon to face either of these cases. Every valid judgment in every department of human knowledge is evolved from the most careful observation of phenomena, the most searching computation of similarities and differences, the most accurate discriminations between them.

It is a crowning absurdity to condemn criticism because it "finds fault" and judges, and to discard it at the behest of a system based upon the most ruthless, tyrannical, and intolerable type of judgment possible to imagine. The bright side of idealistic literary judgments always faces the spectator. He receives the impression that criticism is the pleasant task of choosing superlatives to express incomparable perfection. He comes to admire the idealist's goodness of heart, his never-failing desire to praise and be pleased. What is not exposed is the slaughtered corpses in the rear—the works which, being non-spiritual, do not even enter the range of the idealist's vision. A work condemned by a law, however rigorous, may always be reprieved by an attack on that

---

[44] *The Masters of Modern French Criticism* (1912), p. 377.

law. A work condemned without trial by a proclamation which admits of no questioning is cut down without knowing its crime.

3. When the idealist asserts that the man who, as creator or critic, would gain knowledge of literary values and realities must be the recipient of supramundane experience, he has stated a position which, from the point of view of criticism (i.e., when represented as fact), is untrue and unethical. Such a position declares that the judge of literature must stand totally aloof from both literature and life (an absurd impossibility)—must gaze at both from his station in the ghostly world. The stock in trade of such a judge is that he is not like other men. He has a divine "mission"; he is the utterer of revelations. He does not debate or discuss literary questions; he simply pronounces, like an oracle, the decrees of the ghost. His attitude toward things of this world is one of lofty, occasionally of amused, toleration and condescension. *His* knowledge comes from "insight." He is "deep" because he sees ghosts; whereas the empiricist is "shallow" because he sees objects. The prophet of the spirit has "profundity," because he can dispose of any literary question in the briefest time and with no apparent effort. The empiricist can never attain such "profundity," since he is often puzzled and temporarily baffled by his data, and he is obliged to devote all his effort to his labors with them. It is apparent, surely, that the shallowness and superficiality lie, in truth, on the side of the idealist. By such epithets one may properly characterize his attempt to remove from discussion his personal preferences and prejudices in literature by the assertion that they are encysted in the absolute—that it is not he but the ghost who speaks. Naturally, such preferences, since they are the expression of personal

gratifications, will be opposed in nearly all respects to critical or empirical principles, which are acquired and held impersonally by the critic.

But if this prophetic pose is a pure pretense, why has it so firmly entrenched itself? Obviously, it has great attractiveness for certain categories of people. The mob likes it. The layman hears with approval a declaration that study and training have nothing to do with the power of creating or judging literature, but that the true author and critic are "born that way."[45] Again, it is a position of eminent suitability for those who are unable or unwilling to attain the knowledge of literature and of life which would qualify them as critics. For the position sets no standard of "talent." One has merely to assume an attitude, to strike a pose. Admirable cover is thereby furnished to *poseurs,* dilettants, literary snobs. It is a splendid point of vantage from which paradox lovers may proclaim their dicta: "In a lower sense *this* is true, but in a higher sense the exact opposite is the case"; "The short-sighted critic, judging by mere facts, will conclude *this,* but the true critic, rising superior to the facts, will entirely reverse this decision"; and so on. It is an excellent tilting ground for youthful Hotspurs who rush into the literary field in the vigor of their inspired (i.e., adolescent) enthusiasm, destroy the great majority of literary questions, dictate rapid and unconditional terms of surrender to the remainder (doing so with less

---

[45] Cf. Sir Joshua Reynolds, *Discourses,* VI: "Those who have undertaken to write on our art, and have represented it as a kind of inspiration, as a gift bestowed upon peculiar favourites at their birth, seem to insure a much more favourable disposition from their readers, and have a much more captivating and liberal air, than he who attempts to examine, coldly, whether there are any means by which this art may be acquired; how the mind may be strengthened and expanded, and what guides will show the way to eminence."

difficulty because of their extremely limited acquaintance with them), gaze masterfully over the ruins, and then gallop rapidly off to pursue their titanic careers on other and sterner fields.

But there is another and less sunny side to this picture. If a ghostly prophecy is the deification of personal preferences, then it will naturally conflict with ghostly prophecies formulated by other persons. And when the conflict is joined, what shall judge between the combatants? There is only one standard of appeal—the spiritual organization of the literary seer. *Accordingly, at the first clash of opinion between idealistic judges of literature, all literary discussion is forthwith abandoned.* The debate immediately assumes the following character:

*A.* You are in error because your spiritual connection is either temporarily short-circuited, or because the current which comes through it is not, and never was, of high voltage. Personally, I am sorry for you—etc., etc.[46]

---

[46]A most amusing example of this situation is Charles Lamb's "northern castigation." I quote from E. V. Lucas's *The Works of Charles and Mary Lamb* (1905), vol. 6 (Lamb's letters), p. 213 f.: Lamb, replying to Wordsworth about a gift copy of the *Lyrical Ballads*, enumerated in his letter "several of the passages which had most affected me, adding, unfortunately, that no single piece had moved me so forcibly as the 'Ancient Mariner', 'The Mad Mother', or the 'Lines at Tintern Abbey'. The Post did not sleep a moment. I received almost instantaneously a long letter of four sweating pages from my Reluctant Letter-Writer, the purport of which was, that he was sorry his 2d vol. had not given me more pleasure (Devil a hint did I give it had not pleased me), and 'was compelled to wish that my range of sensibility was more extended, being obliged to believe that I should receive large influxes of happiness and happy Thoughts' (I suppose from the L.B.). . . . . Coleridge, who had not written to me for some months before, starts up from the bed of sickness to reprove me for my hardy presumption: four long pages, equally sweaty and more tedious, came from him; assuring me that, when the works of a man of true genius such as W. undoubtedly was, do not please me at first sight, I should suspect the fault to lie 'in me and not in them', etc. etc. etc. etc. etc. What am I to do with such people?''

*B*. What you say is not true. Quite the contrary is the case. It is you, in fact, who have no insight. And I hesitate to name the motive which actuates you in attacking me—etc., etc.

It can be seen that the terms under which such debates are conducted are necessarily rather personal in nature. They become quarrels of a kind which are ungallantly asserted to be usual among females: they are based, not on principles, but on personal invective. "Flytings" of this kind frequently amuse the spectator as much as they infuriate the principals. But the only matters that need be noted here are these: such arguments are not debates about questions of literature; and they are, by their terms, incapable of arriving at any conclusion other than that afforded by the natural exhaustion of the writers engaged.

The *ne plus ultra* of absurdity is arrived at when the idealist contends that, if the ghost were banished from literature, all enthusiasm would vanish with it. Naturally, when the idealist grants to the ghost all the important values of a work of literature, he looks upon himself, the ghost's spokesman, as the conservator of these values. He thinks of them as essences *apart from* the "earthly" phenomena of literature. Now "enthusiasm," as an abstract term, is the idealist's spiritual special faculty. One does not first have a mysterious power of "enthusiasm" and then begin the study of literature. Enthusiasm *for literature* is something which is the product of the unremitting and fruitful study *of literature*. It accompanies progress in that study; it increases with the individual's knowledge of his subject. If it vanishes when confronted with serious tasks, then it is not worth much: then it has been the enthusiasm of private gratification. As such, it is the lure which attracts the reader in his capacity as reader. But it can have no status as criticism —as reputable and tested information about literature.

The fact that there is no royal road to achievement in any branch of human knowledge is a most fortunate and necessary circumstance. It means that every such branch is a reputable field for the week-day efforts of serious men. It means that a satisfactory vocation can be erected within that field. It means that that branch has attained reputable existence and respectability by erecting standards to bar out the pretender, the dilettant, the fraud. It means, finally, that the results of labors within the field become of directly assessable value to human life.

A valid literary judgment is no different in quality or plane of existence from any other valid human judgment. It has a distinctive subject matter to which it applies the three essential steps of all valid judgments. Author and critic are joint creators of these steps. Since the critic is basically concerned with the all important third step, he must possess the information demanded by that step of those who would work with it. He must possess, that is, the broadest familiarity with both literature and life. He must adopt a method of activity which develops to the full the resources of the special information he possesses. The only method open to him is the empirical or (as it is called) the scientific method.

Will his labors result in causing him to become a "mere plodding college professor," an "academic" critic?[47] What does such an accusation mean? Is there any meaning here other than that necessarily urged by the ghost's jealousy against "material" achievement? Does it mean

---

[47] Cf. Spingarn's *The New Criticism:* " 'What droll creatures these college professors are whenever they talk about art,' wrote Flaubert in one of his letters, and voiced the world's opinion of academic criticism."

that the critic will be a pedant? If so, the accusation is ridiculous. A pedant is one who pursues his labors within his special field in ignorance of the relation of that field to the changing conditions of life. The idealist, who walls off literature from life, is your true pedant. It is impossible for a capable critic to be guilty of pedantry. His labors spring from, they return to, and they are in constant touch with the changing, pulsing, expanding human life of our own day.